DISCURSIVE IDEOLOGIES

DISCURSIVE IDEOLOGIES

Reading Western Rhetoric

C. H. KNOBLAUCH

UTAH STATE UNIVERSITY PRESS
Logan

© 2014 by the University Press of Colorado

Published by Utah State University Press
An imprint of University Press of Colorado
5589 Arapahoe Avenue, Suite 206C
Boulder, Colorado 80303

 The University Press of Colorado is a proud member of
The Association of American University Presses.

The University Press of Colorado is a cooperative publishing enterprise supported,
in part, by Adams State University, Colorado State University, Fort Lewis College,
Metropolitan State University of Denver, Regis University, University of Colorado,
University of Northern Colorado, Utah State University, and Western State Colorado
University.

ISBN: 978-0-87421-935-7 (paper)
ISBN: 978-0-87421-936-4 (ebook)

Library of Congress Cataloging-in-Publication Data
Knoblauch, C. H.
  Discursive ideologies : reading western rhetoric / C.H. Knoblauch.
     pages cm
   ISBN 978-0-87421-935-7 (paperback) — ISBN 978-0-87421-936-4 (ebook)
1. Rhetoric—Philosophy. 2. Rhetoric—Political aspects. I. Title.
  P301.K54 2014
  808.001—dc23
                                   2013048383

Cover photograph © Steve Heap / Shutterstock

CONTENTS

DISCURSIVE IDEOLOGIES

1

THE MEANING OF MEANING

What we believe about words influences the ways in which we live our lives, what we think and say and do. Notice that I'm not referring to our *uses* of language: it's obvious that speaking, writing, listening, and reading have consequences for our lives. What I'm suggesting is rather less apparent: attitudes we have, assumptions we make, beliefs we hold, mostly tacit and unexamined, about what language can do for us, how language works, its connections to the world, the reliability of meaning, the truth-value of different kinds of statements, all affect our lives just as much as, and perhaps even more deeply than, our actual usage. Anthropologist and linguist Edward Sapir, known for his insights into the relativity of representation across languages, argued the error of supposing that "one adjusts to reality without the use of language" and insisted that the "real" world is "to a large extent unconsciously built up on the language habits" of different groups of people. No two languages, he writes, "are ever sufficiently similar to be considered as representing the same social reality" (Sapir 1964, 69). Sapir's observations in linguistics (the study of language) are pertinent also for rhetoric (the study of discourse). That is, what he argued regarding different assumptions about words and reality in different languages anticipates similar distinctions among the multiple, complexly interwoven discourses, or communication practices, that compose social experience in any one language—domestic discourses (the verbal routines of everyday life), religious discourses, scientific, legal, political, medical, artistic, educational, scholarly, and other discourses. These discourses are themselves different worlds of words, albeit within a single language, and they feature, some more self-consciously than others, not just distinct vocabularies, syntactic styles, and registers, but different views of what C. K. Ogden and I. A. Richards (1923) called "the meaning of meaning"—how things are named, what (if anything) is to be regarded as reliably "true," what counts as "proof," how the literal is distinguished from the figurative, who can speak authoritatively, what knowledge is and how it's achieved,

DOI: 10.7330/9780874219364.c001

and myriad other questions. In the most self-conscious of these discourses—religious, legal, or scholarly, for example—one commonly finds competing rhetorical theories vying for authority, with significant consequences attending the ebb and flow of alternative points of view. Ask a Catholic and an Anglican theologian about their contrasting views of the doctrine of transubstantiation, or two lawyers about the "intent" of the framers of the US Constitution, or two literary critics about their readings of "Young Goodman Brown," and conflicts regarding not just meaning but also the meaning of meaning will be quickly apparent.

MEANING AND EVERYDAY LIFE

But let's begin more simply with the familiar discourses of everyday life and consider the tacit rhetorical assumptions of a couple of ordinary Americans whom I will call, for ease of reference, George and Louise. Friday morning, George comes down to breakfast and the newspaper, observes while pouring milk on his cornflakes that the carton says "sell by September 15," which was two days ago, and, fearing the milk may be spoiling, plays safe and empties the carton in the sink. He reads a front-page story on a bond proposal to fund new buildings in his local school district and accepts the objectivity of the report along with the display of evidence supporting the need for new taxes to pay for the borrowing. He's unhappy, however, about Hispanic "aliens" driving up enrollment, and also with school programs that seem to put "multiculturalism" ahead of learning English. Turning to the editorial page, he finds a piece on global warming to be mere opinion, unsubstantiated by facts, its author melodramatic, and decides to withhold judgment until dispassionate science quiets the noise of discordant voices. As for the ad on page 6 hawking "eye-catching cosmetics," he recognizes the manipulative play of words, smirks briefly at the ad's fictions of beauty and sexuality, which he knows were conjured for commercial advantage, and dismisses its claims.

Reaching his office building later in the morning, he glances at the sign in the elevator warning not to exceed a limit of twelve occupants, takes it as an engineer's appraisal, casually estimates the number of his fellow travelers, and rides confidently to his workplace. He spends part of his work time writing proposals to potential business customers that detail how his consulting firm can troubleshoot their management practices and present software solutions. He is confident that his statements are accurate, unbiased, clear, and true, as professional writing is supposed to be, and he trusts that the precision of the language will allow the document to have contractual force if his firm's bid is accepted. Arriving home that afternoon, he sorts his mail, saving a notice of jury duty in two weeks and throwing away a breathless proclamation that he has won a Caribbean cruise, not bothering to open the official-looking envelope. He listens to a phone message from his mother but dismisses her familiar complaint that he "never calls" as an unreasonable plea for attention. In the evening, he watches the televised hearing on a Supreme Court nominee, marking the candidate's views on the first and second amendments. Before bedtime, he amuses himself with a history of the Crimean war; he rarely reads novels and doesn't like poetry. First thing Saturday morning, George, a devout Catholic, goes to confession at his church, admits to the priest that he has failed recently to "keep holy the Sabbath day," and earnestly recites the requisite Hail, Marys and Our Fathers as penance, confident that he has been forgiven. On the way home, he notices a traffic sign saying "No U Turn." He makes a U turn anyway to park in front of his house, interpreting the meaning of the sign as "don't turn unless you're sure there is no oncoming traffic."

Louise follows similar routines, motivated (in part) by equally tacit, occasionally different, assumptions about language. She reads the sale date on the milk carton as an approximation only and decides to keep her milk, sees the bond issue article as an argument motivated by the political slant of the newspaper, and approves the global warming editorial, impressed by the urgency of the writer's prose. She glances at a letter to the editor in which the writer refers to Palestinian militants as "freedom fighters," a label with which she disagrees strenuously, believing that the militants are just plain terrorists. Like George, she sees a cautionary notice in her workplace elevator but regards it not as an example of engineering discourse but as a legal statement protecting the manufacturer from liability if the elevator fails when too fully loaded. She is skeptical about the safety of elevators and often climbs the stairs to her office. She spends part of her workday writing an online human resources newsletter that relies on a friendly, personal touch to maintain a positive image of her company while giving employees valuable information in user-friendly language supported by clever graphics and humorous anecdotes. She has always been grateful to her ninth-grade English teacher for giving her the grammatical proficiency that has made her so successful in her job. Even her diary entries are carefully crafted. After work, she sorts her mail, planning to query an official notice that her electric bill payment is late, worrying about how her mother's letter complaining of loneliness illustrates her failures as a daughter, and opening the same notice George received about a Caribbean cruise package, just in case. Her brother emails that evening, promising to come soon for a visit. She responds with the requisite expressions of eager anticipation, but she knows that he rarely follows through and she isn't particularly interested in seeing him anyway. Saturday morning, she heads for the beach, following directions on her GPS. A sign prohibiting U turns obliges her to go around the block to reach the freeway, which she willingly does because the law is the law.

There may be little, if any, articulate awareness of language directly motivating what George and Louise say, understand, or do. Like the rest of us amidst our ordinary routines, they probably find just thinking to be challenging enough without also consciously thinking about their thinking. Yet they are immersed in language, and their thoughts as well as actions are influenced by a rich array of beliefs and assumptions about words. The beliefs come from lifelong interactions with other people (whoever pointed to a mooing creature and called it a cow "explained" to them that language can name things), from their schooling, including Louise's helpful ninth-grade teacher, and from their practical experience of the world, an experience that has been preshaped, to a greater extent than they probably realize, by their cultural background, language included. What they believe comes to them as settled understanding rather than theory or argument, mostly from the European inheritance of linguistic and rhetorical speculation that has served for centuries as the repository of our cultural common sense about language and discourse. It would take many pages to explain the details and nuances of this common sense, even limited to the thoughts and actions described above, but a sampling of its axioms should be sufficient to make the point. The most important belief George and Louise share is that *language enables people to name, experience, organize, manage, and interact with realities that are different from and "outside" of language*, including a world beyond the self (other people, human institutions, nature) and also a world within the self (feelings, ideas, memories, fears, hopes, imaginings). They presume that language represents these worlds and enables us to function within them. The warning on the milk carton doesn't cause milk to spoil. Rather, milk spoils, and the warning predicts approximately when it will happen. Louise's GPS directions to the beach don't create the road system; they only offer a symbolic rendering and convenient instruction about the best roads to take. For George and Louise, *things precede the names we give them*: real money underlies taxes and bond proposals; physical heat gives meaning to words like *warming* and *cooling*; actual cosmetics come before the ads that promote them. It follows, then, that *the truth and accuracy of language involve a correspondence between words and the worlds to which words refer.* George's professional writing names problems that really exist in a potential client's business operations, and it offers solutions whose validity and practicality can be objectively demonstrated. Louise's representations of her company, and her HR advice to employees, may be judged as true or false by matching them to employees' actual experience. Louise's electric bill is inaccurate because she has paid it. *Substance is always more important than form.* George and Louise don't use the word *rhetoric* very often, but when they do, it's a disparaging reference to language without substance, such as the advertising language George scorns as he reads the cosmetics ad. Louise exploits the clever graphics in her desktop publishing program, but she believes that her PR language is substantial, not mere rhetoric, because it offers real information; it is user-friendly but not misleading or manipulative.

George and Louise also believe in common that *language enables communication.* They communicate with family, friends, business associates, public institutions, service providers, even supernatural beings in George's case, generally confident that what they say is understood. People also communicate with them through talk and through a variety of media, including television, Facebook, e-mail, text messages, blogs, books, newspapers, telephones, letters, business memos, and official documents. They are satisfied that the interchanges, the sending and the receiving, create and maintain valuable, or at least useful, human relationships. George's business writing not only speaks the truth by naming problems and solutions, but it also communicates that truth to a potential client and makes a promise that his company will perform effectively in accordance with the statements in the proposal. The writing must be clear and technically correct, however, in order to be reliable. *Clarity and correctness assure translucent communication,* resulting in social bonds that enable the mutually beneficial conduct of commerce and daily life. Of course, because of the prior belief that *words are subordinate to things,* both George and Louise understand that *actions speak louder than words.* George's business contract is a promise, but it doesn't in itself get the work done. Louise believes that she and her brother know and relate to each other partly as a result of their ability to communicate, but she also knows that what her brother says in his e-mail message must be contextualized by earlier failures to follow through with actual visits. More generally, *what people say must always be evaluated by reference to what is "actually" the case.* That's how we tell the difference between truth, error, and deceit, not to mention the subtler difference between deceit and that socially strategic but ethically complex misrepresentation that enables Louise and her brother to maintain a sibling relationship despite the fact that he doesn't really travel to see her and she doesn't really care. Most of the time, *words need to be interpreted, not just taken at face value,* depending on how much we know about the speaker's intentions and about the communicative context. George and Louise draw different conclusions from the message in the elevator and partly (but only partly) base their actions on what they read. George believes that his mother's complaint about his never calling fails to match the reality of his frequent-enough calls, so he comfortably interprets her statement either as erroneous (in her case, forgetful) or as communicating something different from what it actually says, namely that his mother is lonely. Both George and Louise believe that we cannot only match language to factuality but that *we can look through a verbal statement to perceive the intent of the person who makes it.* They both "know" what their mothers mean, and what the elevator signs mean, and they confidently, though differently, appraise the truth-value of each.

For Louise and George, *different statements have different truth-value,* and they trust them more or less depending on the ways in which they are classified and ranked. George's hierarchy of statements begins with the Word of God. He believes that *there are sacred utterances, like the Bible, that speak to human beings with divine authority* and also that *there are specialized human utterances that have the power to affect supernatural or divine agencies,* including prayers and rites such as Catholic confession. George finds the authority of the newspaper's front-page stories more compelling than the editorials and the editorials more persuasive than the advertisements. The letter announcing his entitlement to a Caribbean cruise is at the bottom of the hierarchy, not just manipulative but deceitful. His mother's message is more reliable than the cruise letter because it doesn't lie but less reliable than the newspaper because his mother's message is more influenced by personal bias. He finds, as most people in our culture probably do, that *there is more truth-value in "realistic" writing, like history, than in fiction writing, that prose is more reliable than poetry, and that argument is more reliable than narrative.* Louise's hierarchy makes room for the value and usefulness of personal, not just "objective," writing because the sincerity of personal writing assures the reliability of its statements. She believes that *writing can portray the self and connect with the inner beings, the selves, of others.* Whether she is writing in her diary, communicating with her mother, or informing her colleagues at work, she has confidence that sincerity is a basis for authenticity, that statements "from the heart" have more value than rhetorical manipulations of seeming objectivity. Louise recognizes that the apparent detachment of front-page articles may conceal a newspaper's political and mercantile agendas, just as the caution sign in the elevator can be more protective of the manufacturer than the riding public, so she interprets both with more skepticism, less trust, than George does. The passionate conviction of the global-warming argument gives its author integrity: she knows where the writer stands. Of course, Louise isn't invariably skeptical about objective narrators. For example, she does not read ulterior motives into the sign prohibiting U turns, accepting the authority of this particular civil discourse without presuming to retain any interpretive license. George, by contrast, regards a commandment to keep the Sabbath as different from a commandment to avoid U turns, although the differential regard is more likely a consequence of rationalized self-interest than a parsing of the degrees of authority implicit in religious and civil discourses. Beliefs about language, whether Louise's or George's or our own, do not have to be philosophically consistent with each other, or consistently applied, and they are always modified by other complexities of human motive and behavior.

Still more beliefs and value-laden assumptions can be mined from this brief encounter with George and Louise. Both of them agree that *the primary value of literacy, the ability to read and write, is mainly practical, allowing the deployment of language skills for social and economic advantage.* George clearly believes, with many Americans, that *"foreigners" should speak our language if they are going to live in our country.* Louise believes that *language is comprised of building blocks (syllables, words, sentences, paragraphs) that are joined together to form ever-more-elaborate statements, and that teaching reading and writing requires learning to manipulate the building blocks from simplest to most complex.* She thanks her ninth-grade teacher for these insights. It is likely that both George and Louise believe that *fundamental realities are the same around the world regardless of language and other cultural differences,* that *talk is cheap,* that really important *public documents—contracts, laws, medical records—are reliable,* and that *immoral writing can corrupt the young and/or ignorant.* One could go on, but my concern is only to underscore the observation with which I began: what we believe about words influences the ways in which we live our lives. Every statement identified by italics in the preceding paragraphs constitutes an axiom from the cultural common sense of the West regarding language and discourse. It belongs to a dispersion of beliefs, values, assumptions, ideas, opinions, practical lore, superstitions, and fragments of formal theory accrued over many centuries, generally below the radar of conscious attention, working in concert (and even in contradiction), to reassure George, Louise, and the rest of us that we can all rely on speech acts. The statements, taken together, comprise a "story" about language and discourse, or rather a collection of stories, an "anthology," whose overlapping themes and narratives preserve a multifaceted picture of communication in our cultural memory. While the stories portraying these beliefs include analytical arguments from linguistics and rhetoric, they are not invariably scientific, consistently theoretical, internally consistent, logical, or even fully articulate. They come from the West's mythico-religious traditions as well as from philosophy, and from experiential lore as well as disciplined knowledge. Their treatment of shared themes varies dramatically from one to another without the demands of proof or consistency expected from scientific or other argumentative discourse. No one story in the anthology has the standing to refute another; their rival accounts simply offer a plurality of understandings. That's why the idea of story more effectively conveys the nature of our common sense about verbal communication than the idea of theory or argument.

The stories function in much the same ways as those in other areas of our cultural knowledge, such as our understanding of what it means to be American, of what comprises the American Dream. We can recall, with varying degrees of self-consciousness, stories about immigration, from the Mayflower to Ellis Island, about revolt against European tyranny, about hard-won political and religious freedoms, about Westward expansion, about the Blue and the Gray, about keeping the world safe for democracy, about progressing from rags to riches through self-reliance, pragmatism, and industry. Taken together, the stories identify and claim to validate "our" shared cultural heritage while also, in their diversity, evoking the complexities, discordances, and irreconcilable differences that make up the American experience. Different individuals and groups emphasize different stories, judging some true and others false, or some meaningful and others not. Not everyone agrees that all the stories are indeed common sense, as, for instance, those that relate mistreatment of Native and African Americans, or those that question whether America is truly a land of opportunity, or those that describe a separation of church and state. As an anthology, the stories reveal not a seamless unity of understanding but a compendium of viewpoints represented in differing treatments of recurring themes. They serve to legitimate those viewpoints, not only providing intellectual and emotional coherence to particular ways of seeing the world but also providing their tellers and listeners with political leverage in the ongoing negotiation of that group's standing or privilege. In general, stories shape the vagaries of actual experience in all areas of cultural life into ideological wholes, confirming fictions that offer historical context, personal and group identification, shared assumptions and values, and rationales for, as well as confidence in, the reasonableness of actions judged to be consistent with their perspectives. The cultural common sense they narrate is pervasive, self-evident, pragmatically effective, immune to falsification, and psychologically necessary for maintaining familiar pictures of the world and routines of human interaction.

Common sense is also, of course, to paraphrase Albert Einstein, the historical record of our prejudices. It is grounded in our oldest, or simplest, or most concrete, or most familiar, or most self-centered experiences (like "the sun rises in the east"), and because it is so serviceable, we generally accept it as authoritative. Yet it is also, in its familiarity, uncritical, and in its faithfulness to local perspective not only limited by that perspective but also unable to sympathize with alternative points of view, finding them wrong, ignorant, or meaningless. Returning to the issue of common sense about language and discourse, Louise's and George's beliefs reveal the influence of narrow perspectives whether they disagree with each other, for example, about the efficacy of religious discourse or share the same views while lacking awareness of vantage points available from other stories in the anthology. Consider the most important axiom they accept in common: the assertion that language names a preexisting world. This belief is neither timeless, nor self-evidently true, nor reliably confirmed by experience, nor unopposed by plausible (if not always intuitively sensible) alternative arguments. The story that relates it has a formal philosophical history, but while it enjoys considerable prestige in the repertory of narratives inscribing our common sense, it does not exhaust Western insight into the relationship between language and reality. To name just one alternative story (shortly, I will introduce more), some philosophers have argued that our sensory experience is already a human interpretation of the physical exteriority surrounding us, that even initial perception, let alone the processes of conceptualization and naming, serves to *constitute* (instead of mirroring or reflecting) the "reality" it presents to us. Words don't point to the world in this view; rather, they make it for us, presenting a "reality" that is comprehensible *as* reality because it is rendered in human terms. This is a transcendental, or romantic, story about meaning, while the more popular story is classical and metaphysical. For many people, and probably for George and Louise, the transcendentalist narrative is less intuitively familiar than the much older account of an intrinsically coherent world that the eye "sees" and language points to. But as later chapters will reveal, it has had a concrete, historical impact on the thinking, speaking, and acting of people who have lived according to the truth of its statements.

RHETORICAL PERSPECTIVES: NAMING

I've argued so far that what we *believe* about language influences how we live our lives. Now I'd like to add that conscious *thought* about language, whether in the domestic discourses of everyday life or in more theorized professional discourses, can be beneficial for those who make the effort. Close reading and formal thinking about the stories that articulate our common sense can allow us to cultivate a curious, reflective, and critically distanced attitude toward the entire anthology as opposed to merely believing or disbelieving individual stories according to the accidental preferences of our experience, upbringing, or education. It means developing a similar attitude toward storytelling itself, appreciating its power to beguile no less than inform anyone who remains uncritical of its crafted illusions of certitude, coherence, and sufficiency. While one cannot live apart from stories, or achieve a transcendent location outside all narrative perspectives, reflective readers can retain the capacity to evaluate the claims of different stories, read new stories as though they too might have the potential to be true, and change their preferences in response to new ideas and experience. The axioms of common sense we've encountered so far belong to plausible European accounts of the nature of discourse that are neither ignorant, nor naïve, nor false—stories that have respectable intellectual pedigrees dating to Greco-Roman times and earlier. But the stories are also different. What I want to suggest is the value of approaching the stories comparatively and critically by reading them, along with others that are less familiar but not less influential, within the various philosophical, rhetorical, and linguistic traditions to which they belong. To do this kind of reading is to achieve perspective on language use, to reflect on the meaning of meaning, and to think about how people act when they participate in discourse. Reading different accounts of the nature and value of discourse doesn't in itself make us better language users, any more than studying ethics makes us better people. But it can enlarge our knowledge of discursive ideologies—those political no less than intellectual commitments that motivate people, including ourselves, to use language in particular ways, react differently to the language uses of others, and draw different conclusions about the authority, value, or significance of language acts. On occasion, this thinking about the meaning of meaning can have not merely intellectual but also practical value for recognizing and modifying ideological convictions—changing our minds about what we think and say and do.

Let's explore this last point in more detail because the knowledge available from conscious reflection on stories about the meaning of meaning is not as academic and esoteric as it might appear. It's true that everyday life, the world of George and Louise, is normally a low-stakes environment for rhetorical reflectiveness: the casual embrace of our personal discursive prejudices is adequate for getting through the day. But language plays many important roles in our lives, and sometimes the stakes are higher than merely the best interpretation of the sale date on a milk carton. Consider the basic, and usually straightforward, act of naming as a case in point. Naming—or representation—is one of the most familiar and important acts that language enables us to perform, and it is usually routine since most names enjoy broad social agreement. Sometimes, however, names are contested, and when they are, the reason is often more than academic: the disagreements can affect people's lives. Louise, for example, disagrees with the letter to the editor that names Palestinian militants as freedom fighters because she is convinced that the militants are terrorists. George refers to the rising Hispanic population as aliens rather than immigrants. Examples of high-stakes naming abound in the world of everyday life: Is someone who reports criminal conduct a police informant or a snitch? Is a social program favoring minority groups affirmative action or reverse discrimination? Is abortion about the right to life or the right to choose? Is evolution about natural selection or intelligent design? Does the practice of allowing people to choose their preferred elementary school constitute neighborhood bonding or segregation? Was the European conquest of the American Indian genocide or "manifest destiny"? Did the admissions policy of the medical school at UC Davis constitute an equal opportunity program or an unfair quota system—as the Supreme Court named it in the lengthy text of its 1978 decision in Bakke v. University of California? (Names can be texts of any size, not just nouns or noun phrases.) What is clear in each of these instances is that contested naming is not a trivial debate. How someone or something is named determines what the person or the thing *is*, and participants in the debate understand that the outcome has public consequences for how people are going to be treated, how people will act, and how the world is going to be understood.

Contested names, like *terrorist* versus *freedom fighter*, bring into sharp relief questions at the heart of any story about discourse. What exactly does a name name? And what is the basis for a name's authority? Any such story includes a theme concerning reference, sometimes proposing, as we have already seen, that words point to worlds outside of language, sometimes contending that words constitute worlds inside the mind, or inside language itself, and sometimes offering mediations of these alternatives. The subtleties of reference are merely intellectual when the name *rutabaga* appears on a grocery list. But names like *literacy* or *freedom* or *globalization* or *ethnic cleansing* transport the intellectual issue into arenas of social, political, and other debate where the assumptions behind naming significantly shape the nature of public discussion. Let's grant Louise her contention that the Palestinians are terrorists, not freedom fighters (since for present purposes her choice is not pertinent to the discussion). What Louise believes about naming does not determine her view of the militants—that view depends on what she believes about geopolitics, or about violence, or about Arabs. But it affects the way she understands the worth or validity of her opinion, the way she responds to alternative points of view, the willingness she may have to reconsider her position, and the strategies she may use to persuade others that her view is correct. Her belief may even affect the authority she enjoys as a namer since that authority depends in part on the social legitimacy of her belief, the number of other people who understand the reliability of verbal statement in the same way she does. Louise is in competition with other namers, and she can't escape the obvious fact that some people see the Palestinians as freedom fighters. How she (or anyone) responds to the dissonance of contested names depends on her assumptions, whether tacit or examined, about what names name and how reliably they do it. Her assumptions constitute a discursive ideology where beliefs about language support, and are supported by, the power arrangements of public discussion.

Were Louise to consult the "anthology" of Western rhetoric, she would discover a surprisingly rich variety of theoretical responses to the question, what do names name? Here is an inventory of abbreviated alternatives, each of which I will introduce more formally, in its particular narrative context, later. One response is implicit in the biblical story of God speaking the world into existence ("God *said*, 'Let there be light'") and then authorizing Adam to name its natural variety. Naming is viewed here as a magical or sacred act, where a supernatural agency composes the "presence" of reality in words. If Louise accepts this view, then the letter writer in the newspaper is incorrect in naming the militants freedom fighters because, in effect, God has provided us with the ability to recognize them as terrorists: the thing is immanent in the name. A second response is that naming is an ontological act, where metaphysical constants (Being) that underlie the world's experiential complexity (Becoming) make it possible to define names with philosophical reliability as they refer to things beyond language. If Louise accepts that view, then the writer is incorrect because we know the definition of *terrorist* and can determine with metaphysical confidence that militant Palestinians fit the definition. Both magical and ontological theories argue that names name a reality beyond themselves, but they differ in supposing either a sacred or a rational basis for the connection. A third response is that naming entails empirical analysis, where the gradual accretion of evidence reveals with increasing precision the appropriateness of a particular representation. Names in this account denote concepts—mental constructs—derived from ranges of experiential information, not fixed realities that exist prior to conceptualization. Through observation and testing, references are established that correspond "objectively" to external experience. If Louise believes this view, then, in principle, the Palestinians may or may not be terrorists, and what we must do to determine the editorial writer's objective truthfulness is gather proof of the viability of the name he prefers.

A fourth response is that naming is an imaginative act in which human needs and predispositions invest experience with meaning. If Louise believes that view, she is obliged to concede that the writer is entitled to name the Palestinians as freedom fighters if his values, assumptions, and experiences of the world make such a conclusion meaningful. But then she is equally free, for the same reasons, to contest the writer's opinion on the basis of her own values. Names in this theory name mental constructs, just as they do in the empirical perspective, but the difference is that meaning is at least as subjective as it is objective. A fifth response is that naming is a social process dependent on the material interactions of language users who name according to the perspectives they share. As such, naming constitutes a political struggle, a kind of collective bargaining, in which opposing groups vie for the authority to control a discourse. The struggle entails the exercise of power, and the group that prevails in the representation sets the terms of meaning. If Louise believes this view, she recognizes the need to invoke or marshal political support for her position in order to resist and challenge the power of the newspaper account. A sixth response is that naming is part of a language game motivated by desire and need that enables us to create humanly satisfying illusions of coherence. The opposition of *terrorist* and *freedom fighter* is a rhetorical fiction, intrinsically mischievous and unstable but used to manipulate debate by appeal to a strategic binary, one term of which is privileged. If Louise believes this view, then she understands that the letter writer's representation may be deconstructed, revealing the manipulative logic that sustains it, in order to subvert a conclusion she finds unsatisfying. Louise knows, however, that her own view is a no less bracketed and tentative judgment because the question is ultimately undecidable by any appeal beyond

the human need to reach some psychically gratifying, albeit imperma-
nent, closure.

Obviously, some of these accounts have enjoyed greater prestige than
others in the discursive common sense of European culture. But all of
them provide bases from which to make and appraise the value of discursive statements. If Louise were to engage consciously in a process of
comparing them, she might recognize that they offer an array of possibilities in the context of which she can identify, examine, confirm, or
reconsider the commitments she brings to the project of naming the
Palestinian militants. If she has been unreflectively assuming, for example, that the issue is settled by rational definition, grounded in a priori
judgments about the behaviors of Palestinian militants, then she's likely
to have been comfortable in the view that the letter writer is simply illogical, failing to understand the definition of *terrorist*. But if she were to recognize that there are alternative possibilities, then her confidence in her
own prejudices might be harder to maintain. If Louise can understand,
say, the competing belief that names are decided by a gathering of objective evidence, then she may also be able to appreciate the reasonableness of a more tentative stance about her opinion that the Palestinians
are terrorists, reexamining both the writer's evidence and her own.
Dissonance in that case might provide a cause for reflection. An awareness of competing perspectives may also help Louise to identify the
commitments, and the strategies of persuasion, that others might bring
to the debate. Is the letter writer implying that his meaning has a metaphysical claim to truth? Louise might have little patience with an appeal
she perceives to be based on fundamentalist conviction. And if the writer
truly believes the militants have been named by God, he is unlikely to
have much tolerance for the error, perhaps even the sin, of believing
they are other than what God has said they are. Or is the writer's opinion
grounded in personal experience of Palestinians and knowledge of their
historical grievances? If he believes that meanings derive from subjective
as much as objective responses to the world, then discussion and subsequent new learning may be possible. Louise's disgust at the violence and
cruelty of the militants' actions may be set against the writer's awareness
of Palestinian economic disenfranchisement and social dislocation in
the interest of negotiating their two points of view.

The matter is not quite as simple, however, as this mechanical illustration suggests. Stories about the nature of naming do not direct, or
even very effectively guide, people's verbal practices. Rather, they inform
practice, comment on it, and provide perspectives from which, self-
consciously, to ratify or critique it. Their distinctive statements on the

theme of naming, understood in the context of the whole anthology, simultaneously make their own persuasive gestures toward believability and offer counterpoint to the gestures of the others. Neither Louise nor the letter writer necessarily professes allegiance to any one of the six perspectives described above. Were Louise to appraise her position, the reason would not be to identify herself as a card-carrying ideologue of some particular stripe but to orient herself among possible options in a way that satisfies her standards of intellectual and ethical inquiry. The rhetorical perspectives represent, as an anthology, a dispersion of conceptual differences, a framework from within which to speculate about the sufficiency of one's beliefs and actions. Being reflective about discursive practice entails evaluating it by reference to all the stories one has encountered about the meaning of meaning, not choosing some preferable option isolated from the dynamic of internal debate and criticism that makes the anthology useful in the first place. On occasions when it matters, as in the case of high-stakes naming, Louise might scrutinize her beliefs and actions, such as her judgment about whether or not Palestinian militants are terrorists, by recalling the implicit conversation of the competing narratives, much as we invoke the stories of our "literary" experience in order to understand the complexities of our life experience. The alternative perspectives do not serve as orthodoxies restrictively governing the activities of language users. The fundamentalist at Church on Sunday morning feels no intellectual inconsistency, let alone remorse, when making a relative judgment at brunch about whether to throw out milk that has been kept past its sale date. Meanwhile, the relativist who finds labeling Palestinians as terrorists to be unreflective, foundationalist thinking might not hesitate to apply a label of her own, like fundamentalist, to the person judged to be so unreflective. Life isn't simple, and neither are stories. The six supposedly different narratives I've proposed as an anthology of Western rhetorical theory, while plausible enough, are themselves collectively a speculative fiction, *my* story about the variety of *those* stories.

RHETORICAL PERSPECTIVES: READING

High-stakes naming is only one arena in which a self-conscious awareness of beliefs about language, or the lack of self-consciousness, can have practical consequences. Another arena is high-stakes reading, where we are routinely required to make judgments about issues of intentionality, the authority or status of a particular text, the ethos of a writer, and the reliability of textual interpretation. Consider the reading of important

public documents, those afforded broad cultural or institutional significance, like the US Constitution, for example. George listens intently to
the televised grilling of a proposed Supreme Court nominee, recognizing that a battle has long raged in the congressional nominating process between those who favor strict construction of the Constitution and
those who argue for readings that adapt to changing historical circumstances. The precise theoretical issue is competing opinions about our
ability to deduce a writer's intent. One position argues for the possibility of identifying original, and stable, meanings across time and space,
presuming that the meanings are lodged in the text itself, accessible
to careful scrutiny. Another argues that original intent is mysterious
at best, that meaning is always located in the interpretive transactions
between readers and texts in specific cultural and historical circumstances. The stakes in this case are just as high as those in high-stakes
naming: Should children be allowed to pray in public schools because
judges claim to understand the literal intent of the framers' injunction
against making laws "prohibiting the free exercise" of religion? Should
people be denied the right to own assault rifles because judges claim
that a contemporary interpretation of "the right of the people to keep
and bear arms" must be modified to reflect the impertinence of an anti-
quated concept of "well regulated militia"? As in the case of contested
representations, the view a justice holds about discourse, in this case
authorial intent, does not resolve an argument about the right to pray
in the classroom or to own an AK-47; rather, it certifies the reasonableness, authority, or power of the position the judge chooses to adopt.
The strict construction argument allows us to say with conviction that
we do or don't accept prayer in public schools because we "know" what
the framers meant. The interpretation argument allows us to say that we
do or don't accept it because we "know" with equivalent conviction that
the constitution is a living document that must be read in the context
of contemporary values and issues. In short, beliefs about what writers,
texts, and readers can or cannot do inspire opposing frames of mind
from within which the arguments for or against school prayer are pursued and evaluated.

Another powerful contemporary example of discursive beliefs driving disputes about the authority of texts is the argument concerning the
Bible as a sacred book whose statements command assent even when
they pertain to the natural or social, not just the spiritual, world. The
discursive question in the case of a sacred book, unlike that of the US
Constitution, is not just the accessibility of authorial intent but, more
important, the ethos of the author, the status of the text as the revealed

Word of God, hence incapable of error or misrepresentation. For some believers, the truths of the Bible are presented literally in direct statement; for others, they derive from interpretive effort. In either case, God and his human agents are the writers; their intentions are pure, if not necessarily clear, and the text has a special power to enable communication between the worlds of the divine and the human. For those who believe in the literal meanings of the Bible, even such technical questions as the age of the earth and the origins of human beings are settled beyond any capacity to reopen them or improve upon their answers through alternative discourses such as geology or evolutionary biology. Even for those who assert the responsibility of readers to interpret the sacred book, and who acknowledge a difference between metaphorical and empirical statement, the theological, or social, or ethical meanings available in the Bible are, in principle, discernible and have the force of moral imperatives, once discerned, whether or not they have efficacy in scientific or other discourses. Meanwhile, there are other possible discursive ideologies from within which to view a text like the Bible. The secular reader may admire and value the Bible as literature without investing it with supernatural authority, or may acknowledge its historical interest and seek to match its stories to archeological or anthropological facts, or may criticize it as mere fable and point out its damaging contributions to ignorance or intolerance. In each instance, the disposition to be religious or not is abetted by alternative discursive beliefs.

Let me continue to clarify the relationship I have in mind between beliefs about words and our other beliefs, as well as our thoughts and actions. It isn't a person's view about the ethos of the Bible that leads to a decision about the truth of faith; rather, it is a commitment to belief or disbelief that conditions someone's understanding of the authority of a religious text. In the same way, it isn't a view of authorial intent that leads to someone's opinion about the meaning of the first or second amendment; rather, the commitment to a particular reading is abetted by an assumption regarding the accessibility of the Constitution's meanings. I'm not arguing that one's views about discourse *cause* other states of belief or dispositions to act. Instead, I'm arguing that those views play a variety of influential roles within still larger states of belief, affect the ways in which beliefs lead to actions, and condition our judgments about the views and actions of others. Whether we are talking about Louise's awareness of the alternative historical theories of representation (naming), or about George's self-consciousness about authorial intent, or about someone else's familiarity with religious and secular views of textual ethos, there are several benefits to the kind of rhetorical self-consciousness I'm depicting. One benefit lies in what we can learn about the motivating premises that people bring to their convictions. A second is more reflective awareness of our own beliefs, as they may be contextualized, and perhaps rendered more problematic, by alternative points of view. A third is the enhanced capacity to critique our own views and even change them if and when interrogation shows them to be faulty or insufficient. And a fourth is freedom from the tyranny of unexamined belief, whether one's own or someone else's. If George naively accepts the strict construction argument about the meanings in the Constitution because he is not familiar with alternative points of view, he risks intimidation by the manipulations of an appeal to higher authority—someone's certainty about what the framers meant. If he naively accepts the interpretation argument, he risks falling prey to the manipulations of an appeal to conveniently self-serving relativism, where someone else's conviction about the meaning of a constitutional amendment is supported by a discursive theory that allows, in principle, for as extravagant an imposition of a reader's will upon a text as is necessary to make it come out right. The contention that meanings are infinitely variable is neither more nor less evidently reliable than the contention that meanings are stable across time. Each view belongs to a discursive ideology that can marshal as many historical arguments, and that requires as much analytical scrutiny, as its alternative.

These qualifications notwithstanding, there are some special circumstances where the relationship between a theory of discourse and the advocacy of a position or an action is more or less directly causal. These circumstances arise most commonly in academic debate—the work of educators and scholars—since those who are specially versed in the language arts not surprisingly cultivate enhanced self-consciousness about the practices of language. In academic and educational settings, the conflicts among alternative discursive ideologies play out in the fuss and feathers of scholarly dispute, in classroom lore and method, in pedagogical theory, in curricular decision making, and ultimately in educational public policy. One ready example is the Great Books debate that has raged on and off for the past century, some people arguing that certain texts deserve iconic cultural status and others arguing that no texts offer meanings so intrinsically stable and timeless that they must be read even by people (often students) who fail to find them relevant or satisfying. The underlying issue in this argument is not the problem of how things are named, as in Louise's view of terrorists, or the problem of authorial intent, as in George's thinking about the Constitution, or the question of ethos in the Bible. Instead, it is the possibility of deriving a universal, reliable meaning, one to which any and all readers will assent, from the statements of a text. After all, the argument in favor of the existence of Great Books must depend on a degree of confidence that they offer the same knowledge to all who read them, a knowledge about the values and aspirations of the culture they inscribe, a knowledge of the attributes of the hero, a knowledge of right conduct and civic responsibility, a knowledge of good and evil. And the problem we inevitably face in the effort to sustain this confidence is the evidence from our own experience that texts do not so readily resolve to universal meanings.

It is a simple matter to show that even the most pedestrian text can have virtually as many readings as there are available readers. If one were to ask a group of readers, no matter their level of skill or sophistication, to write one sentence apiece representing the essential meaning of the paragraph immediately above, one would find versions of the following sentences, among others: *Sometimes a view of discourse leads directly to other beliefs and to actions. Academics have a sophisticated awareness of the problem of reading. Some people believe in Great Books and others don't. Different people don't get the same ideas from a given text. Great Books inscribe the culture. We can't believe in Great Books unless we believe in the possibility of universal meaning. The central problem in the Great Books debate is different from that of debates about naming or authorial intent.* I know that this range is possible, and can be readily extended, because I've asked readers to engage in the exercise. So, the question is not, do readers come to different conclusions about the meaning of a text? The question is, what accounts for the differences? And the answer to that question takes us back to the earlier enumeration of rhetorical perspectives. Here are six ways of accounting for the differences: (1) Some readings are wrong headed because sin and the wiles of the devil have clouded readers' judgments. This is hardly a common position in secular discourse today, but it has worked powerfully during those ages when heretics roamed the land and in circumstances when the text at stake enjoyed greater cultural standing than my paragraph can hope to achieve. (2) Some readings are wrong because readers lack the training or discipline or learning or enlightenment to identify the logical paraphrase that exists at the center of this or any text and that accounts for its coherence. (3) Different readings are right or wrong to differing degrees, depending on readers' familiarity with the context of the text, their knowledge of the author, the genre, the historical moment, the texts on which this text is based, and the prose surrounding this particular paragraph. The more reliable the contextual knowledge, the more plausible the reading. (4) Alternative readings are inevitable, but all readings are plausible in principle because every reader will see the text from a particular vantage point, reflecting personal experience. (5) Isolated readings inevitably vary, but meanings are ultimately social in nature, so a community of readers, with time to compare their interpretations, can reach group consensus that some readings are, for that group at that moment, more acceptable than others. (6) Texts suffer from an extravagant abundance of meaning, and any particular reading reflects the unruly play of signification, signs modifying other signs to produce psychically (not to say practically) necessary, but also misleading and unstable, fictions of coherence.

The interplay of these theoretical options—the conceptual constellation they define—creates the basis for competing arguments about the Great Books, leading to their acceptance or rejection in schools, to particular kinds of teaching (which either limit or multiply the meanings found in texts), to curricula that include or ignore Great Books, and to public policy that ties Great Books or some other set of texts to cultural enrichment or decay, personal growth or alienation, learning or ignorance, and even economic advantage or decline. Feminist critics, looking at the vast array of masculine and Caucasian authors in the traditional literary canon, have self-consciously posed arguments derived from expressivist, sociological, and deconstructive viewpoints (about which more later) in order to challenge cultural hegemony by representing history itself as a text, as a story of struggle in which white males, the political winners, have written women out of the text, erasing their writings even as they erased their bodies. The feminist critical response has been to "revise" the text, to write women back into history by recovering long unpublished or never published women writers, by arguing for the canonical stature of better-known women writers, by identifying women's ways of writing, and by subverting the canon altogether, exposing its self-justifying fictions of heritage, phallocentric superiority, and aesthetic objectivity. Conservative cultural critics, sometimes consciously invoking Aristotelian metaphysics, have in turn responded to such assaults with arguments about Shakespeare's transcendent genius, conveyed through classic works that speak to people of all times and places, regardless of superficial distinctions of gender, race, and ethnicity. They reaffirm the capacity of Great Books to celebrate and pass along to new generations the fundamental verities of Western civilization. These academic arguments are not merely opinionated stances about what or how to teach, with inarticulate assumptions about language lurking unexamined behind the commitments. They are arguments about language itself, constituting a struggle in which discursive ideologies overtly display their competing claims to authority through the expositions of literary, rhetorical, aesthetic, psychological, and educational theory.

SIX STORIES ABOUT DISCOURSE

In all these instances, then—whenever issues of high-stakes naming, intentionality in texts, the ethos of authors, and the accessibility of textual meaning arise in public settings—an awareness of competing theoretical perspectives on language and discourse can offer not just intellectual interest but practical opportunity for more reflective thinking and acting. So, I want to turn now to a review of six alternative Western rhetorical theories with those advantages, practical as well as intellectual, in mind. But before elaborating the six "stories" about the meaning of meaning that I've sketched here in summary, let me add a few additional stipulations and clarifications, beginning with some terms that will come up repeatedly in the accounts to follow. By the word *rhetoric* I mean the theory and practice of public discourse, the arts of communication, argument, narrative, and persuasion. Western rhetoric has two historical dimensions, one philosophical and the other technical, to use the terminology of George Kennedy (Kennedy 1999). I will have little to say about the latter cookbook tradition, but disappointed readers may find recipes aplenty, from the classical *Rhetorica ad Herennium* to the panoply of modern composition textbooks. By *discourse* I mean what Ludwig Wittgenstein (1968) meant by "language game," a system of conventions governing the game's players (speakers, writers, hearers, readers), together with the objectives, strategies, tactics, motives, moves, and rewards that shape its play. Discourse can refer either to language use in general or to a specific set of conventions, those governing legal discourse, for example, as opposed to medical or scientific discourse. Rhetoric is about discourse. By *text* I mean a particular language act, a spoken or written statement that has been constructed according to the conventions of a discourse. The history of rhetoric in Europe is notably a history of the definitions of the word. *Rhetoric* has been defined very restrictively in some theoretical perspectives, the study of "the available means of persuasion," for example, according to Aristotle, who limits its domain exclusively to spoken, natural language in three discourses—the political assembly, the law court, and the ceremonial occasion. But it has also had all-inclusive definitions, where virtually any form of signifying activity—painting, football, cinema, mathematics, ritual, clothing fashions, structures of kinship, dance—not just natural language activity, is regarded as discursive and therefore rhetorical. My definition will encourage a broader range of applications (and therefore of historical writers whose theories I'll regard as rhetorical) than Aristotle would have recognized, including more than linguistic signs, but it will avoid constituting rhetoric as a Theory of Everything to preserve the hope of distinguishing some things from others.

In the chapters to follow, I use the word *story* in the sense of *account* more than in the sense of *fiction*, although I'm pleased to play on the suggestion of fictionality that the word conveys. The six stories, or accounts, that I will read and write (the dialectic is inescapable) cluster around a common theme, which could be expressed as a question: what encourages us to believe that language acts are meaningful? Each story's answer to the question constitutes its elaboration of the theme, its positing of what I will call a "ground of meaningfulness." The stories constitute discursive ideologies, serving to "explain" the nature of language and its uses, its relationships to self and world, announcing the "truths" that permit users to trust the efficacy of discourse. The six stories are titled "Magical Rhetoric," "Ontological Rhetoric," "Objectivist Rhetoric," "Expressivist Rhetoric," "Sociological Rhetoric," and "Deconstructive Rhetoric." Their sequence should not be taken to imply historical progression or intellectual privilege. They simply make up my anthology. In sum, I'll argue that discourse is meaningful in magical rhetoric because of the intrinsic power of utterance; in ontological rhetoric because of the relationship between language and metaphysics; in objectivist rhetoric because of the relationship between language and phenomenal experience; in expressivist rhetoric because of the relationship between language and consciousness or imagination; in sociological rhetoric because of the material intersubjectivity of language users; and in deconstructive rhetoric because of the situatedness of subjects within the intertextuality of verbal statements. Each "ground" serves to distinguish its story about the meaning of meaning from that of the other stories, and each may also be critiqued from any vantage point except its own.

What makes the stories important is the role they play, largely behind the scenes, as discursive ideologies in the discourses that most matter to us as people and citizens: religion, education, public policy, science, law, history, and others. Magical rhetoric informs our sacred books, the Bible, for example, or the Quran. Ontological rhetoric underlies the inerrancy arguments of Christian fundamentalists and also the arguments that Justice Antonin Scalia of the US Supreme Court poses regarding "textualism," his version of the strict construction view of the Constitution. Objectivist rhetoric informs not only scientific and technological discourse but also the No Child Left Behind and Common Core legislation that governs our schools and directs so much attention to educational assessment. Discussions of literacy reflect the differences among several rhetorical perspectives, not coincidentally placing different positions at loggerheads: objectivism supports "functional" literacy arguments; ontological rhetoric informs E. D. Hirsch's (1988) "cultural" literacy; expressivist rhetoric underlies "personal growth" arguments; and sociological rhetoric informs the "critical" pedagogy of Paulo Freire (1969) and Jonathan Kozol (1985). Jean Piaget's (2002) views of child development are objectivist, proposing that infants begin as individual beings and grow through education into social beings; Lev Vygotsky's (1962) views are sociological and propose the opposite, that infants begin as social beings and, through education, gradually differentiate as individuals. Historiography since the seventeenth century has been informed by objectivist rhetoric, emphasizing the empirically based reliability of statements about the past, but counterarguments about the interpretative, unstable, narrative nature of history from Nietzsche to Hayden White have proceeded from the perspective that I'm calling deconstructive rhetoric. Ontological rhetoric offer us conservative values like social stability and enduring truth, objectivist rhetoric valorizes progress through technological ingenuity, expressivist rhetoric emphasizes the importance of the individual and of personal liberties, sociological and deconstructive rhetoric—more radical perspectives by American standards—offer possibilities of political critique and social change. In short, the different assumptions and beliefs featured in these stories work together, and also work against each other, to create the fabric of American public discourse. The stories collectively ratify the meaning of meaning for our culture at this historical moment.

Before proceeding, however, it's important to understand the status of these stories. Simply put, they are my readings of a sampling of texts from the Western rhetorical tradition and occasionally other texts (like the Bible or Karl Popper) that some scholars might not choose to classify as rhetorical at all. I will invoke signatures from the past and present in order to name sources from which my readings/writings derive, but I do not contend that my stories are copies of theirs. Aristotle, Coleridge, and Derrida have told their own stories, whatever they may be, and I tell mine having been provoked by theirs. Including six stories, rather than four or nine, in the anthology has been, philosophically speaking, a somewhat arbitrary decision. It isn't important that there are six but only that the six are different. They are, in the ensemble, intended as a dispersion of intellectual oppositions, linked by appeal to their distinct ways of developing their shared theme. The advantage of the differential accounts is precisely their artificiality, their suppression of the (no doubt numerous) conceptual overlaps one could identify among Aristotle, Coleridge, and Derrida were one disposed to tell a story about continuities instead. In my story, these figures are different, discontinuous, and—inevitably—simplified, offering alternative maps of a conceptual terrain that otherwise would shift and blur beyond all hope of purposeful use. Can we speak of the six stories (or, for that matter, my story about them) as true or false? The answer, which should already have become clear, is a decisive yes or no, depending on what one believes about stories. Some of the six narratives about the nature of discourse depicted here are going to take themselves more seriously, as it were, than others do, and make claims for themselves that others do not. The answer to a question about truth and falsity is yes if the questioner speaks from within a more "serious" perspective that regards the question as meaningful. For example, if one agrees with the conditions of an ontological (say, an Aristotelian) perspective, it becomes both possible and necessary to decide the truth or falsity of other positions. But it's impossible, and indeed meaningless, to speak of deciding the issue from within a deconstructive perspective, where stories amplify but neither falsify nor displace others. My story about these stories, meanwhile, does not claim a transcendent position outside the constellation of perspectives they depict, a seventh, master perspective kept secret throughout discussion of the other six. My own preferred location (at the moment) within the intertextuality of these stories necessitates conceding that it's impossible to remove oneself to a place outside them all in order to judge their sufficiency. We must speak from *somewhere*, and any location conditions what we are entitled to claim.

A final caveat: my anthology is necessarily limited in scope to the extent that a project of reading Western rhetoric is plainly not a project of reading Chinese or Arabic or Indonesian rhetoric. Wherever there is language, there is culture, and wherever there is culture, there is rhetoric—practices of discourse. It follows that there are many stories about the meaning of meaning not encompassed within the cultural framework of the West. The qualification is important, not only because it's true but also because in its truth we're obliged to ponder the long history of colonization that Trinh Minh-ha, who will be discussed in chapter 7, attributes to Western philosophical, logical, rhetorical, and linguistic thought. Restricting my focus to European rhetoric, as I propose to do, arguably risks disparaging other cultural traditions by overlooking them, or worse, appropriating them by appeal to an uncritical assumption that they all somehow derive from European roots. Acknowledging the diversity of world rhetorics while nonetheless restricting my focus to the West, I hope to respect rather than erase cultural difference. It's problematic, on one hand, to exclude other rhetorics without implying myopia or superiority. But on the other hand, the elaboration of a framework of grounds of meaningfulness, understood to be saturated in the epistemological assumptions of European culture, cannot legitimately incorporate rhetorics of other cultures that aren't similarly saturated, except at cost of alleging the existence of rhetorical universals and creating a totalizing narrative in which some handful—however large—of chosen rhetorics becomes the master representation of World Rhetoric. Numerous scholars, notably George Kennedy (Kennedy 1998), have written about and continue to explore contrastive features of the world's many rhetorics. Some have avoided the trap of totalization, although Kennedy himself, overtly pursuing the hunt for universals, has not. I commend their efforts—Han Fei Tzu's theory of audience in forensic oratory is not less significant than Aristotle's. But I also hear the stern warning of Molefi Asante about intellectual imperialism when he insists upon the distinctively African foundations of *nommo*, "the generative and productive power of the spoken word," in *The Afro-Centric Idea* (Asante 1987, 17). He joins Minh-ha in conjuring the specter of the anthropologist whose presumptuous, all-seeing eye—the eye of European objectivism—can recognize "other" rhetorics in no forms beyond those of the West. My stories are local . . . as are all stories.

2
MAGICAL RHETORIC

The story of magical rhetoric is not commonly discussed in histories of Western discourse theory, partly because of the mostly religious rather than secular contexts of word magic and partly because of the proprietary claims of Greco-Roman rhetoric and European enlightenment rationalism. The tradition clearly deserves recognition, however, according to the definitions I offered in chapter 1, where rhetoric is understood as the study and practice of public discourse, and discourse is understood as language in action—speaking, listening, writing, and reading. Magical rhetoric, which may include prayer, prophecy, spells, or incantations (as instances of magical composition), and the interpretation of holy books (an example of magical reading), refers to the discourse of the sacred, a theory and practice of language conditioned by the assumption that the world is, to quote Gerard Manley Hopkins, "charged with the grandeur of God" ("God's Grandeur," 1877). I don't intend the word *magic* to denote verbal trickery or hocus-pocus, or still less to disparage belief by trivializing the Word of God through association with the carnival events of a culture grown jaded about the magical tradition. I propose instead to reclaim an array of meanings derived from study of the nature of religious sensibility—in anthropology, works such as James Frazier's (1959) *The Golden Bough* and Bronislaw Malinowski's (1948) *Magic, Science, and Religion*; in psychology, Freud's (2000) *Totem and Taboo* and William James's (1964) *Varieties of Religious Experience*; in philosophy, Ernst Cassirer's (1955) *Philosophy of Symbolic Forms*; and in history of religion, Mircea Eliade's (1959) *The Sacred and the Profane*. While the complexities of the world of the sacred lie beyond our scope, a gesture of orientation may eliminate any suggestion that magical rhetoric lacks the intellectual or cultural *gravitas* to rub conceptual shoulders with the likes of Aristotle and Kristeva. Briefly, magic derives its power from its immersion in the sacred, a realm of space and time that may or may not be conventionally religious but that is characterized by an aura of felt universality, cosmic order, spiritual power and

DOI: 10.7330/9780874219364.c002

agency, mystery, dread, and awe. According to Mircea Eliade, the sacred is perceived by believers to be the absolute and pervasive fabric of reality "which transcends this world but manifests itself in this world, thereby sanctifying it and making it real" (Eliade 1959, 202). Suzanne Langer refers to magic as a special kind of "language," a form of symbolic action that is "part and parcel of that greater phenomenon, *ritual*, which is the language of religion" (Langer 1973, 49). Ritual, for Langer, is "the formalization of overt behavior in the presence of the Sacred," an "articulation of feelings" peculiar to the circumstances of a profound and enveloping experience of holiness or sanctity (152). The particular feelings of the religious sensibility include, according to Clifford Geertz, "moods we sometimes lump together under such covering terms as 'reverential,' 'solemn,' or 'worshipful' (Geertz 1973, 97), relating to a general sense of sublimity or awe that "springs from entertaining a conception of all-pervading vitality" (98). Consistent with Langer, he regards ritual as "consecrated behavior" (112), a practice giving shape and solemnity to religious belief that "engulfs the whole person, transporting him, so far as he is concerned, into another mode of existence" (120). Magic is one manifestation of this consecrated behavior, a practice of using tokens, images, charms, gestures, or special acts of language to influence people, events, or the natural world or to summon or beseech supernatural agencies.

Ernst Cassirer, a neo-Kantian philosopher whose work frequently explores the nature of myth, argues that magic requires the conviction that the natural, human, and supernatural worlds are all concretely, immediately, and intensely interrelated. Magic is always "sympathetic," he writes in *An Essay on Man*, for human beings "would not think of coming into a magical contact with nature" if they were not already convinced that "there is a common bond that unites all things." Citing an ancient Stoic concept of the "sympathy of the Whole," he insists that we cannot grasp the power or efficacy of magic by framing it within rationalist traditions dominated by metaphysical or mechanical concepts of space, time, individuation, and causality. It is obviously illogical to presume that some mysterious action at a distance between two dissimilar objects is taking place when a voodoo doll's defacement causes pain to an actual human being or when a prayer's intercession is credited with a healing effect. Magic erases distance, temporality, and difference, conceives the multiplicity of the world in terms of underlying unity, and understands that the apparent "separation . . . between the different kinds of natural objects is, after all, an artificial, not a real one" (Cassirer 1965, 94). Once understood that everything affects and influences everything else, that there is a "breath diffused throughout the universe which imparts to all things the tension by which they are held together" (95), there is no longer a limitation on what may serve as cause and what may constitute its effect, what may temporally precede or follow, what might be designated present or absent. When all times and spaces are blended, there is only here and now. Hence, prophecy, for instance, which is a species of magical rhetoric, is not foretelling the future but rather witnessing an eternal present. Cassirer illustrates this unity of space and time by appeal to ritual festivities among tribes in the Trobriand Islands, where during the "sacred season" the people are joined by their spirit ancestors, who sit "perched in the trees" watching younger members of the tribe conduct magical dances and rejoicing with them in the harvest. The dancers are "fused with all things in nature," they are in social communion, and "their joy is felt by the whole of nature and shared by their ancestors." For the duration of the dancing, "space and time have vanished; the past has become the present; the golden age of mankind has come back" (95). In the "sympathetic" atmosphere of the sacred, objects, physical movements, and words become charged with magical powers. In the case of magical language, whether naming or mythic story, prayer, or incantation, a word is so entwined with its reference, so embedded in a world of intimate verbal and nonverbal relations, as to have power to evoke and influence whatever it is linked with, whether thing, being, or event, because the name and the thing are effectively extensions of each other. Magical rhetoric, then, is a view of discourse that presumes, within the sphere of the sacred, that words—names, incantations, oaths, curses, prophecies, prayers, blessings, and covenants, among other usages— affect the world beyond language, influence people and things, create supernatural effects, control events, and gain supplicatory access to the infinite: "Nothing resists the magic word" (110).

Obviously, magical rhetoric does not belong to the routine world of daily life, and it has only specialized impact in modern European culture compared to the pervasively rational discourses that have come, over centuries, to condition our ordinary (Western) experience. That doesn't mean, however, that magic is no longer a relevant form of rhetorical practice. Geertz points out that no human being, in any culture, lives in the realm of the sacred all the time. Magic has always been identified with special times or situations, as much so for the Trobrianders as for us. In our culture, magical rhetoric continues to seize the imagination, articulate the beliefs, and stimulate the reverence and awe of contemporary believers, although, to be sure, people react in different settings with varying degrees of seriousness, including sincere conviction, token regard, and even amusement. It finds most earnest voice, as it always has, in religious ritual: people read the Bible as the Word of God; they listen reverently to the sermons of ministers; they sing hymns of praise; they pray and believe their prayers are heard; they are ritually named, and sometimes renamed, in baptismal and confirmation ceremonies; some of them, specially ordained as priests, are privileged to say "This is my body" and bread is transubstantiated, or "I absolve you" and a penitent's sins are forgiven; in some religions, bishops have authority to make *ex cathedra* pronouncements that cannot err in spiritual matters. Other language acts transport the aura of magical language from the sacred into the profane: people say grace at meals; witnesses swear on a sacred book to affirm their truthfulness; people sing the national anthem; public servants take oaths of office; politicians erect monuments to the Ten Commandments; children intone the pledge of allegiance to affirm their patriotism; people visit astrologers; they pray for rain; at death, relatives carve their names on stone slabs. "The dispositions which religious rituals induce," Geertz explains, have their most important impact "outside the boundaries of the ritual itself as they reflect back to color the individual's conception of the established world of bare fact" (Geertz 1973, 119). We don't all react with equal seriousness to magical acts of language, and some of us react with skepticism to them all. But large numbers of people continue to engage in those acts with great sincerity, and even the most jaded may well resort to prayer in times of stress, or "swear to God" to insist on their honesty.

THE BIBLE

In magical rhetoric the ground of meaningfulness is the intrinsic power of utterance, a reverential or awe-filled belief in the interanimation of language and the world, where words do not merely correspond to some independent reality but rather fuse with it so completely that the enunciation of names is equivalent to the control of things and the influencing of events. There is no better extended enactment of this view of language than what can be found in the Bible, that ancient storehouse of myths, legends, songs, prayers, parables, and teachings that has stood for centuries as the sacred book of Judeo-Christian culture. "In the beginning was the Word," says the Gospel according to John, "and the Word was with God, and the Word was God. He was in the beginning with God; all things were made through Him. . . . In him was life, and the life was the light of men. The light shines in the darkness, and the darkness has not overcome it" (1 John :1–6 [Revised Standard Version]).

John's statement precisely identifies the source of verbal meaningfulness in the domain of the sacred as the intrinsic power of words, and it is remarkable for several reasons. First, as a gloss on Genesis, it proclaims that language was present at the beginning, not a mere instrument that God created subsequently for human use but a power coeval with God. Language is the "voice" of God's will by which the world was spoken into existence; it is the vocabulary and syntax of reality. Hence, language does not merely name preexisting things but instead creates them through the divine act of naming. Second, as the passage goes on, there is a rich fusion of *Word* and *God*: initially, language is a distinct medium, a "being" related to God ("in the beginning was the Word"); then, it is identified as God's "voice" ("the Word was with God"); and finally it is equated with God, literally divine on its own terms. Third, the unified reference, God/Word, is identified not only as the creator of nature but also as the inspiration of human life, the "light of men" whose vitality is a beacon leading human beings through the darkness of the world. Fourth, there is a suggestion, evolving through the passage, of the correlation of God/Word with the incarnate Christ, the Word among men, the incarnation not only of God but of language as well. "And the Word became flesh and dwelt among us, full of grace and truth" (I John:14). This is not an occasion for interpretive riffs regarding the theology of John's Gospel. Whatever theological import experts might ascribe to the intersections of *God* and *Word*, we offer here only the straightforward, secular interpretation that the Gospel's opening passage testifies to the authority of language, establishes its affiliation with divinity, reassures believers that it continues to connect them to divinity, and praises the role of language in illuminating their path through the darkness.

The Bible is, throughout, a cornucopia of ideas about the magical or divine properties of language, rendered for the most part in dramatic form. It's an inexhaustible repository of commands, blessings, oaths, prophecies, namings, hymns, promises, laws, orations, prayers, covenants, chants, incantations, curses, lies, and temptations, all providing a tacit commentary on the intrinsic power of utterance. Moreover, the Bible, when conceived as a sacred book, is itself an act of language with powers that separate it from other texts. The Bible finds its own mythic origins in God's verbal covenant with the Israelites, described in Exodus, when the "two tablets of the testimony" are initially "written with the finger of God" (Exodus 31:18). More important, after Moses destroys the first set of tablets, appalled at the Israelites' idolatrous behavior, God initially promises to write a second edition: "I will write upon the tables the words that were on the first tables, which you broke" (Exodus 34:1).

But when God and Moses come together again on Sinai, God directs Moses to do the writing instead: "Write these words; in accordance with these words I have made a covenant with you and with Israel." After forty days and nights, Moses "wrote upon the tables the words of the covenant, the ten commandments" (Exodus 34:28). The power of God's writing is now, through the mythic account, transferred to humanity, the resulting "scripture" a human artifact although its writer is inspired by God. The holiness of this sacred scripture is symbolized in God's subsequent instruction to "make me a sanctuary"—a "tabernacle" that will contain the "ark of the testimony"—so that, as the people of Israel continue their journey to the Promised Land, "I may dwell in their midst" (Exodus 25:8). God provides elaborate instructions for the manufacture of the tabernacle (Exodus 36–40), and once this house for the Word of God is built, the text clearly emphasizes the magical properties associated with the sacred writing. A "cloud covered the tent of meeting, and the glory of the Lord filled the tabernacle," and from that time forward "throughout all their journeys," whenever the cloud surrounded the tabernacle, "the people of Israel would go onward," but whenever the cloud was absent, they would remain until its return; the "cloud of the Lord was upon the tabernacle by day, and fire was in it by night, in the sight of all the house of Israel" (Exodus 40:38). This sense of the awful presence and power of the sacred book is frequently echoed in the New Testament (sometimes called the new covenant), no less than in the Old, as in the conclusion of the Gospel according to Luke: "Then he said to them, 'These are my words which I spoke to you, while I was still with you, that everything written about me in the law of Moses and the prophets and the psalms must be fulfilled. Then he opened their minds to understand the scriptures, and said to them, 'Thus it is written . . . '" (Luke 24:44–45).

"Myth," Langer observes, "is the indispensable forerunner of metaphysics" (Langer 1973, 201), a narrative, dramatic, prelogical rendering of beliefs about the coherence and unity of the world, the nature of humanity, and the purposeful relationship between human beings and the cosmos. The expressive form of the passage from John's Gospel clearly suggests mythic rather than philosophical thinking, with its oracular voice, mingling of human and divine, framing of origins, and evocation of metamorphosis (the transubstantiation of the Word). Similarly mythic in form are the dramatic narrative of the Tablets, symbolizing the origins of law, coauthored by God and humans, and the magical representation of the Ark of the Covenant, leading the Israelites on their epic journey surrounded by signs of the presence of God. Yet these mythic renderings also anticipate discussions of theology, ontology (the nature of being), psychology, ethics, natural law, philosophy of language, semantics, and other theoretical issues. What we find in the Bible is a web of such stories, metaphorical statements that will be reworked over time into philosophical concepts but which contain in themselves rich explorations of theoretical questions. The issue of naming is a good example, represented in Genesis as a story about God's creative power, later to be understood philosophically as one of the most important functions of linguistic signs. Genesis is clear that creating and naming are equivalent. A verbal command initiates the process of creation ("God said, 'Let there be light'"), ordering the world into existence, and subsequent verbal actions distribute the world into its array of forms, species, and functions ("God separated the light from the darkness"[Genesis 1:3–4]). Through additional creative utterances, he formalizes the distinction between light and dark ("God called the light Day, and the darkness he called Night" [5]), identifies "evening" and "morning" (5), and finally, "seasons" and "years" (14), thereby creating time, a measure, initially, of the succession of his creative acts. He proceeds to name into existence, and similarly differentiate, the "waters" and the "firmament," and then the "vegetation" of the firmament, including its genera and species ("each according to its kind" [11]), and then "the lights in the firmament of the heavens" (14). Finally, he names "the beasts of the earth according to their kinds" (25). There is, of course, a familiar semantic theory dramatized here, that words *denote*, thereby enabling the designation and distinction of things. But the implication in this series of creative assertions is more interesting, consistent with a magical theory of language: that things do not actually become things until they are named. The word constitutes the thing in the process of calling it forth.

This is not to suggest equivalence between the view in Genesis and such later, subjectivist philosophical perspectives as Cartesian rationalism and Kantian idealism, where language is also conceived to play an active role in constituting the world. We'll discuss later some parallel thinking that reveals the truth of Langer's observation about myth serving as the prelogical foundation of metaphysics, such as Samuel Coleridge's (1965) invoking of Genesis to describe human creativity in *Biographia Literaria*. But in the mythic world of the Bible there is not the least suggestion of the rational concept of human subjectivity that will come eventually to bedevil skeptical European philosophy. One consequential difference (among others to be discussed later) is that there is no mediation in the Biblical naming myth between *word* and *thing*, no idea or notion or concept, no *human* consciousness forming the meaning of the word. In Genesis, God is the omnipotent, encompassing subjectivity from which the world proceeds, and language is the voice of God, in effect equivalent to God Himself. God does not think the world into existence and then name it: God *said*, "Let there be light." We have as testimony to the direct relationship between name and reality both the narrative in Genesis and the interpretation in John: "the Word was God." Language is neither denotative (signifying things) nor connotative (signifying the human valuation of things) since both of these functions presume the human mind's mediating, ideational activity. To be sure, the connotative function is dramatized in some of the speech acts that surround the naming process in Genesis. For example, as the world of things is differentiated over the succession of six "days," God sees that his creation is "good," particularly the animate world of living beings, fish, birds, and animals, the "swarms of living creatures," so He "blesses" the living world, saying "Be fruitful and multiply" (Genesis 1:22). This blessing signifies not the brute fact of the world's existence but its importance in the eyes of God, suggesting that language not only names but also evaluates, stamping things with judgments of approbation or disapproval, creating hierarchies on the basis of the favor bestowed on different categories of things. But finally, the biblical story of naming is mythic, not analytical, and its clear emphasis is the magical, not merely the semantic, power of language, whether creating the world in Genesis or creating the new church in Matthew 16:17–18, when Jesus renames Simon Bar-Jona as Peter, the "rock" (in Greek, *petra*), founding Christianity by uttering a magic word.

Following the naming and blessing of the animal kingdom, God speaks "man" into existence, fashioning humanity "in the image of God," and not only blesses this god-like being but also declares that he shall "have dominion" over the rest of the world (Genesis 1:26–28; 5:1–2). To enable human control of the world, God passes the power of naming to the first man (significantly, Adam is not actually named as such, that is, known by a proper name, until after the Fall). God brings "every beast of the field and every bird of the air" before man "to see what he would call them," and whatever name he gave, "that was its name" (Genesis 2:19). This is, of course, a second naming—a human naming by contrast to the initial divine naming—much as, later (though for different reasons), the Tablets of the Testimony are first written by God and subsequently by Moses. In each case, we see a ritual passing of God's verbal power to human beings. Both man and human language are equally formed "in the image of God." Significantly, man's naming of the richness of the living world takes place in the context of a passage about his loneliness—"it is not good that the man should be alone"—and about God's intent to "make him a helper fit for him" (Genesis 2:18). According to the logic of the passage, God gives language to human beings, not only as a means of controlling the world but also as a means of alleviating isolation, that is, creating kinship and social bonding. Only, it seems, through the process of verbally identifying the range of life does it become clear to God that no creature yet meets the requirements of a companion for man. And so, God makes that companion and brings her before man, who then, just as he had named all other creatures, now names her, saying, "This at last is bone of my bones and flesh of my flesh; she shall be called woman" (Genesis 1:23). She is called "woman" (in Hebrew, *ishshah*), the passage explains, "because she was taken out of man" (in Hebrew, *ish*), suggesting at once not only that man and woman are joined in kinship as they are joined in their names but also that man "has dominion" over her by having pronounced her name, just as he had pronounced the names of other living beings.

The story about the creative potency of language that dominates the first two chapters of Genesis takes an interesting turn at the beginning of the third chapter, which introduces the first example in the Bible of the persuasive power of language—oratory, in effect—but which associates that persuasiveness not with God's commanding or man's naming but with the "subtle" speech of the serpent (Genesis 3:1). The Bible does not explain what accounts for the serpent's ability to speak, but no sooner is woman created and named than the serpent cajoles her to violate God's commandment not to eat of the tree of the knowledge of good and evil. There are evident symbolic parallels in the passage: a fatal tree in an otherwise perfected garden, a snake in the midst of God's living creation, suggesting in mythic terms the dangerous complexity of the world, for all its wonder and promise. And in the serpent's speech there is another parallel, a dangerous complexity to language as well, which Plato (1975), for example, explores, from a different perspective and cultural tradition when, in *Gorgias*, he decries the capacity of an unscrupulous orator to mislead the ignorant or inattentive with words that appeal to self-interest instead of righteousness. Through the serpent's oratory, the Bible mythically portrays a latent mischievousness in language, the negative power of words to deceive and beguile. The serpent assures woman that she "will not die" from eating the forbidden fruit (Genesis 3:4). God does not want human beings to become godlike themselves, he explains, and that is the selfish reason for denying access to this tree alone: "God knows that when you eat of it your eyes will be opened, and you will be like God, knowing good and evil" (5). The cunning of the serpent's "argument" lies in the manipulation of human weaknesses, including woman's curiosity, her vanity at the prospect of being "like God," and her innocence of the world. The woman's fall into sin leads God to a new use of his verbal power, one he has had no previous occasion to exercise, and that is the power of the curse. First, he says to the serpent, "Because you have done this, cursed are you . . . above all wild animals" (14); then, by verbal decree, he visits the pain of childbirth on woman, and finally, he condemns man to mortality ("you are dust, and to dust you shall return" [19]). Creation itself, God says, has been corrupted by sin: "Cursed is the ground because of you" and "thorns and thistles it shall bring forth to you" (17–18). All of this human disaster (itself brought about by verbal curse or command) has arisen from false uses of language, initially because the serpent orator has beguiled woman and subsequently, as God explains to man, "because you have listened to the voice of your wife" (17). Only at this point in the story, following God's condemnation of human beings to the pains of mortality, does the Bible refer to man as "Adam" [17] (in Hebrew, *ha-adamah*, "the ground") and does Adam assign a proper name, "Eve," to his wife "because she was the mother of all living"[20] ("Eve" suggests the Hebrew, *hawwah*, a reference to "life"). Their lapsarian, mortal condition now marked by their human names, Adam and Eve give birth to subsequent generations, which Genesis goes on to recognize by means of a record of their names (Cain, Abel, and Seth, the sons of Adam; Enosh, Kenan, Mahal'alel, and their descendants): "This is the book of the generations of Adam" (5:1).

The Bible's ambivalence about the magical power of language is reiterated later in Genesis through the myth of the Tower of Babel, which suggests that the serpent was not altogether wrong about God's jealous defense of his prerogatives. As chapter 11 explains, "the whole earth had one language and few words," a condition that enabled these early generations of Adam to band together efficiently in social groups. They make a decision to "build . . . a city," including "a tower with its top in the heavens," so that human beings can "make a name for [them] selves, lest [they] be scattered abroad upon the face of the whole earth" (Genesis 11:4). When God sees the tower in progress, a potential triumph of human cooperation, he observes that the proud builders are "one people," that they "have all one language," and that "this is only the beginning of what they will do" (6). Recognizing the power of language, and the god-like capabilities that speech can provide to human beings, God resolves to "go down, and there confuse their language, that they may not understand one another's speech" (7). He then "scatter[s] them abroad," leaving behind the unfinished construction, which is subsequently called Babel because, the passage explains, "there the Lord confused the language of all the earth" (9). Obviously, the literal function of the myth is to account for the diversity of the world's languages, but the richness of the story derives from its association of language with the power of God, and its portrait of a jealous God punishing human beings for their arrogance in using his divine instrument not merely as a vehicle for social interaction but to exalt themselves by building a tower with its "top in the heavens." The parallels between the Babel story and other accounts of language in Genesis and Exodus are noteworthy because a common motif is the before-and-after depiction of a divine gift altered by human transgression. Language is diversified at Babel as a punishment for pride. Earlier, speech is passed to human beings in the Garden, but human beings share with the serpent in its abuse: Eve by listening to false rhetoric, then persuading Adam to join her in sin, then blaming the serpent for her own choices ("the serpent beguiled me"), and also Adam for accepting Eve's false rhetoric, then weakly blaming Eve and even, indirectly, God himself, for his choices ("the woman whom thou gavest to be with me, she gave me fruit of the tree, and I ate" [3:12]). Human naming power is diminished and, as a result, is no longer a means of creating the eternal vitality of the living world but is only a means of recording the "generations of Adam" (Genesis 5:1) as they pass away, leaving nothing but their names behind. The wicked serpent passes to human beings the false gift of verbal deceit, just as God had passed the gift of verbal truth. Later, in Exodus, the gift of writing, characterized initially as "the finger of God" (Exodus 31:18) on sacred stone, is passed to Moses as a human instrument following the idolatrous behavior of the Israelites. It is now powerful when "inspired" by God but no longer powerful merely because a human being chooses to write.

Nonetheless, for all the ups and downs of verbal communication between God and humanity, and between one person and another, in the Bible, language retains its magical properties, capable of blessing the righteous and promising them God's favor, cursing the wicked, appealing to God's mercy, giving people special power or authority through names, and doing great deeds through rhetorical skill. God makes a promise to Noah: "I will never again curse the ground because of man" (Genesis 9:20); God also establishes a "covenant with [him] and [his] descendants" (8), making a divine promise about the future prosperity of the chosen people. God makes the same covenant with Abram, providing him a magical name, Abraham: "For I have made you the father of a multitude of nations" (17:5). Abraham persuades God, through inspired oratory, to spare the virtuous in Sodom, astonished afterwards at his own verbal audacity ("I have taken upon myself to speak to the Lord, I who am but dust and ashes" [18:27]). God renames Jacob, saying, "Your name shall no longer be called Jacob, but Israel, for you have striven with God and with men, and have prevailed" (32:28). Moses complains about the burden God has placed on him to persuade the Pharaoh to release the Israelites, saying, "I am not eloquent . . . but I am slow of speech and of tongue," but God answers, "Who has made man's mouth? . . . Now therefore go, and I will be with your mouth and teach you what you shall speak" (Exodus 4:10–12). Later, Moses defends the sinful Israelites by making use of his rhetorical power to move God to be merciful: "O Lord, why does thy wrath burn hot against thy people, whom thou hast brought forth out of the land of Egypt?" (32: 11). God provides laws to the Israelites in Leviticus, and names the generations of the chosen people in Numbers, telling Moses and Aaron: "Put my name upon the people of Israel, and I will bless them" (Numbers 6:27). Job's lamentations move God to relieve his sufferings, and Job's prayers protect his friends: "My servant Job shall pray for you, for I will accept his prayer not to deal with you according to your folly" (Job 42:8). David's psalms proclaim that the world is suffused with language, that the heavens themselves "are telling the glory of God," that "their voice goes out through all the earth, and their words to the end of the world" (Psalms 19:4). The psalms also speak of teaching magical knowledge through "the words of my mouth," uttering "dark sayings from of old," telling "things that we have heard and known," passing to the "coming generation the glorious deeds of the Lord . . . and the wonders which he has wrought" (78). Whether symbolized by God's covenants and commandments, the oratory of Abraham and Moses, the teaching of the prophets, the working of miracles, the parables of Jesus, or the pastoral work of Jesus's disciples, who, when they preach "in [Jesus's] name," are given power to "cast out devils" and "speak with new tongues" (Mark 16:17), a consistent theme from the Old Testament through the New is the intrinsic power of utterance to affect the world, speak to God in supplication, and convey God's teachings to the chosen.

TERESA OF AVILA

Magical rhetoric comes in many flavors, but its model in Judeo-Christian culture is prayer. Often too restrictively understood as petitioning a supernatural being, prayer in the fullest sense is a communion with the sacred through the mediation of language, an experience of spiritual transcendence that entails losing the self in an act of acquiescence to the power of God. No one explores the discursive environment of prayer more richly or subtly than Teresa of Avila (1515–1582), the sixteenth-century Spanish nun, mystic, and Catholic saint who, together with John of the Cross, also cofounded the mendicant order of Discalced Carmelites. Instructed by her father confessors to write about the visions, supernatural revelations, and intense meditations that were so manifest in her public devotions, Teresa dutifully composed *The Book of Her Life*, a narrative whose initial political function to assure the doctrinal orthodoxy of her mystical experience was quickly eclipsed by the edifying religious value of her observations about the rhetoric of prayer as practiced at the highest levels of spiritual consciousness. Teresa distinguishes between the "vocal prayer" of her convent—chanted communal recitations following set formulas (from the Our Father and Hail, Mary to extensive litanies, novenas, and liturgical ceremonies, especially the Mass), and "mental prayer"—a contemplative inner speech where the voice of God, the Word of God, stills the intellect, silencing the human speech that proceeds from conscious thought. She depicts a progression of four stages of prayer beginning with spoken performance and concluding in a mystical communion that is at once speechless and yet wholly engrossed in conversation with God. She also distinguishes the characteristics of speech proceeding from the voice of God from the voices of human beings and from the voice of the devil, the latter always eager to beguile the naïve or the ostentatiously pious with counterfeit messages.

Teresa compares prayer to the work of cultivating a garden, likening the stages or degrees of prayer to the various means by which the garden can be watered (Teresa of Avila 2008, 61ff.). The most arduous recourse is drawing water from a well while the least arduous is relying on rainfall. The first, a mechanical exercise of hauling individual buckets, parallels the effort and limited results of vocal prayer (the first degree) in watering the soul, while the second, a natural, essentially passive reliance on rain, parallels the fourth degree, a complete enriching of the soul through mystical union with God. Relying on an aqueduct rather than a well for cultivating the garden means more water with less labor, but it is also still mechanical rather than natural, paralleling therefore the second degree of prayer, in which initial, halting efforts are made to quiet the rational faculties—and with them the vocal speech that proceeds from intellect, memory, and volition—in order to hear the voice of God and attend to his presence. Watering the garden by means of a river

or stream is more natural than watering from a well or aqueduct, corresponding therefore to the third degree of prayer, where the faculties
are even less intrusive, allowing the soul to be more naturally attuned to
the experience of the sacred. But the third means of watering is not as
completely effortless as rainfall and the third stage of prayer falls short
of complete beatific union. The irony in Teresa's simile is only apparent: vocal prayer in its prescribed repetitiveness is, to be sure, simple
to master while mental prayer, the speechless communication of the
mystical state, requires intense focus over years of exacting discipline.
But Teresa's point is that the hardest work is the early work of quieting
the mind, dissociating from the distractions of everyday life (even in a
convent) in order to achieve a condition of readiness to hear the Word.
Vocal prayer occurs in the midst of those distractions and requires a
strenuous effort of will to block them out while also remembering the
formal conventions of the rosary or the breviary. "Beginners in prayer,"
she explains, "must tire themselves in recollecting their senses" (i.e.,
concentrating on ritualized performance) because "they are accus-
tomed to being distracted." This "discursive work with the intellect"—
the conscious observance of the formalities of public prayer—"is what is
meant by fetching water from the well" (62–63). By contrast, the natural condition of the soul is stillness and passivity before the Word: "In
mystical theology . . . the intellect ceases to work because God suspends
it. . . . What I say about not ascending to God unless He raises one up is
language of the spirit" (69).

Consistent with a belief in the intrinsic power of language that is the
hallmark of magical rhetoric, Teresa's explanation of the three stages of
mental prayer places all authority in the divine Word, experienced as a
communicative union with God, eliminating intellectual activity—"to
compose speeches and search for ideas" (Teresa of Avila 2008, 90)—
in favor of an absolute receptiveness and acquiescence. Prayer and the
experience of God are virtually indivisible. The person who prays is
submitting to the power of the Word, does not rationally use language
to summon or beseech God but instead comprehends God's presence
through the act of contemplation. In the second degree of prayer, the
first move toward mental, as opposed to vocal, expression, "His Majesty
is beginning to communicate Himself to this soul." Teresa refers to this
stage as the "prayer of quiet" (81), where the soul is preparing itself for
the Word. God, she says, "desires that this soul understand that He is
so close it no longer needs to send Him messengers but can speak with
Him itself and not by shouting since He is so near that when it merely
moves its lips, He understands it" (83). By the third stage of prayer,

which Teresa describes as a "sleep of the faculties" (95), the soul "utters many words . . . in praise of God without thinking them up, unless it is the Lord who thinks them up" (97). The soul begins to approach union with God. Finally, in the fourth degree, the condition of mystical apprehension, prayer is synonymous with divine union—the word made sacred. More important, Teresa does not speak of the mystical condition as ineffability, somehow beyond language; on the contrary she says that "You have so loved us that we can truthfully speak of this communication which You engage in with souls" (106). Prayer, the power of the word, albeit divorced from intellect and speech, is the environment in which mystical union is achieved.

Because the snares of the Devil are many and various (as perhaps are also the snares of father confessors), Teresa is careful to explain the experience of communication with God (through visions and revelations as well as prayer) by distinguishing it from other acts of language. Given the suppression of the intellect during periods of intense mental prayer (contemplation), she concedes that there is opportunity for self-deception and/or diabolical intervention. But she insists that there is no mistaking the divine utterance: "The words are very explicit but are not heard with the bodily ears, although they are understood much more clearly than they would be if heard. . . . In the case of these words God addresses to the soul there is no way of avoiding them . . . they make me listen" (Teresa of Avila 2008, 161). The difference between words coming from God and words coming from human beings, including the self, is that, in the first case, the words are intuitively and compellingly *heard* while in the second they are rationally, sometimes argumentatively, *composed.* Self-deception is possible when statements are formed through the intellect, but Teresa insists that one can identify those statements by noticing the conscious work involved in their composition. In words that come from God, "the experience is as though we were listening to a very holy person . . . who we know will not lie to us." These words "bear with them such majesty that even though one does not call to mind who it is that speaks them, they make one tremble." Moreover, "such long sentences are said so quickly that much time would have been necessary to compose them, and in no way does it seem to me that we can then fail to know that they are something we do not fabricate ourselves" (164). At such times, she goes on, God speaks to the soul in a language "that belongs so to heaven" that it "makes the intellect become aware" as though "the soul has other ears with which it hears, and God makes it listen." In the most intense mystical experiences, there is even greater intuitive understanding, although still through a form of "locution"—"that

divine language in which it seems the Holy Spirit was speaking" (249)—
where even an awareness of listening disappears, leaving only a sense
that "there is nothing more to do than to enjoy . . . for the soul sees that
in an instant it is wise" (178–79). As for diabolical interventions mas-
querading as the speech of God, Teresa reassures her confessors that
the soul both recognizes and resists the devil's tricks by appeal to the felt
sense of the truths of sacred scripture, where conformity to or deviation
from scripture makes evident the source of the speech. "When locution
comes from the devil it seems that all blessings go into hiding and flee
from the soul, in that it is left displeased and agitated and without any
good effect." Teresa concludes with the conviction available to someone who accepts the presence of God in and through the power of his
Word: "It seems to me that whoever has experience of the good spirit
will understand" (166–67).

ERNST CASSIRER

The Bible, understood as a sacred book communicating the Word of
God, and Teresa of Avila's practice of contemplative prayer serve as
compelling examples of magical rhetoric. But there are also illuminating philosophical accounts of magical rhetoric, not themselves part of
the magical tradition but commentaries upon it from other rhetorical
perspectives. Ernst Cassirer (1874–1945), for instance, sympathetically
describes mythic thinking, and what he calls "word magic," in a number of provocative arguments, including *An Essay on Man, Language and
Myth*, and the monumental, three-volume *Philosophy of Symbolic Forms*.
The second of these works, *Language and Myth*, is a summary review of
the analysis of prelogical thought that he elaborates at greater length in
Symbolic Forms, and it can serve as a distillation of Cassirer's point of view.
Cassirer is himself a neo-Kantian philosopher (as such, a proponent of
what I will later discuss as expressivist rhetoric), whose overarching the-
sis is the development of consciousness and modes of symbolic representation (conceived as dialectically constitutive of each other) from mythic
to scientific thought. As Susanne Langer points out in a brief translator's preface to *Language and Myth*, Cassirer's work on "the odyssey of
the mind" is distinguished by the seriousness with which it treats forms
of human conception and representation that previous philosophy had
simplistically considered to be ignorant, irrational, and superstitious
(Langer 1946, viii). For Cassirer, mythic thought is *non*rational without
the value judgment implicit in *ir*rational, a primordial means of fashioning the coherence of the world that depends on immediate, emotional,

and figurative responses to experience rather than distanced, logical responses. If the latter are embodied in the discourses of science and philosophy, the former are embodied not only in the discourse of myth but also in dreams, and according to Cassirer, in still-vital Western traditions of religion, art, and poetry, all of which place a higher premium on metaphorical than on factual representation.

Cassirer argues that myth articulates an animate, passionate world in which feelings, desires, needs, and fears are symbolically objectified as responsive agencies, gods, demons, or other personifications that humanize the natural world, including heavenly bodies, sky, earth, water, day and night, animals, plants, and natural phenomena, from lightning bolts to the changing of the seasons. It is a dramatically charged, emotionally rich account of the ways in which human beings of a given culture imagine themselves situated in the world, "a particular way of seeing" that "carries within itself its particular and proper source of light" (Cassirer 1946, 11). The mythic imagination focuses on "the sensible present," the immediate, palpable experience of nature without concern for sharply demarcating its objects; it is "captivated and enthralled by the intuition which suddenly confronts it" (32). Since this concrete experience is acontextual, it is unclassified, an object not of distant contemplation but of spontaneous emotional engagement (33). The function of myth is not primarily to differentiate but to interanimate human experience. Hence, the mythic world is synthetic rather than analytic, possessing a fluidity of substance and form in which objects are distinct but not separate and may freely metamorphose. Myth responds to human need, specifically the need for sympathetic association with everything in nature, all things suffused with the atmosphere of the sacred. The whole is prior to the part, a spiritual or magical oneness prior to any distribution of local identities. Cassirer illustrates with an explanation of certain features of Indo-Germanic mythology, noting that, in the *Avesta* (the sacred texts of Zoroastrianism), Mithra is not a sun god but rather a "spirit of heavenly light," suggesting that "the worship of light as an undifferentiated, total experience preceded that of the individual heavenly bodies, which figure only as its . . . particular manifestations" (14). The parallel with Genesis is striking. God creates light on the first day but doesn't create the sun, moon, and stars until the fourth day, leaving the rational mind to wonder where light was coming from in the absence of these differentiated sources. The point is that light does not have a source apart from God. Light in itself, the vanquishing of darkness, the origination of the cosmos, has more encompassing value than any local manifestation, so it is represented as the first gift from God, while specific illuminated bodies, far from preceding light in a rational relationship of cause and effect, are merely individuations of God's gift. Mythic conception initially grasps "only the great, fundamental, qualitative contrast of light and darkness," comprehending it as "one essence, one complex whole" from which "definite characters only gradually emerge" (14).

The vehicle that enables the presenting as well as differentiating of the mythic world is symbolization, an imaginative act dramatized in the Genesis myth when God names light, thereby forming cosmos out of chaos, and then individuates the sun, moon, and stars along with the other manifestations of being that emerge with the coming of light. The symbol, according to Cassirer, is not an imitation or arbitrary designation of a preexisting object but rather an "organ of reality," the means by which "anything real becomes an object for intellectual apprehension, and as such is made visible to us" (Cassirer 1946, 8). He insists that "the mythical form of conception is not something superadded to certain definite elements of empirical existence; instead, the primary 'experience' itself is steeped in the imagery of myth and saturated with its atmosphere" (10). The charged world of the sacred, symbolized by light, preconditions the apprehension of objects and events so that their emergence is not a translation into the language of the sacred but is an already magical identity of signifier and signified within sacred space and time. This insight is important for understanding what it means to say that mythic language creates and governs its objects. Mythic language presents "separate and individualized forms only insofar as it 'posits' them, as it carves them out of the undifferentiated whole of its pristine vision" (14). The world does not appear as a distribution of phenomena, "things and processes, permanent and transitory aspects, objects and actions," which are subsequently mapped by language; instead, "language itself . . . initiates such articulations, and develops them in its own sphere" (12). The enunciation and the reality are fused; there is no space between the symbol and its meaning (58). The central belief of mythic consciousness is that "name and essence bear a necessary and internal relation to each other," that a name does not merely denote its object but that "the potency of the real thing is contained in the name" (3). This potency is what Cassirer calls "word magic" (44), the power to create and control by naming.

Cassirer tracks "word veneration" through several cultures, not only the Judeo-Christian (where the Gospel according to John deifies language), but in Egyptian theology, in a Polynesian creation hymn, in the Bundahish (the Zoroastrian account of creation), in Chinese culture, among the Algonquins, and in Indian religious thought, where, according to the Hindu *Vedas*, "Vac," the power of spoken language, is exalted even over the gods themselves: "On the Spoken Word all the gods depend, all beasts and men; in the Word live all creatures . . . the Word is the Imperishable, the firstborn of the eternal Law" (Cassirer 1946, 48). The power of the Word, transferred from gods to human beings, is evident in the ritual aspects of naming, from the anointing of pharaohs in Egyptian culture (where the new Pharaoh's names each convey specific, divine attributes [49]), to the Christian ceremony of baptism, where personal names are sometimes chosen by reference to saints, holy persons whose names have become associated with spirituality. As Cassirer explains, "Even a person's ego, his very self and personality, is indissolubly linked, in mythic thinking, with his name" (49–50). Our names constitute our individuality, our distinctive being, much as the stars are individuated against the backdrop of the light. They ground us in the present and identify our links with the past (as in the Bible's naming of the generations). Some names can evoke reverence and fear, as in the case of the Hebrew name for God, which some Jews take care never to pronounce out of veneration and dread. They can summon forth, as in the Gospel according to Matthew, where Jesus says to his disciples, "For where two or three are gathered in my name, there am I in the midst of them" (Matthew 18:20). In word magic, the immediacy of the name merges with the immediacy of what is named, such that "the conscious experience is not merely wedded to the word, but is consumed by it. Whatever has been fixed by a name, henceforth is not only real, but is Reality" (Cassirer 1946, 58). Given the proper circumstances, this magical potency extends beyond names to include other acts of language as well; in prayer, for example, formulaic words, uttered with ritual care (as in the case of the Lord's Prayer, which Jesus directly teaches to his disciples in the Gospel according to Luke 11:2–4), have power to reach out to God. The priest at a Roman Catholic Mass uses similarly sanctified language to turn bread and wine into the body and blood of Christ. In such verbal acts, a "magic circle" surrounds the utterance, a sacred moment that gives words unusual efficacy. Referring to the Vedic books, Cassirer notes that the priest who makes a holy utterance "has to observe the most meticulous detail—any deviation . . . would void the potency of the prayer" (78). Spells and incantations in nonreligious, magical settings often observe similar ritual precision, tacitly confirming that it is not language that constitutes the domain of the sacred, but rather the sacred that conveys power to appropriately specialized uses of language.

Cassirer discusses word magic and the mythic imagination primarily in the context of religious belief or else by reference to cultures that do not valorize rationalist and empirical thought. But he also suggests some additional importance to myth and magical rhetoric in parallels he finds between the views of discourse in those traditions and certain Western theories of metaphor and literary language. There are two distinguishing features of myth, already discussed, that relate it evidently to views of metaphor associated with European romanticism—the post-Kantian tradition to which Cassirer himself belongs. One is its capacity to project human need and desire into the world of nature, representing phenomena in humanly comprehensible symbolic forms, a fusion of mind and experience that Samuel Coleridge (1965, 145) refers to as "the coalescence of subject and object." The second is a creative tension in mythic thought between similitude and difference, where individuation lacks the definitude of rational categories of thought so that phenomena, in their concreteness, are readily fused together in organic syntheses against the backdrop of belief in the unity of all things, the luminous fabric of the cosmos. The tendency of rational thought, Cassirer explains, is to create analytical distance between the mind and its objects of attention by a process of differentiating and classifying, where the object "fits into the sum total of phenomena, yet remains set off from them as something independent and singular" (Cassirer 1946, 89–90). A logical concept, fixed within a network of generic and specific relations, "has a certain 'area' that belongs to it and whereby it is distinguished from other conceptual spheres." While there may be overlapping of these spheres, each "maintains its definitively bounded location in conceptual space" (90). The tendency of mythic thought is precisely opposite, featuring "the representation of subjective impulses and excitations in definite objective forms and figures" (88); in other words, mind and object are unified through the mediation of symbol, while the immediacy of the "objective form" captivates attention and resists logical placement within a system of conceptual differences. Cassirer describes this resistance as "the law of the leveling and extinction of specific differences" (91), where any one thing may evoke another, where any singularity manifests the whole. "The part does not merely represent the whole, or the specimen its class; they are identical with the totality to which they belong" (92). He calls this identity the "magic of analogy" (91), where logically dissimilar things are imaginatively synthesized. The fusion of differences characteristic of myth is precisely, also, the action of metaphor, where, as in Eliot's *Prufrock*, evening can be represented as "spread out against the sky," as though it were an independent being, and then compared to "a patient etherized upon a table" ("The Love Song of J. Alfred Prufrock," 1920). Literary language, like mythic language, evokes "the magic of analogy" to transform experience into a responsive, humanized symbolic representation.

The symbolic projection of consciousness into experience is essentially Cassirer's philosophical rendering of what the Bible represents mythically as the creation of the world. Poets, in other words, also create worlds when, metaphorically speaking, they borrow the divine power of the Word for human purposes. This parallel, far from originating with Cassirer, actually has a long European genealogy. Samuel Coleridge (1965, 167), like Cassirer much indebted to Kant, explicitly relates divine and human creativity in chapter 13 of *Biographia Literaria*, where he writes that imagination is "the living power and prime agent of all human perception . . . a repetition in the finite mind of the eternal act of creation in the infinite I AM." Coleridge is not *thinking* mythically here, but is, like Cassirer, asserting the potency of language by linking word magic intellectually with the romantic conception of expressivity (to be discussed in chapter 5), understood as the forming of objective experience through the mind's own active symbolic processes. Coleridge's parallel of divine and human creativity is echoed centuries earlier, although less affirmatively, in Plato's *Ion*, where the ability of the poet, the prophet, and the "pronouncer of oracles" is a gift from the gods, enabling them to conjure divine truths in pleasing artistic forms and move audiences with magical verbal powers. Socrates attributes these powers to "inspiration," portraying the poet as "out of his senses," a "light and winged and holy thing" who has "no invention in him until he has been inspired . . . and reason is no longer in him" (Plato 1953, 534b). "Inspiration" (from Latin *inspirito*, meaning literally "to breathe into") is, according to Socrates, a form of possession, where "God himself is the speaker" and the poets "are only the interpreters of the gods" (533c). Plato offers an intriguing depiction of the relationship between poet and audience, a rare insight into magical rhetoric from the vantage point of the hearer or reader of sacred utterance. He likens the "divinity" moving through the poet to "the stone that Euripides calls a magnet," commonly known as the "stone of Heraclea." The poet is first inspired by a muse, and then from this inspired individual "a chain of other persons is suspended, who take the inspiration" (533c). By means of this chain of spectators, all enchanted by the music of the artist, "God sways the souls of men in any direction which He pleases, causing each link to communicate the power to the next" (535e). The "magnetism" of poetic enthrallment suggests the "magic circle" that Cassirer describes in the ritualized language of the sacred, where an atmosphere of intense communal excitement (which Socrates describes by reference to dancing "Corybantian revelers" or "Bacchic maidens") attends the divinely inspired language of the poet.

Socrates is, however, profoundly uncomfortable with the poet's capacity to move people through mimetic art (as we will see in chapter 3), finally electing to banish the poet from his ideal society (Plato 1960, 607) for the poet's arousal of dangerous passions. He speaks with rather anxious ambivalence about divinely inspired, poetic language, unwilling to regard it disapprovingly (as he does the cynically self-interested prose of sophists like Gorgias), fearful perhaps of antagonizing spiritual agencies, yet unable to commend the irrationality of the poet and the dubious moral effects of poetry in a state dedicated to reason (Plato 1960, 606–608). Plato struggles, arguably, to reconcile the magical rhetoric that still resonates in his culture with the rationalist rhetoric that Greek philosophy is, at that very moment, coming to enshrine as the dominant discourse of the West. Precisely *because* of the connections between mythic and literary expression, Plato appears to fear the power of an art that speaks with the voice of God while yet exalting uncontrolled emotion, the whirling Bacchic maidens, over logic. Plato's ambivalence will frequently reappear in European literary thought as writers attempt to explain the acknowledged power of poetry without approving the excesses of imagination. It is clear, for example, in Bede's description of the art of the poet Caedmon in his *Ecclesiastical History of the English Nation,* where the poetic voice is similarly characterized as a gift from God but also regarded with suspicion until Caedmon's personal sanctity is affirmed. Caedmon's poetic gift resembles the oratorical gift that God bestows on Moses in Exodus after Moses first complains that he has no ability to speak. A mysterious person appears to Caedmon in his sleep, asking him to sing, and Caedmon says, "I cannot sing." When the "person" insists, Caedmon follows his instructions "and presently [begins] to sing verses to the praise of God, which he had never heard." On awakening, Caedmon, at that time a brother in the monastery at Whitby, goes immediately to Abbess Hilda to acquaint her with what has happened, and she promptly assembles a group of "learned men" to hear of his dream, listen to his verses, and "give their judgment what it was, and whence his verse proceeded." Presumably, given Christian recollection of the rhetorical interventions of the serpent in Eden, Caedmon's eloquence might as readily have derived from diabolical as divine influences. Fortunately for him (one surmises), the learned men conclude "that heavenly grace [has] been conferred on him by our Lord," that he did not acquire "the art of poetry from men, but from God," and that only poetic expressions of the truths of sacred scripture "[suit] his religious tongue" (Bede 1970, 205–08). The spontaneous creativity of poetic art, when its source is divine inspiration, has a power derivative of the Bible's sacred word to speak truth with God's voice. But that power, in an age when theology rather than myth had come to constitute the cognitive underpinnings of religion, could have suspicious origins and, in its emotional appeals, deleterious effects.

For the romantic Coleridge and the Kantian Cassirer, the resemblances between mythic and poetic language are more enthusiastically portrayed than they are in the writing of Plato and Bede, arguably because Coleridge's and Cassirer's portrayals are less complicated by still-vibrant recollections of the powerful but enigmatic, potentially demonic world of magic. Yet Coleridge and Cassirer begin from the same underlying parallel: an expressivity, whether mythic or poetic, that presents an intensely immediate, emotional, metamorphic, and captivating truth of human experience wholly inaccessible to the measured logic of rational discourse. If there is a modern, secular legacy of magical rhetoric beyond the special conditions of religious experience, it may plausibly lie in the intuitions of wholeness amidst difference, the reconciliations of discordant ideas and feelings, the interanimation of subject and object associated with the aesthetic effects that theorists like Cassirer attribute to the metaphorical language of poetry. What is missing, of course, is the efficacy of the word, the intrinsic power of utterance to affect the world beyond it. Poetry, as Cassirer understands it, only simulates magical rhetoric because it exerts no control over the images it conjures. But what remains of the ancient, creative power of magic is the "aesthetically liberated" capacity of metaphoric language to fashion a world of illusion and fantasy no longer "mythically bound and fettered" to the gods and demons of its creation but free to give voice to "pure feeling" through a mode of symbolic action that is neither unself-consciously superstitious nor stultifyingly logical. As Cassirer concludes (Cassirer 1946, 98–99), myth and word magic, which had once "confronted the human mind as hard realistic powers," now create psychological rather than supernatural realities, employing the "sensuous forms of word and image" in a discourse of deliberate intellectual play, a free exercise of ancient verbal magic for rejuvenating the spirit rather than propitiating the spirits, substituting aesthetic excitement for reverential awe.

3

ONTOLOGICAL RHETORIC

PLATO

The dominant rhetorical tradition of ancient Greece and Rome, from Plato (429–347 BCE) to Quintilian, is characterized by a view of discourse that is arguably the antithesis of magical rhetoric, proposing, in essence, that language is all humble rather than all powerful. The reason for its humble status, even in disciplines (like logic and rhetoric) at the heart of liberal-arts learning, is the belief that the reality named by language is intrinsically coherent independent of verbal mediation. Plato's theory of discourse, for example, is consistent with his view of other human mediations of the world-in-itself: why settle for a knock-off when you can have the real thing? And so Plato is a good place to begin an introduction to the perspective that I call "ontological" rhetoric. The *Republic* repeatedly distinguishes between Being (the Ideal) and Becoming (the Actual), two distinct orders of reality, hierarchically arranged, the first generating the second and providing its variety, coherence, and purposefulness. The world of Being is a *meta*physical plane ("above nature"), variously called the plane of the Good (Plato 1960, 507b), of the Beautiful (507b), of ideal pattern (472c), or, famously, of Ideas or Forms, after the Greek *eidos*. Becoming is a physical plane, the familiar world of the senses, characterized by appearance rather than reality, change rather than permanence, decay rather than eternal perfection, shadows rather than things in themselves, and opinion or illusion rather than knowledge. Socrates underscores the difference between the eye's power to perceive the "daylight" of knowledge and the sun's power to create that daylight (508d), not wholly to disparage human mediations of Being but to insist on the priority of the metaphysical over the physical and to avoid the error of supposing that a knowledge of manifestations of the Good is equivalent to the Good itself (509a). The *Republic*'s well-known cave metaphor (514 *f.*) makes the distinction clearly by characterizing the human condition as degrees of imprisonment in a world of semi-darkness dominated by the appearances of things, shadows thrown on a

DOI: 10.7330/9780874219364.c003

wall by flickering firelight. Most human beings inhabit the cave either as prisoners chained to illusion or as prisoners tyrannized by a dependence on belief rather than knowledge. A few courageous souls are able, by the use of reason, to escape these conditions and clamber out of the cave, representing the upward progress of the mind through education, but their eyes are unaccustomed to light and they mistake their perceptions of objects made visible by the sun as the ideal forms of true knowledge. Only a very small, elite group of human beings perseveres to achieve the capacity for pure intellection, which for Plato is akin to mystical understanding, no longer dependent on mediations but instead intuitive and ineffable. This group is comprised of "philosophers," who discipline themselves in the fierce daylight outside the cave until they are able to apprehend the sun directly, representing the contemplative experience of the plane of true Being.

Since most human beings are unable to achieve Socrates's ultimate PhD, the capacity for direct, unmediated apprehension of the world of Forms, he directs his educational attention primarily to the befuddled undergraduates still clambering out of the cave and to the mediations of reality they persistently mistake for true knowledge. One such mediation is art, which Socrates discusses late in the *Republic* (Plato 1960, 595 *f.*) by appeal to an argument he gradually extends to all human depictions of the world. Socrates offers a representational or "mimetic" theory of art (after *mimesis*, the Greek word for "imitation"), suggesting that the painting of an object, let's say a table, constitutes an imitation at two removes from the plane of ideal forms. Since the gods first conceived the idea of Table, it follows that the carpenter who makes an actual table resembling the governing form is imitating the gods. When an artist then depicts the physical table on a canvas, the depiction is an imitation of an imitation, no better than a mirror image (596d) of the material object and, as such, only a distant likeness of the original idea. Socrates extends the example of the table painting to literature as well in the *Republic*, observing that the tragic poet works similarly at two removes, the action of the play imitating action in the human world which in turn imitates an ideal of action on the plane of metaphysical truth (597e). He concludes with a generalization that all kinds of representational mediation are necessarily distant from the truth because none of them can do more than hold a mirror up to the phenomenal appearances of things (598b). His discussion of the nature of language, in the dialogue called *Cratylus*, and his two dialogues on rhetoric, *Gorgias* and *Phaedrus*, consistently and unsurprisingly parallel the discussions of art and literature in the *Republic*, all governed by the same mimetic assumption.

Plato's theory of representation offers an example of the ontological story of the meaning of meaning, where language derives its power to signify from its relationship to an intrinsically and purposefully ordered, that is, teleological, exteriority. The ground of meaningfulness in the ontological point of view is metaphysical truth, the rational principles, or sometimes mystical intuitions, that comprise a coherent universe "above nature," governing both nature itself and also the mediations that comprise our knowledge of nature, including the signs, grammar, and representational acts of language. Plato is confident, although nervously confident, that the most carefully wrought, philosophically correct assertions of language are true because they point to things in the material world (including objects, actions, relationships, institutions, values, and other references), which in turn summon to mind the ideal forms from which they derive. At the same time, however, the authority of discourse depends on maintaining the priority of knowledge over words. Language is never more than an imitation of its objects, words mirroring impressions of things in the soul, which are themselves copies of things in nature, which in turn are derived from the plane of Being. Not only is language, at best, only *distantly* related to the plane of Being, but it is also nonessentially related. The verbal "mirroring" of materiality is irrelevant to the reality of the physical world because that world exists prior to and independent of naming. Moreover, language is limited in the quality of its representation by the distortion inevitably present in a humanly constructed "mirror": that is, words as human constructs are intrinsically flawed and have grown ever more debased over time as languages have changed and multiplied, distancing users from the truth of first names. Finally, whatever utility language may possess for imitating the physical world, it cannot directly manifest the metaphysical order from which materiality derives. Plato's version of the ontological story begins (logically but not chronologically) with *Cratylus*, where the issue is the intrinsic unreliability of words, then proceeds to *Gorgias*, where the issue is the mischief and deceit of public speaking, then reaches its highest complexity in *Phaedrus*, where the issue is the truth of discourse, including a discomfiting but provocative footnote on the problem of literacy.

CRATYLUS, GORGIAS, PHAEDRUS

The foregrounded concern of *Cratylus* is whether words are natural or conventional signs, whether they are necessarily related to their referents (as smoke is naturally the sign of fire) or only arbitrarily related (as the color red is, in some cultures, conventionally a warning). Socrates would prefer to conclude that words are natural signs, a view that, if proven, would strengthen the bond between words and things. However, after an extended, arguably whimsical, attempt to identify necessary relationships between various names—of men, gods, heavenly bodies, natural elements, seasons, important ideas—and their corresponding referents in reality, he is obliged to concede that his forays into speculative etymology "are quite outrageous and ridiculous" (Plato 1970, 426b). He fails to find a satisfactory path backward to a truth of first names where the essence of something is traceable in its verbal representation. By the end of the dialogue, the arbitrariness of verbal signs is a disconcertingly necessary conclusion justifying Socrates's fundamental mistrust of language as a vehicle for the pursuit of reliable knowledge. This conclusion is hardly surprising, however, in light of the mimetic perspective that governs his thinking: the very idea of representation as mirroring has preordained his skepticism. What is essential for Socrates is the distinction between names and things, where "things have some fixed reality of their own" (386e), each with an "essential nature" (423e), names are "instrument(s) of teaching and of separating reality"(388c), these instruments are a "vocal imitation of that which is imitated" (423c), and "the name is one thing and the thing of which it is the name is another" (430a). Ideally, Socrates argues, the truth of names (385b *f.*) should lie in the correctness of their depictions of the "nature of the eternal and the absolute" (397b); ideally, the name maker "grasps with his letters and syllables the reality of the things named and imitates their essential nature" (424b). This relationship between name and thing (whether natural or conventional) ought to have been forged "aloft among the gods" (408c). But the reality is that we cannot be confident of the divine credentials of name makers because first names, and the subsequent evolution of language, are lost to history. Perhaps "the gods gave the earliest names," or perhaps we got them from "some foreign folk" who are "more ancient than we are" (425e), or perhaps it is simply "impossible to investigate them because of their antiquity" (426a). What is clear to Socrates is that the "original words" that preceded modern speech have been "completely buried by those who wished to dress them up," people "who care nothing for truth," and who, throughout time, have changed the originals "until finally no human being can understand what in the world the word means" (414c). He is obliged to concede that the question of the reliability of first names is effectively moot, so the only recourse for the philosophically disciplined mind is to concern itself primarily with things in themselves, recognizing that, while our dependence on words is unavoidable, we put them to best use when we subordinate them strictly to our preverbal knowledge of the truth. Surely, he says, no "man of sense" can put "his soul under the control of names" or name makers to the point of "affirming that he knows anything" (440c). Better to learn from the truth "whether the image is properly made" than to attempt to learn from the image "whether it is itself a good imitation," or still less attempt to learn "the truth which it imitates" (439a).

The separation that Socrates maintains between things in themselves and words as images of things accounts, in *Gorgias*, for his animosity toward sophists who put talk ahead of knowledge, using it to manipulate weak minds for unscrupulous purposes, but also for a guarded hope late in the discussion that those who profoundly know their subjects can represent them ethically and usefully in discourse. Plato sets up the dialogue's argument by appeal to three foils, Gorgias of Leontini, a popular sophist of the era, Polus, a student of Gorgias, whose youthful arrogance encourages Socrates's strongest critiques, and Callicles, a friend of Socrates whom Gorgias encourages in the debate, suggesting that he has some sympathy for Callicles's point of view. Socrates believes that Gorgias maintains a cynical attitude toward truth and communication based on Gorgias's public boast that his skill at public speaking enables him to defend any position on any subject with equal persuasive authority. The gist of Socrates's response, delivered sharply to the foolish Polus, who has goaded him into offering his opinion of rhetoric as an "art," is to differentiate between the "knack" (Plato 1975, 463b) of the rhetorician, whose only interest is persuasion without regard for the truth, and the authentic knowledge of the philosopher. There is no need for an orator to know the truth, he asserts; it is sufficient that the orator has "discovered some device of persuasion" that can make him appear "to those who do not know to know better than those who know" (459b). Far from being a true art, like politics or medicine, rhetoric is a mere "habitude," a routine behavior like cooking or hair dressing, whose aim is "flattery," the gratification of an audience, with no regard for "the real nature of the things it applies" (464e). Warming to his task, Socrates inveighs against the "rascally, deceitful, ignoble, and illiberal nature" of activities intended to deceive people "by forms and colours, polish and dress" before eventually calming himself and resolving to seek the restraint of more logical argument in order to "avoid prolixity" (465b). Later, responding to Callicles's more temperate discussion of the value of the active, political life (where rhetoric is useful), he explains that the problem with orators is that, instead of "speaking always with a view to what is best" in order to improve the citizenry through their speeches, they are content with "gratifying the citizens . . . sacrificing the common weal to their own personal interest," by appeal to "base mob-oratory" (502e). One cannot help but recall, in this reference, the "mob oratory" that resulted in the death of Socrates. Plato, like his mentor, had determined, by the time *Gorgias* was written, to forsake political life in favor of a purer, philosophical calling, where reasoning need not debase itself in the messy, unscrupulous give and take of public discussion. By the conclusion of the dialogue, Socrates, evidently conveying Plato's own commitment to philosophy over Athenian politics, manages a small concession to the usefulness of rhetoric, depicting the ideal orator as a "man of art and virtue," a philosopher first, whose skill at words is matched by knowledge of his subject. This true orator, far from the pragmatically opportunistic Gorgias, "applies to our souls the words that he speaks" with a view always to explaining "how justice may be engendered in the souls of his fellow-citizens" (504e).

If *Gorgias* is, at times, a rant, it's an instructive one for underscoring the consistency of Plato's mimetic theory of discourse. The hierarchical relationship between things and words in *Cratylus* is precisely paralleled here in the relationship between knowledge and oratory. In the ontological perspective, the meaningfulness of language is founded on the stability (but also instability) of its reference to the intrinsically coherent world outside of language. Unlike the magical perspective, where words create and have power to control things, here the truth of things determines the truth of words. When speech reliably mirrors the truth of things, it effectively moves the souls of hearers to beneficial understanding. When it fails to mirror properly, its statements are recognizably false or erroneous by appeal to correct understanding of what always, in any case, remains meaningful in itself, the reality beyond the mirror—the metaphysical order from which all other meaning derives. The trouble with rhetoric, compared to Socrates's preferred philosophical discourse, is that its business is to move people, not to educate them. Philosophy respects the priority of things over names, taking as its province the rational display of truth. The rhetorician, too, respects that priority—whenever "he" is also a philosopher. But what makes the rhetorician effective *as* a rhetorician, the ability to move people, has no direct relationship to the philosophical determination of truth and error. The skills that enable a knowledgeable and honest orator to convey the truth in pleasing language equally allow an ignorant or unscrupulous one to achieve base purposes by manipulating the same verbal effects. Since rhetoric and philosophy have different means and ends, the scrupulous orator must accept a personal responsibility to think well before speaking. The trouble is, that responsibility is a moral imperative that rhetoric, strictly as a mode of discourse, is not obliged to enforce.

What makes *Phaedrus* more interesting than *Gorgias*, and the richest of the dialogues dealing directly with language and discourse, is Plato's ambiguous dramatization of the concerns he seeks to consider philosophically. The dialogue is a written text about people talking and writing about the arts of talking and writing. What Plato means to say about rhetoric, positive as well as negative, is enacted, not just uttered, by the two characters, Socrates and Phaedrus, in company with the absent third character, Lysias, who is present in and through his speech. The characters form a love triangle, and their motives are tangled. They talk about rhetoric by talking about love. Or perhaps they talk about love by talking about rhetoric. The views of love in the three speeches, one by Lysias, one a partial revision of Lysias by Socrates, and one (presumably) constituting Socrates's "true story," are transparently self-serving, not just Lysias's naughty pitch for the advantages of a nonlover's lack of commitment, but also Socrates's lyrically erotic myths about the god of love. All three speeches seek to create favorable impressions of the speakers, both of whom appear to have designs on the affections of Phaedrus and an interest in creating unfavorable impressions of a rival. Socrates's initial critique of Lysias's speech (Plato 1956, 234 *f.*) is beneath him, a writing teacher's huffy marginal comment about lack of originality and poor organization: "He has said the same things two or three times over." Socrates's own first speech (237 *f.*), ostensibly an improved rewriting of Lysias's text, cleverly sidesteps Lysias's cynical championing of the nonlover, but it is calculated to strut his superior organizational skills, beginning with a proper introduction, forecasting the matter at hand, defining important terms, summarizing along the way. His sin lies in the intent more than the deed. He is obliged to deliver the speech with his cloak covering his head, a frank admission of the ulterior motive influencing his behavior. Fear of impiety toward the gods finally obliges him to stop short of the conclusion and to upbraid himself for participating in such a "dreadful" enactment of texts—Lysias's speech, certainly, but also his own, "the speech you made me utter" (242 *f.*). His second speech is then undertaken as an act of contrition to mollify the god of love, but not before appealing to Phaedrus to urge Lysias, that roué, to cleanse his conscience also, and only after inviting Phaedrus to cuddle up while he speaks the truth about love. "Where is the lad I was addressing?" he asks. "I want him to hear this too" before "yielding to the nonlover." "He is always here at your elbow," Phaedrus responds, "whenever you need him" (243e). Socrates's lyrical second speech, with its discussion of the "divine madness" of the lover and its frankly sexual depiction of the soul that "gazes upon the beauty of its beloved" (251c) may indeed be his truth, but it is hardly a disinterested truth. The interplay of motives, texts, and subtexts is a postmodern garden of delights.

That said, while the second speech is intended to move Phaedrus (which is, after all, the business of rhetoric), it is also intended as a philosophical statement, pleasing to the gods. The dialogue's ontological view of the meaning of meaning parallels the theory in *Cratylus* and *Gorgias*, both in the second speech and the commentary that follows. Socrates alludes in that speech to the "region beyond the skies" of which no poet has ever sung, a metaphysical realm "without colour or shape, intangible but utterly real, apprehensible only by intellect" (Plato 1956, 247c). In this realm, immortal souls "behold absolute justice and discipline and knowledge," not the knowledge that is "attached to things which come into being . . . but the absolute knowledge which corresponds to what is absolutely real" (247d). Socrates's ensuing conversation with Phaedrus about a truly ethical art of rhetoric, where the wisdom of the speaker is embodied in structured, harmonious speech, presumes a mimetic relationship between the order of the cosmos and the order of a text. There is nothing "disgraceful" in writing speeches; the disgrace comes from writing badly (258d). The speaker should acquire knowledge before turning to the art of oratory (260e) and then should speak honestly, rather than manipulatively, about what he knows (261). The resulting speech should seek to imitate the order and elegance of that "region beyond the skies," displaying an "organic shape, like a "living being," lacking neither head nor feet, with "a middle and extremities so composed as to fit one another and the work as a whole" (264c). The ideal speech fuses moral and aesthetic values, integrity, harmony, balance, unity, propriety, clarity. As it happens, Socrates can think of no better example of such a speech than the one he has just delivered. Lysias's effort—"your friend's speech" (264d)—is "opposite" in sentiment to Socrates's view of lovers and nonlovers, and it contains a "number of features" that one would "profit by not attempting to imitate." His own speech, by contrast, endeavoring to speak honestly about the madness of the lover, may have "hit upon some truth," resulting in "a not entirely unconvincing speech, a mythical hymn which celebrates in suitably devotional language the praises of Love" (265C). One is tempted to imagine that Socrates has won the argument and the boy in a single stroke, a perfect harmony of philosophical and carnal ambitions, all achieved through the art of rhetoric.

The most striking observations in the later part of this conversation are not those related to oratory (which are conventional iterations of classical theory) but instead those that concern written discourse. *Phaedrus* inaugurates a discussion of the problem of literacy that will haunt European culture for the next two thousand years. What makes writing and reading problematic, according to Socrates, is that, unlike speaking and listening, they presume no immediate social bond uniting writer and reader in a common effort to identify, or at least negotiate, and communicate the truth. While the advantage of writing may be its ability to transcend spatial and temporal boundaries, its greater deficiency is an absence of that immediate, collaborative interrogation of statement that oral discourse enjoys, where the speaker can ask, "Do you understand?" and the listener can ask, "What do you mean?" Socrates relates the story of the god, Theuth, who brings the gift of writing to the Egyptian king, Thamus, persuaded of its power and value. Thamus responds, however, by observing that the gift is "not a sure receipt for memory and wisdom," as Theuth claims (Plato 1956, 274e), but on the contrary is an instrument that will cause people "to cease to exercise their memory and become forgetful," relying on "external signs" to recall "things" instead of on their own "internal resources" (275a). What's worse, Socrates goes on, is that writing is mute, appearing to promise meaning yet unable to explain what its meaning is. Writing is like painting in its eerie detachment from living communication: when an observer queries the seemingly human forms in a work of art, they "maintain a solemn silence." This silence is merely frustrating when the observer of a painting or the reader of a written text is knowledgeable and wise, but it is mischievous when the painting or the text falls into the hands of the ignorant. Writing cannot "distinguish between suitable and unsuitable readers" but instead "circulates equally among those who understand the subject and those who have no business with it" (275e). Socrates recommends instead what Phaedrus calls "the living and animate speech of a man with knowledge," compared to which writing is a mere "shadow" (276b). Not only is writing limited in its ability to speak the truth by its tertiary remove from the place where truth resides (i.e., an imitation of speech, which is an imitation of things, which are imitations of forms), but it is also unable to control its meanings to ensure that readers correctly understand what it seeks to communicate. These conditions attend even the best writing, where truth is honestly sought. What of writing that is poorly achieved, or erroneous, or intentionally deceitful? Plato's anxiety about the problem of literacy will be dramatically validated centuries later when, after the printing press is introduced into Europe in the sixteenth century, the Bible becomes accessible to readers who, unlike the clergy, do not have the writings of the fathers of the church to serve as a framework for interpreting biblical statements. What happens is effectively what Plato predicted: the meanings of the Bible are dispersed, modified, and corrupted, culminating in the Protestant Reformation. It seems that even God's Word, with apologies to Moses, is poorly served by print.

ARISTOTLE

Compared to Plato, Aristotle (384–322 BCE) has the unhappy reputation of making up in thoroughness for what he lacks in grace. Aristotle's rendering of the ontological story differs from Plato's in its strategies, where doggedly linear logic takes the place of narrative, in its tone, where we are never uncertain about Aristotle's certainties, and also in the details of the metaphysical ground of meaning, where his taste for the concrete and pragmatic has provided philosophers with many happy hours of debate over the differences between realist and idealist epistemologies. But for our purposes, his story, thematically, is notable more for its similarities than its differences, identifying, as Plato's did, an intrinsically coherent exteriority prior to perception and language and advancing a similarly mimetic view of the priority of things over ideas and ideas over words. Aristotle states the matter with characteristic definitiveness in *On Interpretation*, the second book of the *Organon*, arguing that spoken words are "symbols or signs of affections or impressions of the soul"; that written words are signs of spoken words; and that, while speech and writing differ across nations and cultures, "the mental affections themselves," that is, the ideas that words denote, "are the same for the whole of mankind, as are also the objects of which these affections are representations or likenesses, images, copies" (Aristotle 1973, 16a4–8). To put the whole story together, though, one must follow a thread of reasoning that runs with relentless consistency throughout Aristotle's works: through *Physics* and *Metaphysics*, where he describes the rational order that governs the world; through the books of the *Organon*, his contributions to logical theory, where "scientific" knowledge and discourse are described; through *Rhetoric* and *Poetics*, where practical forms of discourse are examined; and elsewhere besides. By the end of the tour, one has discovered something curious about Aristotle's story, though perfectly consonant with a mimetic perspective. Compared to Plato, he actually has very little to say about language, even in works that might be supposed to feature language as a centerpiece. In Aristotle's account of the meaning of meaning, language is, in important respects, invisible, particularly so in higher (scientific) forms of discourse. Where it rises to visibility, as in the later part of *Rhetoric*, its manifestation as "style" is famously dissed as a necessary, but in principle unfortunate, concession to "the corruption of the audience."

Aristotle's metaphysical world lacks the mystical dimensions of Plato's, but it serves the same function as the ground of discursive meaningfulness. Furthermore, Aristotle's confidence in its reality conditions a habit of mind that frames every topic, every discussion, across the considerable breadth of his philosophical work, his ethical, political, and even zoological texts no less than the logical and rhetorical. An indirect but illuminating demonstration of its impact on Aristotle's thinking may be found in the *Rhetoric* in an obscure byway where Aristotle is discussing the argumentative "topoi" (to which we'll return later) that are appropriate to forensic oratory (the discourse of the law court). He is talking about what motivates people to behave immorally of their own free will, and raises the question, "Why do people break the law?" His peculiar answer is that "vice and weakness" are what cause lawbreakers to "make the choice of harming and of doing bad things," going on to explain that "if certain people have one depravity or more it is in relation to this [depravity] that they are in fact wicked." An "underlying vice" of cowardice, for example, leads someone to abandon comrades in battle, while a vice of short temper causes another to commit an assault (Aristotle 1991, 1368b4). Aristotle's opinion that cowardice *causes* cowardly behavior should occasion a double take. Consider how people of our own time and place might respond to a parallel question concerning why a particular woman murdered her husband. One person might suggest that she murdered her husband because he abused her, another that she wanted to collect on his insurance policy, a third that her lover made her do it. By contrast, Aristotle's answer is that she murdered her husband because . . . she's a murderer! (Husband killing is the sort of thing that murderers do.) Such a pronouncement strikes some modern minds (many, one hopes) less like an explanation than a prejudice— akin to "explaining" the poor school performance of a Mexican child living in poverty by appeal to the a priori judgment that Hispanics are lazy. The logic that drives this type of argument is that general truths, a priori categories, or universal assumptions determine our understanding of specific situations. This logic recurs throughout the *Rhetoric* (and elsewhere), as when Aristotle confidently asserts that "the virtues and actions of those who are superior by nature are more honorable, for example those of a man more than those of a woman" (1367a22); or later, "the young and the rich are given to insults" (1379a); or still later, "it is a source of indignation . . . for a lesser person to dispute with a greater one" (1387a). Regrettably, ontological rhetoric, the hallmark of which is reasoning from metaphysical constants, provides an intellectually respectable rationale for stereotypes that would be comic in its circularity if it weren't so earnestly and dangerously applied as an instrument of oppression. I recall an Internet site that precisely characterizes Aristotle's metaphysical point of view. The site offers imagined responses of famous philosophers, artists, and literary writers to the question, why did the chicken cross the road? Aristotle's response is that it's the nature of chickens to cross the road.

Most of the details of Aristotle's metaphysical world are irrelevant to our purposes, but a few are worth noting, not only to account for his theory of discourse but also to anticipate the critique of his theory that will be posed many centuries later in the empiricist arguments of Arnauld, Descartes, Locke, and others. A good starting point is with the teleological nature of the experiential world, that is, the logical organization and purposefulness that the world of Being imposes on the world of Becoming. In *Physics*, Aristotle introduces four "causes" that account for that teleology: the agent cause, the material cause, the formal cause, and the final cause (Aristotle 1961a, 194b18*f*). The agent cause of a particular table, for example, is a carpenter; the material cause might be wood; the formal cause is the idea of a table, represented perhaps in a blueprint or diagram; and the final cause is the purpose for which a table is made—perhaps to eat or work on. The agent cause of a particular speech is the orator; the material cause, human speech; the formal cause, the logical structure of the argument; and the final cause, the deliberative, forensic, or epideictic purpose of the speech. The agent cause of "the world" is an "unmoved mover" (conventionally, God); the material cause, the physical substance of the world; the formal cause, genera and species that group and interrelate the things of the world; and the final cause, whatever might have motivated God to create the world in the first place. The illustrations here are cursory, but they serve to characterize the framework of causality and logical necessity that, according to Aristotle, makes the world coherent in all its manifestations. That material coherence exists prior to acts of perception, cognition, or verbal representation. Hence, in *Categories*, which is the first book of the *Organon*, Aristotle says that any object, any "perceptible," must exist before it can be perceived, so that "if you cancel the perceptible, you cancel the perception as well." The act of perception necessitates, first, a body perceived, and only second, "the subject perceiving," for "such things as water and fire, out of which are composed living beings, exist before any such things and prior to all acts of perception" (Aristotle 1973, 7b27–8a13). The mind is essentially a passive receiver of perceptions, in other words, and those perceptions enter the mind not as sensory stimuli that the mind must sort and otherwise act upon but as already meaningful wholes (the material table, for example). He writes in *Metaphysics* that "intellect finds its fulfillment in being aware of the intelligible" and enjoying the intelligible "as its possession"; mind and the intelligible, he adds, once in contact with each other, "are the same" in the sense that knowledge, the "possession" of what is observed, is the conceptual image or copy of what was originally perceived (Aristotle 1952, 1072b15*f*).

Another dimension of this patterned, logical necessity, where the observable world is mirrored as knowledge in the mind, is introduced elsewhere in *Categories*, where Aristotle undertakes the description of the "predicaments" and "predicables." The predicaments are "categories" that enable the logical sorting of the experiential world into objects, "perceptibles," as well as the variety of qualifications, conditions, relations, circumstances, and other attributes that can be applied to them. There are ten categories, including substance, quality, quantity, relation, time, place, action, passivity, condition, and position. Hence, a human being (substance) may also be female (quality), one of three together (quantity), the mother of the other two (relation), present at this moment (time), in a room (place), laughing (action), being served a martini (passivity), slightly inebriated (condition), and sitting down (position). There are five predicables, including genus, species, property, accident, and specific difference (quiddity). The predicables locate objects in groups, differentiate them from other objects, and identify their important and less important characteristics. Hence, Louise is a human being (species) and an animal (the genus that includes the human species), is warm blooded (property), has two legs (accident), and has the capacity to reason (specific difference). Properties belong to things necessarily (Louise could not be human if she were not warm blooded), while accidents belong nonnecessarily (she could be a different color and still be human). Most important, Louise's species is fundamentally differentiated from all other species by its capacity to reason, which is the property of properties, the "specific difference," or what medieval philosophy called the quiddity of that natural being. Aristotle's concept of specific difference is the linchpin of his metaphysics, identifying the essential being of an object, its intrinsic meaningfulness unmediated by any act of perception, cognition, or representation. It is also the concept that Locke (1965) will challenge in his *Essay Concerning Human Understanding* in the process of telling an entirely different story about the meaning of meaning.

The connection between this arcane metaphysical architecture and Aristotle's theory of discourse is closer at hand than it might appear, in fact quite immediately at hand to the extent that his discussion of perception, the predicables, and the predicaments takes place in the *Organon*, a traditional grouping of his treatises on logic that is finally about scientific (in the sense of rigorously logical) discursive practice. Basically, the books of the *Organon* explain how logical assertions and argumentative chains of assertions, the substance of discourse, map onto the knowledge of the world that human beings derive from perception. The first book is *Categories*, which concerns the terms of logical propositions (subject and predicate); the second is *On Interpretation*, which concerns the forming of the proposition, defined as a statement that is either true or false; the third is *Prior Analytics*, which concerns the forming of deductive inferences in syllogisms, taken to be the most rigorous kind of argument; the fourth is *Posterior Analytics*, which concerns the substance of scientific knowledge (in the sense of syllogisms whose conclusions are necessarily true); the fifth is *Topics*, which concerns the substance of dialectical, or nonnecessary syllogisms; and the sixth is *On Sophistical Refutations*, which concerns invalid syllogisms that only appear to demonstrate their conclusions. In brief, consistent with a mimetic theory of discourse, the forms of propositions and syllogisms, which are acts of pure intellection, follow logical rules for relating the metaphysical predicaments and predicables that are the substance of knowledge, while the grammatical forms of language map onto propositions and syllogisms, giving visible shape to argument: all human beings have the capacity to reason; Louise is a human being. The test of the truthfulness of an argument, again consistent with a mimetic theory, is the quality of the relationship between its statements and the realities of the world to which they refer (if Louise is an aardvark, the argument fails). As Aristotle (1973) says about propositional truth-value in *On Interpretation*: "It is by the facts of the case, by their being or not being so, that a statement is called true or false" (4b10).

If we take Aristotle's discussion of syllogistic reasoning in the *Organon* as a metaphor for his notion of how knowledge is acquired and disseminated through discursive practice, two points are noteworthy as anticipations of how some later stories about language and discourse will diverge from his. The first concerns the view of knowledge implicit in the idea of the syllogism, a line of reasoning that proceeds from a general premise (like all human beings are rational) to a particular conclusion. The movement of a syllogism is downward into the store of knowledge in the sense that the conclusion is only a more specific instance of the general truth of the major premise. Syllogisms don't add to knowledge by making new knowledge; they only explore the latent details of what is already known: if we know that human beings are rational, we know that Louise is rational presuming she is human. The implication is that knowledge, in effect the world's collection of major premises, is stable and bounded, a system of truths that can be endlessly refined, qualified, or exemplified but not fundamentally altered. For Aristotle, these truths come from a store comprised of the substance of philosophy, history, ethics, politics, epic literature, drama, poetry, oratory, and religious books that are collectively the archive of classical Greek culture. The syllogistic metaphor of stable knowledge will undergo significant revision in the Renaissance, when the movement of reasoning comes to be likened to the chains of geometric reasoning, outward toward new entailments, new connections, indeed new knowledge, rather than downward, from major premises to necessary (but smaller) conclusions. The second point about Aristotle's discussion of reasoning in the *Organon* has to do with the linguistic representation of propositions. While logical assertions may be embodied by sentences, they are not the same thing as sentences and do not require verbal form for their existence. It is in that sense that language is effectively invisible in Aristotle's thinking. What makes a proposition logical is the lawful attribution of a predicate to a subject, an attribution that could be represented symbolically (all A is B) without a sentence formulation, or an attribution that could take different syntactic forms, or an attribution that could be described over more than one sentence. A crude analogy (minus the rigor of the true proposition) may be found in the relationship between an essay and its outline. The logical essence of an essay's argument, according to this theory, may be found in the outline, which is then embodied in the sentences that comprise the whole text. When language returns to visibility in the stories of Locke and others, Aristotle's assumptions about the nonlinguistic nature of thinking will be challenged (the expression *purple unicorn*, for instance, is more evidently an adjective followed by a noun than it is an accident predicated of a substance), with dramatic consequences for theories about discourse and about the nature of knowledge itself.

In *Rhetoric*, Aristotle explores practical, as opposed to scientific, discourse, where everything he describes elsewhere about metaphysics, necessary knowledge, propositions, and syllogisms is adapted, but not fundamentally changed, to suit the pragmatic realities of public (hence, nonscientific) discussion, including the political assembly, the law court, and other (epideictic) social occasions. Consistent with the mimetic tradition, he represents the forms of public discourse as an imitation of the more technically rigorous logic of scientific thought but also as an inevitable falling away from the ideal of necessary knowledge that purely logical thinking can achieve. He calls rhetoric the counterpart of "dialectic" (Aristotle 1991, 1354a), where dialectic is the practical-world equivalent of logic and enthymeme the practical equivalent of syllogism. The concern of dialectic is to derive pragmatically logical arguments through disputation (the accused is guilty for these reasons; the accused is innocent for those reasons), and rhetoric is then concerned to present the competing arguments to audiences. Rhetoric turns *probably* but not *necessarily* true lines of reasoning (enthymemes) into arrangements of verbal statements, which are designed, by the skill with which they are composed and performed, to persuade audiences of the truth of the propositional content they display. Aristotle is quite clear that while practical knowledge cannot achieve the certainty of scientific knowledge, the forms of rhetoric are ideally modeled on the forms of logic so that practical knowledge approaches, without achieving, the reliability of necessary knowledge. He writes that "it belongs to the same capacity both to see the true and [to see] what resembles the true," insisting that human beings "have a natural disposition for the true" and that those who are well practiced in the rigors of achieving scientific knowledge also possess a commensurate ability to arrive at reliable opinions (what Aristotle calls "doxa"). Moreover, he contends that the enthymemic argument is the rhetorical equivalent of the syllogistic argument, different in its less-structured movement from one proposition to the next but parallel (though not equal) in its ability to arrive at legitimate conclusions. The truly knowledgeable mind that is "best able to see from what materials, and how, a syllogism arises" will have equivalent talent to compose enthymemes "if he grasps also what sort of things an enthymeme is concerned with" (1355a11).

As in *On Interpretation*, where the sentence is only "accidentally" related to the proposition, so in the *Rhetoric* language is well down the list of Aristotle's significant issues when discussing "the available means of persuasion" (Aristotle 1991, 1355b). The essence of rhetorical theory is identifying the resources available to the orator for forming effective arguments, and most of the *Rhetoric* is accordingly taken up with the appeals to ethos (the character of the speaker), pathos (the audience), and logos (the argument itself) available for each of the domains of rhetoric. Foremost among the means of persuasion are the artistic proofs, which are arrayed as "topoi" (Greek for "places") from which prototypical lines of reasoning (story lines) or forms of argument (like definition, or comparison) may be derived, and which are grouped together under the heading of "invention" ("heuresis"). The concepts of invention and topos serve as compelling demonstration of the point of view of a mimetic theory of discourse. *Invention* does not denote what the word routinely suggests to our post-Enlightenment sensibility, namely, the creation of a radically original argument or text. Neither does *topos* suggest a device that somehow taps the psychological wellsprings of creativity. Aristotle's topoi are *places* in the storehouse of cultural knowledge, whether the mind of the orator or the books—the epics, tragedies, histories, political speeches, philosophical works—that comprise the culture. In short, they are applications not to creativity but to memory. Their use in new speeches represents a reworking of familiar themes, story lines, and formal arrangements. Remember that mimesis refers to imitation, not originality: what is valued, both philosophically and aesthetically, is the familiar made fresh, the time-honored reinvoked, the old stories retold, the general truth reexemplified, "what oft was thought but ne'er so well expressed." Meanwhile, the work of invention is not explicitly linguistic work: it is rational inquiry into "the available means of persuasion." Language, for Aristotle, comes third in line after the invention and arrangement of proofs (where proofs have the same extralinguistic reality that propositions have in logic), foreshadowing the sequence of "canons" that Cicero will identify for Roman rhetoric; invention (where arguments are retrieved); disposition (where they are arranged); elocution (where they are rendered in formal language); memory (where mnemonic devices are employed to aid the orator in recalling the parts of the speech); and action, or pronunciation (the physical mannerisms, voice inflections, and other techniques for dramatizing the speech). Hence, the very partitioning of the *Rhetoric* illustrates how much work Aristotle imagines an orator must accomplish before getting to the tedious business of translating the "speech" into language.

Aristotle writes about language out of characteristically compulsive thoroughness and with a sense of impatient indulgence of the realities of human weakness. He opens his discussion of style by observing that the first, and greater, part of the *Rhetoric* concerns "that which comes first by nature," namely, "the facts from which a speech has persuasive effect." The details of style and delivery (the speaking of the speech) come next, not only in the sequence of issues to be treated in an account of rhetoric but also in the making of a speech (Aristotle 1991,

1403b). The "facts" do not derive from acts of language but from acts of rational disputation. One might suppose that Aristotle is simply distinguishing between doing research for a presentation and then, subsequently, preparing the text. But his explanation of the subordinate status of language in the art of speech making suggests that there is something deeper than merely this pragmatic division of labor. We must pay attention to delivery, he writes, when dealing with matters of opinion, "not because it is right but because it is necessary." Ideally, "true justice" should require nothing more than debate "by means of the facts themselves" so that "everything except demonstration is incidental." What makes the choices of diction, style, and delivery important is "the corruption of the audience." Facts appeal to the mind, but words appeal to the emotions, and moving the audience is as important in practical discourse as convincing it. "Expression," therefore, "has some small necessary place in all teaching" because "to speak in one way rather than another does make some difference in regard to clarity, though not a great difference," and words are "forms of outward show" that are needed "to affect the audience" (1404a).

Predictably, Aristotle's focus in the section on style and delivery is on clarity, the means by which lexical and syntactic choices assist the display of "facts." Language is a form of adornment, the dress of thought, more effective (and affective) as it is more becoming to the occasion. He says, famously, in *Poetics* that "the perfection of style is to be clear without being mean" (Aristotle 1961b, 1458a22). His observations about style emphasize the three p's, purity, propriety, and perspicuity, which medieval grammarians will later discuss as the "doctrine of decorum" (Aristotle 1991, 1405a *f*; Aristotle 1961b, 1457b *f*). Purity concerns the familiarity or currency of usage, where common words and expressions are generally preferable to "strange" words, foreign borrowings, exotic words, and new coinages. Propriety concerns the appropriateness or aptness of words and expressions. Hence, Aristotle criticizes Euripides for using the expression "king of the oar" to describe a proficient sailor because "the word 'king' goes beyond the dignity of the subject" (Aristotle 1991, 1405a29). Perspicuity (clarity) refers to the transparency of reference, the ease with which one can discern the facts as they are reflected in words. Decorum suggests an interplay of ethical and aesthetic considerations, since the orator's (or poet's) responsibilities are both to speak the truth and to speak it memorably. Aristotle's discussion of "metaphor" is revealing in this regard since for Aristotle metaphor is nothing more than an especially pleasing form of adornment, the jewelry on the dress of thought, enhancing clarity by adding "sweetness and strangeness" (1405a). He invokes images of dress in the discussion of metaphor, explaining the need for appropriateness. of verbal effect through an example of the clothing proper to young and old men. A "scarlet cloak" is "right for a young one," but hardly for one who is older. A metaphor is simply a substitute of one term or expression for another in order to enhance otherwise prosaic representation. As Aristotle explains in *Poetics*, the artist might substitute a metaphorical reference to "10,000 deeds" in place of a more conventional reference to "many deeds," or might refer to "the evening of life" based on an analogy between the stages of life and the stages of the day. For Aristotle, metaphor is essentially a logical exercise, the substitution of a species term (*10,000 deeds*) for a generic term, for example, or an analogy (Aristotle 1961b, 1457b *f*). It is far from Wordsworth's "spontaneous overflow of feeling" since clarity of reference—a true reflection in the mirror of language—remains the dominant value. Language is finally most effective when it is least obtrusive and least reliable when it draws the most attention to itself.

Like Plato, Aristotle is primarily, if not exclusively, concerned with spoken language, and mostly from the vantage point of the speaker. This is hardly surprising given the values and beliefs of ontological rhetoric. Speakers are at the nearest remove from the truth of things-in-themselves, mirroring the world in language, responsible primarily for ensuring that the mirror is free of distortion. They are the initial mediators of things by means of words, the closest to the truth of their subject matter, and, presuming impeccable ethos, the most reliable actors in the spectrum of verbal practice. Listeners are next in the hierarchy of reliability since, while they are obliged to mediate the relationship between what they hear and what they know or seek to learn, they have the advantage of being able to interrogate speakers about the truth of their statements. Third in the hierarchy come writers, who have an additional burden of translating the signs of spoken language into the signs of written language, holding a mirror up to a mirror, one additional remove from the "presence" of things. And finally, lowest in the hierarchy, come poor readers, obliged across distances of space and time to gauge the relationship between marks on a page and animate speech, speech and propositions, propositions and things. Plato and Aristotle have little directly to say about the art of reading, partly because of their philosophical values and partly, no doubt, because reading, which presumes access to written texts, was an uncommon practice among Athenians of the fifth century BCE. Their position, however, given the logic of a mimetic theory of discourse, is as inescapable as the last proposition in an Aristotelian enthymeme. If the material world reflects the truth of the ideal world, and a (knowledgeable) text reflects that truth, then a reading of the text, if it is a competent reading, identifies the truth of the text. The disciplined art of reading entails correctly retrieving the propositional content of a text, the logical paraphrase at the heart of its pattern of sentences. Readers are not free to make meanings of their own; they are obliged to pursue meanings that are latent in what they read. And there can only be one true reading, a necessary inference from Aristotle's law of contrariety, which states that a thing cannot both be and not be at the same time and in the same respect (Aristotle 1952, 1005b *f*). A reading cannot be both true and false, and if it is true, then no other can be simultaneously true. Alternative readings result from intellectual incapacity, laziness, or perversity, while reaching the truth of the text (or correctly identifying its error) is both an intellectual labor and a moral imperative.

ST. AUGUSTINE

But these are my own inferences, not explicit lines of Platonic or Aristotelian thinking. The art of reading becomes a chapter in the European story of ontological rhetoric only later, after a text appears on the cultural landscape whose meanings are compelling enough, and whose appeal is broad enough, to make textual interpretation an important intellectual and social problem. That text, of course, is the Bible, and one vastly influential investigation of the techniques of biblical exegesis, from which we may derive an ontological theory of reading, is Saint Augustine's *On Christian Doctrine*. Situated at the intersection of Greco-Roman and Judeo-Christian cultures, Augustine (354–430) is both rhetorician and priest, trained in the arts of language before his conversion to the faith. After his conversion, subsequent ordination, and eventual installation as bishop of Hippo, his greatest pastoral challenge, as a teacher of other priests along with the lay faithful, was the correct reading of the sacred book. The challenge was complicated by the fact that heretical readings were posing a significant problem for the unity of the early church; one could find a Manichean or Gnostic lurking behind every bush. And it was further, more personally complicated by Augustine's own earlier infatuation with the tales of pagan Greece and Rome, whose substance he found to be antithetical to the truths of the Christian faith, but whose techniques of storytelling, whose reliance on narrative, dramatic rendering, and figurative language, are disturbingly similar to those of the Bible. He laments in *Confessions* that he had wasted his youth reading those pagan books, preferring "empty romances to more valuable studies," beguiled by "the wooden horse and its crew of soldiers," which made "an enchanting dream, futile though it was." He recalls his early education: "I was obliged to memorize the wanderings of a hero named Aeneas while . . . I failed to remember my own erratic ways. I learned to lament the death of Dido . . . while all the time I was dying, separated from you, my God and my Life." Now that he has seen the light, he understands that, "while curtains are hung over the entrances to the schools," they are not so much "symbols in honor of mystery as veils concealing error" (Augustine 1961, I:13). Turning to the Bible, he discovers that, while its "gait [is] humble," the "heights it reache[s] [are] sublime." It contains "something . . . at once beyond the understanding of the proud and hidden from the eyes of children"; it is "enfolded in mysteries" (III:5). He concedes that there had previously been passages that "struck [him] as absurd," but goes on to say that, once he "had heard reasonable explanations," he came to regard them as "of the nature of profound mysteries." The Bible has a "deeper meaning in which its great secrets are locked away" (VI:5). The challenge, however, is how to interpret these mysteries and understand the deeper meanings when the surface meanings in Bible narratives, parallel in their dramatic, metaphorical representations to stories in the pagan texts, appear sometimes, at the literal level, to be "absurd."

The organization of *On Christian Doctrine*, Augustine's effort to theorize exegesis, reveals the strategy he will use to identify and stabilize the meanings of the sacred book. In keeping with an ontological theory, he intends to "speak of things as such first and of signs later" (Augustine 1958, I: iii). Accordingly, the first book of *On Christian Doctrine* is a review of the truths of the Catholic faith as established by the writings of the fathers of the church (Tertullian, Saint Ambrose, Saint Jerome, and Augustine himself, among others). The second book offers a theory of signs and the truth of propositions, the third book is an analysis of figurative passages in the Bible, and the final book is a discussion of eloquence, applicable to pulpit oratory. Augustine's intent is essentially to anchor the meanings of one text in the meanings of another believed to be more philosophically transparent—that is, to ground understanding of the Bible in the propositional substance of the new Christian theology. The problem with sacred scripture is that some passages are "covered with a most dense mist" so that "many and varied obscurities and ambiguities deceive those who read casually." Augustine explains that God speaks metaphorically in order to "conquer pride by work," obliging the faithful to earn their understanding by close, exegetical analysis.

"What is sought with difficulty," he explains, "is discovered with more pleasure." The Holy Spirit, he says, has "magnificently and wholesomely modulated the Holy Scriptures" so that those who labor in hunger for the truth may find both "open places," where the text of the sacred book speaks plainly but also "obscure places" that may "deter a disdainful attitude" (Augustine 1961, II:vi). The difficulty for Augustine and his priests is that, while the Bible always speaks the truth, unprepared lay readers do not always correctly perceive it because of ambiguities in the Bible's "signs." Anyone who "understands in the Scriptures something other than that intended by them is deceived, although they do not lie" (I:xxxvi). So, the resolution of the difficulty lies in referring Biblical statements to the logical propositions of Church doctrine. Of interest, the priority Augustine establishes is not, then, from the Bible, as the Word of God, to Church theology, but rather the reverse. Faced with the spread of Manichean heresy, he shackles the power of the sacred book, as described in chapter 2, in the chains of rational thought. And from his day to modern times, Catholicism, by contrast with Protestant Christianity, has tended to maintain the same priority, insisting that the mysteries, metaphors, and stories of the Bible be read against the backdrop of official doctrine.

Using reasoning similar to Aristotle's, Augustine argues that the Bible's statements have logical propositions at their core that their superficial verbal form may sometimes embellish to inspire the faithful and other times obscure to strengthen commitment to faith by obliging readers to overcome textual challenges. In keeping with an ontological theory, the test of a good biblical reading is its correspondence to the a priori truths of the faith. Augustine says that "the truth of valid inference," that is, the conclusions we derive from correctly interpreting signs, is "not instituted by men" but is instead "perpetually instituted by God in the reasonable order of things." For example, "the person who narrates the order of events in time does not compose that order himself"; rather, the text's order mirrors the order of things in nature. Similarly, someone who shows "the natures of animals, plants, or minerals does not discuss things instituted by men," nor does someone who "describes the stars or their motions" (Augustine 1961, II:xxxii). Truths exist independent of discourse and determine, therefore, the reliability of statements. Biblical statements may appear to be unreliable because they fail on the surface to correspond to the truth. But the Bible cannot lie. Therefore, its metaphorical or otherwise ambiguous statements, appearing to contradict "the reasonable order of things," must be interpreted until they reveal the propositions of Church doctrine. Augustine provides a telling example of this reasoning in Book III, where he undertakes to explain the interpretation of metaphorical passages. The rule for determining whether or not a Biblical statement is figurative is to evaluate its surface meaning to see if it accords with Christian theology. If a statement "commends beneficence" or "condemns vice," then it is literal; if it does the opposite, then it can only be figurative. The Bible says, for instance, that "except you eat the flesh of the Son of man, and drink his blood, you shall not have life in you." Since the statement appears to recommend cannibalism, "it is *therefore* a figure" (italics added). The rule, then, for proceeding to understand this statement is that "what is read should be subjected to diligent scrutiny until an interpretation contributing to the reign of charity is produced" (III:xv–xvi). A cynic might object that this view of interpretation conveniently forces all readings, not to mention all readers, to conform to orthodoxy, someone's privileged representation of the way the world is, if they are to be regarded as "legitimate." And indeed, judged from perspectives other than the ontological theory of the meaning of meaning, it does precisely that. But for believers, for Augustine no less than for Plato and Aristotle before him (and for a great many others after them as well), the truths of a metaphysically ordered universe offer human beings a hope that the chaos, danger, evil, and irrationality of the world of Becoming are indeed comprehensible by reference to something purposeful behind them, and that discourse, for all the lies and errors it propagates because of human weakness, may also enjoy, at its best, some modest authority to shine a light in the darkness.

ANTONIN SCALIA AND HELENE CIXOUS

Ontological rhetoric sponsors the Western epistemological perspective sometimes referred to as essentialism—a belief that the world's "deep structure" exists independent of the means of naming it, which leads to a further belief that verbal and other forms of representation, correctly managed through the practices of composing and comprehending, serve as windows through which to perceive the realities they denote. While the genealogy of ontological rhetoric may be seen in the intersection of Greco-Roman and Judeo-Christian discourse theory, the essentialism at its heart spans the collective centuries of European philosophy and remains as powerful an influence on rhetorical practice today as it was in fifth century (BCE) Athens and first century (CE) Carthage. It's tempting to assume that essentialism, sometimes also called foundationalism or fundamentalism, exclusively supports conservative ideology, where values of permanence, stability, and tradition (certainly the values of Plato, Aristotle, and Augustine) serve to regulate superficial conditions of indeterminacy and flux. But in fact, liberal and even radical ideologies seeking the alteration of some status quo can promote essentialism with the same zeal. Ontological rhetoric proceeds from an attitude about the nature of the truth, not from the political valence of a particular conviction: right to life and right to choose can evoke equivalent doctrinal enthusiasm from their advocates. Supreme Court justice Antonin Scalia (1936–) and French feminist Helene Cixous (1937–), otherwise strange bedfellows indeed, make this point in their similarly essentialist arguments about discourse, the nature of reading in Scalia's case and the nature of women's writing in the case of Cixous. Scalia's theory of "textualism," which defends a conservative belief in the determinacy of meaning, and Cixous's theory of "ecriture feminine," which offers a radical critique of phallocentrism, display equivalent confidence in ontological realities underlying their representations.

Textualism is a hermeneutic that presumes both the existence of a univocal, unchanging, public understanding of the meaning of a text and the possibility of access to that understanding, even at different historical moments, through rigorous close reading. It's the equivalent in legal discourse of the argument for explication de texte that characterized New Criticism in the literary theory of the mid-twentieth century. It's also an argument that hopes to assuage Plato's fear of writing by liberating it, as he did not, from the interpretive ravages of reading across space and time. In *A Matter of Interpretation: Federal Courts and the Law*, Antonin Scalia (1998) argues for the possibility of necessarily correct readings of statements in the US Constitution based on accessible knowledge of common-sense verbal usage in the eighteenth-century social milieu of the framers, readings which may serve today as the basis for judicial decisions in particular cases. Like the New Critics, Scalia denies access to authorial intention, insisting therefore that he does not subscribe to "strict construction" constitutional arguments that claim an awareness of what the framers meant to say. But in application, his distinction between textualism and strict construction lacks a substantial difference because the claim to know with certainty what the words mean nevertheless establishes a necessity of reference—a determinate meaning—based on the framers' choice of one construction over an infinite range of alternative possibilities. If the framers used a particular expression, it's reasonable to conclude that they used it deliberately. And if we know the expression's contemporary reference, then, unless the framers made a diction error, we can be confident of what they intended. In his ruling in *District of Columbia v. Heller*, which asserts a Second-Amendment right to possess a hand gun in the home even when unrelated to service in a militia, Scalia's (2008) textualist approach begins with an assumption that "the Constitution was written to be understood by the voters; its words and phrases were used in their normal and ordinary as distinguished from technical meaning" (3) and then sets out to establish the common meanings of key terms and expressions through fifty densely but narrowly logical pages of comparative semantic analysis. He concludes, for example, after comparing multiple uses of the constitutional phrase "right of the people" that, taken together, "these instances unambiguously refer to individual rights, not 'collective' rights, or rights that may be exercised only through participation in some corporate body" (5). Hence, the right to possess firearms applies personally to each member of a militia, not just to the militia as a government entity. Scalia's treatment is reminiscent of Augustine's analysis of metaphor—where knowledge of the true meaning of a statement precedes rather than results from its close inspection. The cause-effect relationship between Scalia's well-publicized prior commitment to the right (his included) to own firearms and the logical necessity implied in his reading of the language of the Constitution is, outside the worldview of ontological rhetoric, unmistakably biased. Within that worldview, however, the constitutional language is clear to Scalia because the essential right of individuals to possess handguns is self-evident and unassailable.

Some critics have characterized Helene Cixous's depiction of a feminine mode of writing in *The Laugh of the Medusa* as a rhetorical contrivance enabling Cixous to interrogate phallocentric values such as rationality, authority, argumentation, logic, and linearity, which have historically marginalized women as writers. Defense of Cixous's strategy as a deconstruction of the hierarchical binary man/woman is certainly plausible in light of Cixous's long friendship with Jacques Derrida and his influence on her thinking. She makes various gestures in her text to suggest a Derridean critique—ostensibly denying the ontological status of women's discourse ("it is impossible to *define* a feminine practice of writing" [Cixous 1976, 883]) and suggesting in her regard for Jean Genet that "inscriptions of femininity" (878n3) may not be unique to women. At the same time, however, she does not make the double move characteristic of Derridean critique, which we'll explore in chapter 7, where a binary is first inverted and then ultimately *sub*verted. The subordinate term of her binary is one she's obliged to invent for herself: women's writing in opposition to men's writing. Then, having invented it, she is mostly content to argue both its difference and (at least for women) its priority, never seeking to overthrow the binary itself in order to propose a writing that is not gendered. The fact is, her political project—the liberation of women as speaking subjects—arguably makes the subversion of the binary a self-defeating strategy, entailing the reappropriation of women's expressiveness within a new representation of writing that denies the role of gender as a formative principle. But the consequence of retaining the binary is an essentialist rendering of woman as well as women's writing, manifest in Cixous's invocation of what is most explicitly and materially female—the female body.

Medusa is an exhortation to women, silenced for centuries by social, political, and economic oppression, to "write their bodies," and Cixous's ontological claim is that the writing of women is as organically different from the writing of men as the vagina is different from the penis. While she insists that she doesn't want "to confuse the biological and the cultural" (Cixous 1976, 875), her point is that she doesn't want the physical and psychological intimidation of "conventional man" to be mistaken for a cultural necessity. Meanwhile, her argument depends on an unwavering identification of woman and body, women's writing and women's bodies, enabling a metaphorical opposition of womb and phallus. "I write this as a woman, toward women. When I say 'woman,' I'm speaking of . . . a universal woman subject who must bring women to their senses and to their meaning in history" (875–76). "Write!" she says. "Writing is for you, you are for you; your body is yours, take it" (876). The entire history of writing, she asserts, "is confounded with the history of reason," a tradition of "self-admiring, self-stimulating, self-congratulatory phallocentrism" (879). It's a history of the writing of men, "the builders of the analytic empire" (892), whose mode of expression Cixous describes variously as "linear," "objectivized," "generalized" (881); comprised of "partitions," "classes," "rhetorics," "regulations," and "codes" (886); preoccupied with "successiveness" and "connection" (888); and committed to "opposition," "hierarchizing," and "the struggle for mastery" (893). Women's writing by contrast, arising from a "desire to live self from within, a desire for the swollen belly, for language, for blood" (891), is indistinguishable from their unique sexuality, an intrinsically female (pro)creativity, an aesthetic practice interwoven with "a passionate and precise interrogation of . . . erotogeneity" (876). When a woman speaks in public, she doesn't do so as a disembodied mind: she "throws her trembling body forward; she lets go of herself, she flies; all of her passes into her voice, and it's with her body that she vitally supports the 'logic' of her speech" (881). The "true texts of women—female-sexed texts"

(877) Cixous likens both to singing—"first music from the first voice of love which is alive in every woman" (881)—and also to flying—"flying in language and making it fly," taking pleasure in "jumbling the order of space, in disorienting it, in changing around the furniture, dislocating things and values, breaking them all up, emptying structures, and turning propriety upside down" (887). What is obvious in Cixous's urging of women to "write through their bodies" (886) is the essentially gendered nature of her understanding of writing, an ontological understanding that serves as metaphysical foundation for her feminist political engagement. As with Scalia, albeit at the other end of the political spectrum, core conceptions and beliefs, represented but not created through language, are the ground for Cixous's work on behalf of the liberation of women's voices.

4

OBJECTIVIST RHETORIC

DESCARTES

Rene Descartes (1596–1650) begins his *Discourse on the Method of Rightly Conducting the Reason and Seeking Truth in the Sciences* by describing his mistrust of books. Reviewing the course of his own early learning, he identifies the knowledge to be gained from books, including famous deeds learned from history, pleasing but impossible events from fiction and poetry, powers of eloquence from rhetoric, quantitative processes from mathematics, exhortations to virtue from moral treatises, the path to heaven from theology, learned disputation from philosophy, and professional skills from law and medicine. His catalog symbolically identifies the substance of that stable, bounded repository of cultural knowledge in which Aristotle had grounded the unassailable major premises of his syllogisms and enthymemes. But Descartes introduces the ancient library of wisdom mostly to disparage it: the fanciful embroideries of history and fiction; the uselessness of works on rhetoric and poetics since they address "gifts of nature rather than fruits of study"; the limited practicality of classical mathematics, "good only for the mechanical arts"; the failure of ethics treatises to identify "an adequate criterion of virtue"; the irrelevance of theology since the road to heaven is "just as open to the most ignorant as to the most learned"; and the futility of speculative philosophy, which has failed to produce "anything which is not in dispute and consequently doubtful and uncertain." As for professional literature, law, medicine, and other arts, "since they took their cardinal principles from philosophy," itself unreliable as a ground for learning, "nothing solid could be built on so insecure a foundation" (Descartes 1960a, 7–8). By the end of his studies, he finds himself "saddled with so many doubts and errors" that all he can be certain of is the extent of his ignorance (5). Not only are the books themselves faulty but so too are the means, specifically the conventions of logical inquiry, by which all this traditional knowledge had been produced and mined for its inexhaustible subtleties. In examining the arts of logic, he explains, he

DOI: 10.7330/9780874219364.c004

had been obliged to conclude that "its syllogisms and most of its other methods serve rather to explain to another what one already knows, or even . . . to speak freely and without judgment of what one does not know, than to learn new things" (14). In his dismissal of both the content of ancient knowledge and the classical instruments of speculative inquiry, Descartes strikes at the heart of Aristotle's philosophy, its assumption that the truth of human understanding and argument—the substance of discourse—is anchored in, and in turn reflects, a bedrock of ontological certainty.

The ancient books had reliably archived the axiomatic assertions of Western culture, had held the mirror up to nature, catching in reflection the array of metaphysical absolutes (Being) that supports the coherence of the phenomenal world (Becoming). Truths of genus, species, and specific difference, of time, space, motion, cause, and effect were mirrored in physics, metaphysics, and logic. Ethics mirrored the golden mean between behavioral extremes; politics testified to the intrinsic hierarchies of human aptitude and class privilege; mathematics and music celebrated the harmonics of nature, the music of the spheres; rhetoric organized discursive memory; and history as well as literature captured the deeper meanings of human events, dramatizing the values of the culture in stirring narrative. There was never an expectation of learning new things; there was instead the satisfying illumination or exemplification of timeless truths, an endless glossing of what was already known, an application of general principles to particular circumstances, or an aesthetically pleasing restatement of what "oft was thought but ne'er so well expressed." In seeking something called "the New," Descartes creates not a specific knowledge in one field of study but an altered concept of knowledge itself, together with a changed understanding of what it means to compose discourse. He rejects Aristotle's syllogism as a metaphor for writing and learning, where the direction of inquiry is "down" into the store of accumulated wisdom. In its place, he proposes an "outward," voyaging, expansionist, and progressive ideal of composition, beginning with a critical attitude toward abstraction and characterized by a painstaking observation of phenomenal experience that leads by accretion to ever-newer knowledge. He resolves to "seek no other knowledge than that which I might find within myself, or perhaps in the great book of nature," emphasizing a pragmatic intelligence, "thinking about the things around me so that I [can] derive some profit from them" rather than speculating, like "a man of letters in his study," on empty ideas that have no practical value, but that serve, "the farther they are removed from common sense," merely to show off his "wit" in making them appear plausible (Descartes 1960a, 8–9). He proposes a discursive practice that emphasizes four intellectual values. The first is skepticism, "never to accept anything as true unless I [recognize] it to be certainly and evidently such." The second is analysis, "to divide each of the difficulties which I [encounter] into as many parts as possible, and as might be required for an easier solution." The third is method, "to think in an orderly fashion . . . beginning with the things which [are] simplest and easiest to understand, and gradually and by degrees reaching toward more complex knowledge, even treating, as though ordered, materials which [are] not necessarily so." And the fourth is inclusiveness, "always to make enumerations so complete, and reviews so general, that I would be certain that nothing [is] omitted" (15).

Descartes turns decisively away from Aristotle's metaphysical self-confidence and toward a studied uncertainty and caution, comparing himself to a "man who walks alone in the darkness," resolving to go so slowly and circumspectly that "if I [do] not get ahead very rapidly I [am] at least safe from falling" (Descartes 1960a, 14). He claims to pattern his deliberate method on the strategy of "travelers, who, finding themselves lost in a forest, must not wander about . . . but should go as straight as they can in the direction they first select" in order to arrive "at some destination" (19). The journey images are important because they metaphorically link learning to a step-by-step progression away from ignorance and toward the truth, a "new" truth that is not intuitively, rationally, or timelessly present to the mind as ontological certainty but that must be constructed—composed—laboriously in time, with inevitable missteps along the way. Descartes argues that "truth can be discovered only little by little" (52) as researchers move methodically from the known to the unknown, and from the simple to the more complex, by means of chains of assertions grounded in previous inquiry and pushing ever forward toward the next discovery. Scientific knowledge is not only cumulative but also, in its emphasis on self-critique, inevitably collective and public, an ever-ongoing task, not for the closeted, armchair speculator but for groups, and generations, of researchers actively searching out the mysteries of the world. Because the process is deliberate and halting, dependent on trial and error, no one singly completes the journey. Setting the standard for scientific inquiry as a collective practice, Descartes resolves "to publish faithfully to the world the little which I [have] discovered," encouraging others to contribute in their turn "to the experiments which must be made." By this means, "later investigators could begin where the earlier had left off" so that "mankind would combine the lives and work of many people, and would go much further

than any individual could go by himself" (46). The result is less comprehensive than the settled understanding of the ancient world, the next
assertion ever beyond the horizon of contemporary learning, but the
knowledge of experiment is shared, reliable, and progressive, featuring
a gradual but certain improvement, never possible from speculative philosophy, in the array of practical applications by which human beings
might become "masters and possessors of nature." Knowing the "nature
and behavior of fire, water, air, stars, the heavens, and all the other bodies which surround us," he is convinced, it will be possible in time to
"employ these entities for all the purposes for which they are suited"
and also to invent "an infinity of devices" with which to improve the life
of society (45).

By proclaiming the superiority of an experimental, progressive, and
pragmatic knowledge based on observation over the bookish knowledge
of the ancient world, Descartes writes an early chapter in a new story
about the meaning of meaning, one that displaces metaphysics as the
ground of meaningfulness and puts in its place a concept of phenomenal experience, that is, sensory and other "factual" information derived
from nature and everyday life. Objectivist rhetoric is comprised of empirical inquiry, driven by a cycle of hypothesis and experiment, which leads
to defensible assertions linked to previous, similarly tested assertions in
a temporally evolving pattern of data-driven argument. The objectivist
rhetorician both seeks facts and makes statements whose validity can
be determined by appeal to facts. Since "the truth of the hypotheses is
proved by the actuality of the effects" (Descartes 1960a, 55), facts serve
at once as the source and test of meaningful discursive representation,
the foundation of scientific learning. But for all of Descartes's emphasis
on experiential observation, what is just as striking as his introduction
of a new story about meaningfulness is the style and voice of its presentation. The character of Descartes's own rhetoric is unmistakable in the
profuse deployment of first-person singular pronouns, beginning in the
earliest paragraphs of the *Discourse*: "I have never fancied"; "I have often
wished"; "I know of no other qualities"; "I am disposed to believe"; "I
will not hesitate to avow"; "I have already reaped"; "I have been accus-
tomed to think"; "I nevertheless derive the highest satisfaction"; "I conceive myself to have already made"; "I have chosen." The text is suffused
with the rhetoric of autobiography, and its narrator is strikingly self-
preoccupied. To be sure, it's not the taste for autobiography in itself that
stands out as original or distinctive—Montaigne is only the most obvious
of the many writers during the European Renaissance who are smitten
with the intricacies of their own minds. But what is distinctive here is

that the *Discourse* so ostensibly seeks to identify a mode of inquiry and a theory of knowledge that depend on skepticism and objectivity. From the first pages of the *Discourse*, Descartes introduces a tension between the desire to ground knowledge in observation and a preoccupation with the character of the observers themselves.

This tension is not, however, to be attributed simply to a perverse authorial narcissism; it is in fact intrinsic to the shift of reference that occurs when Descartes turns away from ontological and toward objectivist rhetoric. One can imagine him asking such questions as What are 'facts' anyway? Where do they come from? What does it mean to 'observe' and make statements about facts? For Aristotle, our understanding of everyday life, the world of Becoming, is derivative, anchored in the stable world of Being, which human rationality can directly apprehend in and through ever-shifting phenomenal experience. Aristotle's "mind" is a "passive affection," as he explains in *On the Soul*, receptive but not constitutive. It receives into itself the form of any object of perception: "It is not the stone which is in the soul," he writes, "but its form" (*De Anima* 1907, 431b29–432.). Having rejected metaphysics as the anchor of reality, Descartes is obliged to substitute an alternate source of the coherence of empirical experience, which he locates in the intellective action of the observer, whose reactions to the data of perception— the forming of ideas, the constructing and testing of hypotheses, the developing of lines of thought—is what enables knowledge to emerge. Knowledge is not present as such to perception, as Aristotle had argued. Instead, it must be built from the particulars of observation. Descartes realizes, for example, that not everything presented to the mind by the senses is necessarily accurate (consider the diminished size of an object when seen from a distance, or the broken appearance of a pencil when viewed in a glass of water). Moreover, whatever is determined to be factual does not in itself constitute knowledge (since it must be associated with other facts in the statements of a pattern of argument). What produces knowledge, therefore—and here Descartes draws a fateful philosophical distinction—is the human mind evaluating sensory information in the course of methodical inquiry. Human consciousness is the site of that skeptical attitude, analytical regard, orderly inquiry, and rigorous inclusiveness that together constitute the new objective "method." Learning is the consequence of systematic cognitive effort to sort, arrange, and identify the significance of observational information. What is perceived as sensory data, the material world beyond the thinking subject, becomes the stuff of scientific argument only as cognition acts upon it, takes it in, relates it to previous experience, and shapes it into mental constructs, that is, ideas, assertions, and lines of thought. In objectivist rhetoric, cognition discovers the logic of nature through discursive construction and rigorous empirical analysis.

Descartes's psychologizing of knowledge is fateful because it leads him to commit an historic epistemological blunder: in the context of creating scientific method, he accidentally creates the "self." More precisely, he reifies two philosophical concepts, neither of which had existed independent of the other in ontological rhetoric, the subject and the object, opening, as a consequence, an unbridgeable chasm between consciousness and materiality. "I think," he famously (and dubiously) declares, and "therefore, I am." Two implications are embedded in this axiom. First, the world of cognition differs essentially from the world of material existence: "This ego, this mind, this soul, by which I am what I am, is entirely distinct from the body and is easier to know than the latter." Moreover, "even if the body were not, the soul would not cease to be all that it now is" (Descartes 1960a, 24–25). Second, not only is ego different from body, but it is also prior to body, the very means by which materiality can be perceived and rendered intelligible in the first place. The domain of the subject is comprised of ideas, while the domain of the object is comprised of physical "data," the "thingness" of which is different in kind from the mental constructs by means of which the mind composes knowledge. Whatever an idea may be, it is certainly not a thing because it has no sensory aspect; and whatever a thing may be, it is certainly not an idea, both because of its thingness and because its existence is independent of the will of the subject. In *The Meditations Concerning First Philosophy*, Descartes (1960b) labors to explain the irreconcilable opposition his objectivist argument has created, in the process increasingly—and ironically—emphasizing the importance of the subject even as he underscores the observational nature of reliable knowledge. "Everything which I have thus far accepted as entirely true and assured," he insists, "has been acquired from the senses or by means of the senses." But he adds an important qualification: "I have learned by experience that these senses sometimes mislead me" (76). While he is confident that his own reality as a conscious subject "is necessarily true every time" he "pronounce[s] it or conceive[s] it in [his] mind" (82), he grows increasingly skeptical that we can "know anything certain about material objects" (118). Materiality without mind is meaningless, while consciousness, even in the absence of the material, is rich in meaning, not only aware of its own existence and the existence of God but also possessed of certain innate "modes of substance" that condition the perception of physical reality, among them "ideas of duration and number" as well as "extension, shape, location, and movement" (101). Finally, for Descartes, it is only the more reliable existence of the subject that makes the existence of the object scientifically plausible. There is reason to conclude that materiality exists even though certainty of its nature and significance must remain elusive, only because there is "present in my mind a certain idea of corporeal nature" (114). The "passive faculty of perceiving" cannot account for the meaningfulness of experience and "would be valueless" to him if it weren't for "another active faculty capable of forming and producing these ideas" (133). The track of Descartes's reasoning is as clear as it is discomfiting. An argument that begins with the priority of observation ends ironically with a conclusion about the mind's own action as the agency that alone produces knowledge.

European culture has been writing and reading the objectivist story with unparalleled enthusiasm over the nearly four hundred years since the appearance of *Discourse on Method*, enjoying the technological no less than intellectual prosperity available from the potent inquiries of theoretical and experimental science. Objectivist rhetoric has become the dominant discursive theory of modern times, not only in scientific inquiry but in its applied derivatives, like medicine and engineering; in those less-rigorous discourses that seek to emulate scientific method, such as the behavioral sciences and economics; in sociopolitical discourses, notably education, where curricular engineering and behavioral assessment imitate empirical ideals; and in the popular imagination, which regards objectivity as a benchmark of truthfulness. But there is a serpent, it appears, in every garden, and Descartes's new intellectual Eden contains an epistemological worm that has been eating ever since at Western confidence in knowledge and discourse alike. True, the new method promises a steady increase of knowledge. But what kind of knowledge? Certainly not the stable, comprehensive, logically necessary knowledge of Aristotle. While Descartes's knowledge is progressive, it is also forever partial. While repeated experiment strengthens its authenticity, the same process of experiment can invalidate it at any time. While it is grounded in fact, its substance is finally an interpretation that changes over time as new facts are discovered or old ones reevaluated within altered conceptual frameworks. Cartesian dualism isolates the subject in a realm created and governed by its own activities, populated with its own ideational substance, leaving the object an inert and unresponsive exteriority, alienated from consciousness and accessible to it only through the mediation of ambiguous artifacts of mind—ideas represented as mathematical or linguistic signs, clothed in the sometimes superficial trappings of disinterested observation (from tables of statistics to statements without personal pronouns). Objectivist rhetoric is finally, as Descartes formulates it, paradoxical at its core because what exclusively enables objectivity is the prior existence of subjectivity. The triumph of scientific inquiry has come at a higher philosophical cost, therefore, than Descartes, or discourse theory after him, might have preferred to pay, in the form of an epistemological tangle that has replaced the ontological certitude of the ancient world with a pervasive modern doubt about the nature of knowledge that extends far beyond the merely formal skepticism of Descartes's new method. With Cartesian dualism, the Age of Belief begins to slide inexorably toward the Age of Anxiety.

LOCKE

In *Essay Concerning Human Understanding,* John Locke (1632–1704), representing the different but related perspective of British empiricism, reasserts the ground of meaningfulness that defines objectivist rhetoric, declaring that "we will make greater progress in the discovery of rational and contemplative knowledge" if we reject mere speculative opinion and search for it "in the fountain, *in the consideration of things themselves*" (Locke 1965, 56). But Locke, reacting against the argument of Cartesian rationalism in favor of innate "principles and ideas," which he believes would only reestablish the prejudices of philosophical abstraction, makes a counterclaim about the priority of sensory information in the production of scientific knowledge. He challenges Descartes's view of the proactive agency of the subject by claiming that the mind works initially only with the data that observation presents to it: "The senses at first let in *particular* ideas, and furnish the yet empty cabinet," then the mind, "growing familiar with some of them," stores them in memory, abstracts them to form general or species concepts, tags them with names, and finally employs them as "the *materials* about which to exercise its discursive faculty" (35). By insisting that the mind is only reactive, rather than proactive, in the making of knowledge, Locke substitutes a radical (one might say naïve) empiricism in place of Descartes's rationalism, establishing the second of two intellectual poles between which objectivist arguments have continued to oscillate into modern times, positivism at one pole contending that nothing is scientifically intelligible that is not grounded in empirical fact, and idealism at the other contending that even the "fact" is already a symbolic representation dependent on interpretations of sensory stimuli. But what is particularly interesting about Locke's empiricism is less its view of where knowledge originates than its depiction of the vehicle by which knowledge is ultimately constructed, which for him is natural language. Descartes had spoken in a limited way about the role of mathematics, or more precisely geometry, as the "language" of scientific discourse, likening his new method to "those long chains of reasoning, so simple and easy, which enabled the geometricians to reach the most difficult demonstrations" and wondering whether "all things knowable to men might not fall into a similar logical sequence" (Descartes 1960a, 15). But for Locke, the problem of how empirical inquiry progresses from sensory stimulation to rational picture of the world is dramatically focused on the mediating role of human language. What had been virtually invisible for Aristotle is for Locke a compelling focus of attention—a focus that obliges him, more than Descartes, to grapple with the paradoxical relationship between observation and interpretation. In his theory of language, he effectively reproduces Cartesian dualism, only coming to the sovereignty of the subject by appeal to the innateness of verbal conception.

After spending considerable energy in the opening books of the *Essay* denying the existence of innate ideas and then explaining his alternative view of how perception works, how ideas are formed, how simple ideas differ from complex ones, and how we distinguish real ideas from the "fantastical," Locke makes an announcement, closing Book II, that stunningly reorients the direction of his argument, in the process turning Aristotelian discourse theory, as it had been articulated in the *Organon*, topsy-turvy. "I find that there is so close a connection between ideas and WORDS," he writes, "that it is impossible to speak clearly and distinctly of our knowledge, which all consists in propositions, without considering, first, the nature, use, and signification of Language" (Locke 1965, 225). Arguably, through its referral of propositional knowledge to the philosophy of language, no assertion in intellectual history more dramatically challenges the tradition of Aristotelian metaphysics. And Book III of the *Essay*, which Locke titles simply "Of Words," goes on to inaugurate an extended, still energetic, debate in Western rhetoric concerning the role language plays not merely in denoting reality but in constituting it through the interrelationship of consciousness and materiality. To be sure, there had been earlier rumblings about Aristotle's error in mistaking words and grammatical relationships for ontological realities. The Port-Royal logician, Antoine Arnauld, had taken up the theme in his *Art of Thinking*, published nearly thirty years earlier than the *Essay* and undoubtedly influential in the development of Locke's position. Challenging the value of Aristotle's ten categories or predicaments,

discussed in the previous chapter, Arnauld observes that the categories hinder rather than help logical thought because they are wrongly
regarded as "established by reason and by truth" when in fact they are
"mere words" and as such "only arbitrary classifications which do not
contribute any clear or distinct idea of things to the mind" (Arnauld
1964, 43–44). Locke takes his cue from this demotion of metaphysics to
verbal illusion, expanding Arnauld's critique more destructively from
the predicaments to the predicables, especially "specific difference," in
the course of an extended examination of how words enable the forming of ideas and thereby help to create pictures of the world.

Locke begins with a seemingly harmless observation that words, in
their immediate signification, represent "ideas in the mind of him that
uses them" and also "ideas in the minds of other men, with whom they
communicate" (Locke 1965, 31–32). But he moves quickly toward complexity by noting that people too often wrongly suppose "the words to
stand also for the reality of things," an error that results from miscon-
ceiving the relationship between things, which are singular, and ideas,
which are general. Ideas are derived from composites of things, words
represent only ideas, and neither words nor ideas signify singular entities in nature. A necessary consequence is that the generalized meanings of verbal ideation "belong not to the real existence of things; but
are the inventions and creatures of the understanding, made by it for its
own use" (235). Words can denote only the species "essences" of things
("substances" in Locke's terminology), those marked features of the
phenomenal world that conceptualization fixes and names in the course
of grouping together sensory and other material information as determinate ideas. In the case of more complex and abstract ideas ("mixed
modes")—an idea like adultery, for instance—the mind "takes a liberty
not to follow the existence of things exactly," instead connecting various ideas from different conceptual categories under a single abstract
word (242–43). In such instances, which are linguistic commonplaces,
"the mind searches not its patterns in nature . . . but puts such together
as may best serve its own purposes, without tying itself to a precise imitation of anything that really exists" (244). What is plain, here, is that
Locke, for all his effort to ground knowledge in empirical observation,
is obliged to concede a gap between the world of sensory information
and the world of verbalized idea that widens more and more dramatically as one moves from the simplest possible ideas (which are, even
then, not equivalent to things) to those abstract concepts, relationships
among generalizations, and lines of reasoning that would properly be
called knowledge. His version of realism, far from reasserting the sturdy

reliability of objectivist inquiry by eliminating the apparent subjectivism of Cartesian innateness, only reintroduces the subject/object dichotomy by revealing the gulf between materiality and any form of verbal/ideational representation.

But Locke has only begun to explore the depths of subjectivity. When he turns to discuss the names assigned to natural "substances," he introduces a concept that will decisively repudiate Aristotle's ontological discourse theory while creating new epistemological challenges for objectivist rhetoric as well. He calls the concept "nominal essence," formulating it in the context of a critique of the central feature of Aristotle's metaphysical order of nature, the notion of quiddity or specific difference. Recall that in chapter 3 specific difference was described as the most important of the five predicables in Aristotle's theory of logical attribution, including also genus, species, property, and accident. Specific difference is that property of a substance that distinguishes it essentially from all other substances, providing its intrinsic autonomy as a thing. Considering the substance named gold, Locke describes "a body yellow, of a certain weight, malleable, fusible, and fixed," all properties accessible to observation. Remembering his Aristotle, Locke proceeds to say that the "real essence" of this object, its quiddity, is "the constitution of the insensible parts of that body, on which those qualities and all the other properties of gold depend." Unfortunately, however, this essence, being "insensible," is not available to observation, which means that we cannot know it in any way consistent with a strictly empirical theory of learning. All we can know is "that abstract idea to which the name is annexed," the verbal idea of gold, which, Locke concludes, is "all the essence of natural substances that *we* know" and which Locke goes on to call "by a peculiar name, the *nominal essence*, to distinguish it from the real constitution of substances" (Locke 1965, 247). The concession here is striking, for it not only eliminates the abstract self-sufficiency of gold as substance in an ontological theory of knowledge but also severely compromises the link to empirical reality available from an objectivist theory. Locke expands the insight, seemingly unaware of the implications, suggesting that "to talk of specific differences in *nature*, without reference to general ideas in names, is to talk unintelligibly" (249). Pushing the point still further, "it is clear, that our distinguishing substances into species by names, is not at all founded on their real essences; nor can we pretend to range and determine them exactly into species, according to internal essential differences" (253). By this point, Locke has effectively conceded that what we know of the world, indeed all we know, is our own language-based conceptions, a view that takes him to the brink of linguistic and cultural relativism by the end of the chapter: "If we will examine it, we shall not find the nominal essence of any one species of substances in all men the same" (255).

The Aristotelian world-in-itself has clearly disappeared in Locke, and even the objectivist world-in-itself (in the sense of an intrinsically rule-governed physical system) is troublingly indemonstrable, an always partial, uncertain achievement based on the presumption that there must be a substantial essence somehow motivating the derivation of the nominal essence accessible as human knowledge. That does not mean, however, that Locke denies the possibility of scientific knowledge. On the contrary, he comes to his position as an empiricist nonetheless, albeit one who is obliged to concede the epistemological dualism that empiricism has introduced. It's important to differentiate between the objectivist perspective and what chapter 5 will call the expressivist theory of discourse. Neither Locke nor Descartes before him has the least doubt that scientific rhetoric makes statements about the world that are based on fact, supported by the aggregation of fact, and tested by appeal to fact. Expressivism, by contrast, takes the view that autonomous activities of mind project the "world" (i.e., the aggregate of meanings we call the world) through deployment of an array of signs and symbolic modes, fashioning coherences that respond primarily to human desire and need. In expressivist theory, while large masses of cold salt water, for example, are *there*, available to human perception, what establishes their human value is packed into the complexly metaphorical signification of the word *ocean*. To the extent that Descartes and Locke accentuate the role of the subject, it is only to identify the challenges of denotation and empirical reasoning in order primarily to urge the need for skepticism and diligent self-critique regarding the conduct and results of scientific inquiry. Expressivism glories in subjectivity, suggesting, in its emphasis on the power of imagination, a latter-day version of magical rhetoric, only rewritten for agnostics. Objectivism, on the other hand, concedes the messy amalgam of logic, emotion, opinion, superstition, historical error, prejudice, ulterior motive, and outright irrationality constituting the subject but struggles to bring it under the control of a rigorous, analytic theory of composition. Hence, Locke's response to having seemingly cornered himself in epistemological relativism is to dedicate the rest of Book III to a close examination of the "imperfection of words," the "abuse of words," and the "remedies of the foregoing," seeking to distinguish between the more careful, hence more objectively reliable, language of science and the imprecise language of everyday use. His recommendations are insufficient, as later contributions to objectivist rhetoric (privileging mathematics over ordinary language) will show, and they are woefully unoriginal, reiterating the empty do's and don'ts of school grammar: "use no word without a signification"; use words in a way that is "clear and distinct"; employ only common usages where possible; and define terms (286–95). But the intent, however unsuccessful, is to salvage verbal discourse for scientific purposes by offering strategies to make it really, *really* clear. At its best, Locke insists, language can serve as a neutral conduit, an instrument, for empirical lines of reasoning.

Having explored issues of conceptualization and verbal denotation, Locke moves on to develop his empiricist theory of knowledge and "discursive reasoning," the composing of scientific argument. Knowledge is simply "the perception of the connection of and agreement, or disagreement and repugnancy, of any of our ideas" (Locke 1965, 299). He acknowledges the epistemological problem inherent in the conclusion that "the mind knows not things immediately, but only by the intervention of . . . ideas" but argues that "the actual receiving of ideas from without," the perception of sensory stimuli, "gives us notice of the existence of other things" (352). There are two types of ideas "that we may be assured agree with things." The first are "simple ideas," basic conceptions of the world directly proceeding from our sensory experience, like "whiteness" or "bitterness," that provide the empirical starting point for all subsequent knowledge. The second are "complex ideas," which he calls "archetypes of the mind's own making," purely formal ideas, like those of mathematics or logic, that derive their reliability from an internal consistency that can be mapped onto the empirical world. The "ideal existence" of triangles, for example, will "hold true" necessarily "when they have a *real existence* in matter" (321). "Substances" (like gold) are the most problematic concepts for science because they involve compilations of sensory experience, formed as mixed ideas the components of which different observers may sort and emphasize differently. "In the knowledge of bodies, we must be content to glean what we can from particular experiments," where "our senses" must be "warily employed in taking notice of their qualities and operations" (367). Our complex ideas of them "must be such . . . as are made up of such simple ones as have been discovered to co-exist in nature" (324). Locke echoes Descartes in depicting rational discourse as a chain of assertions, grounded in and tested by observable fact, moving steadily forward from the known to the unknown. At every step, it is necessary "to perceive the immediate agreement of the intervening ideas," and this "intuitive perception" must be "carried out exactly in the mind" through the many proofs required in "long deductions" (307). Like Descartes, Locke repudiates the syllogism as an appropriate argumentative model because it neither begins in observation nor uses empirical experience in order to inquire after new knowledge. Instead, anticipating later developments, he commends the discourse of mathematicians, who "by a continued chain of reasonings, proceed to the discovery and demonstration of truths that appear at first sight beyond human capacity" (363). By means of such a method, the metaphorical equivalent of a lab report or a scientific article, Locke is confident that knowledge "may be carried much further than it has hitherto been," provided that scientists "with freedom of mind, employ all that industry and labor of thought, in improving the means of discovering truth" (310).

KARL POPPER

French rationalism and British empiricism, represented here in the work of Descartes and Locke, have particular value for the sharp distinction they both draw between the objectivist and the ontological stories of the meaning of meaning, in which the opposition of grounds of meaningfulness could not be more evident than in the assault on Aristotelian metaphysics by appeal to a standard of rigorous physical observation. But these early renderings don't begin to exhaust the complexities or applications of objectivist rhetoric. Later versions, strongly influenced by Kant and German idealism, as well as structuralism, pragmatism, and logical positivism, among other intellectual movements, demonstrate how its assumptions and practices have evolved, not only in science but in many other areas of modern culture. Objectivism has become the dominant, most pervasive, and most trusted discourse theory of our time, sustaining our deep confidence in progress, dispassionate analysis, "facts," practical knowledge, technological inventiveness, and other values besides. But it has moved far beyond Descartes's rudimentary scientific method and Locke's naïve realism. A good example of modern objectivism may be found in the work of Karl Popper (1902–1994), a distinguished twentieth-century philosopher of science and a proponent of "scientific realism." Popper begins his argument in *The Logic of Scientific Discovery* with a dramatic repudiation of the most basic idea that people hold about empirical science, namely the notion that science is inductive, that it proceeds from singular experiential observations and culminates in general hypotheses, theories, and laws. Popper (2007, 3) unhesitatingly confirms the objectivist ground of meaningfulness, making clear in his opening sentence that the scientist "constructs hypotheses, or systems of theories, and tests them against experience by observation and experiment." But the sentence requires close reading because it carefully avoids two erroneous beliefs that are common to induction theory, one concerning the starting point of empirical inquiry and another concerning its end. He does not contend that science is unconcerned about experiential facts, but he significantly redefines the role of observation. And he does not contend that science is uninterested in general assertions, but he reconceives the relationship between those assertions and the physical world.

Taking first the issue of observation, Popper invites readers to consider a simple thought experiment (Popper 2007, 88): imagine being directed at this moment to begin recording your sensory experience. Where would we start, what experience would count, and how would we know when it's exhausted? The problem is reminiscent of the comic situation in Laurence Sterne's (1940) novel, Tristram Shandy, published between 1759 and 1767 as a critique of the theory of associational psychology, where Tristram is overpowered by sensory impressions flooding in on all sides and is therefore unable to write about his life, or even effectively live it. Suppose further that a very large, minutely detailed list of experiences has been formed. What scientific knowledge would it constitute, what starting point for systematic inquiry, what conclusion about the world? The point is clear, although it appears to contradict the traditional understanding of scientific method. Science is driven not by information, Popper insists, but by problems, questions, and points of view that prompt the search for information. In induction theory, observation motivates the scientist to generalize; in Popper's methodological argument, a trial generalization motivates the scientist to observe. Popper calls his theory the "deductive method of testing" because the new role for observation is to evaluate hypotheses empirically after, and only after, they have been advanced. The second issue, regarding the end of science, is more interesting philosophically, and it turns on a problem that Locke had posed, namely the relationship between verbal conception and empirical experience, one he had tried to resolve by urging weakly that scientific language be as clear as possible. The problem is not clarity, Popper shows, but rather the inherent difference between "sensation" and verbal conception. He writes that "we can utter no scientific statement that does not go far beyond what can be known with certainty 'on the basis of immediate experience.'" Every statement uses "*universal* names (or symbols, or ideas); every statement has the character of a theory, of a hypothesis." He cites a simple example: "Here is a glass of water." This statement "cannot be verified by any observational experience" because the universals that it contains—glass, water—"cannot be correlated with any specific sense-experience." A sensory experience is a unique event, one of a kind, while the statement refers only to generalized concepts that are essentially subjective value judgments, one about containers and one about liquids (Popper 2007, 76). The consequence of Popper's line of reasoning is stunning—that science cannot make direct, affirmative statements about the phenomena of the physical world.

Having dispatched the induction argument, Popper develops his own theory of scientific method by appeal to what he calls the "criterion of demarcation," which he refers to as "falsifiability," for all properly empirical argument. He explains that the criterion of demarcation for positivistic theories, which retain assumptions about induction, is that any empirical statement must be "capable of being finally decided," that is, objectively verified as true or false. But the problem, as he described above with respect to the assertion about the glass of water, is that scientific statements cannot be positively affirmed by appeal to observational experience. The belief that such affirmations are possible he calls "psychologism" (Popper 2007, 75), a subjective attitude or feeling that something is true. This subjective response "can never justify a scientific statement" (24) and is indeed incompatible with science, the hallmark of which is objectivity. His conclusion is logically inescapable: "Theories are, therefore, *never* empirically verifiable" (18). But if scientific statements, and scientific systems, cannot be positively affirmed, they can nonetheless be "falsified" by means of rigorously empirical tests. "What characterizes the empirical method," he insists, "is its manner of exposing to falsification, in every conceivable way, the system to be tested." Invoking a Darwinian metaphor, he says that the idea is to identify the system "which is by comparison the fittest, by exposing them all to the fiercest struggle for survival" (20). Theories are "nets cast to catch what we call 'the world': to rationalize, to explain, and to master it" (38). Falsifiability is the criterion for deciding "whether or not a theoretical system belongs to empirical science" (57), and falsification is the method by which a theory's chances for survival are either enhanced or reduced. A theory is empirically tested (i.e., subjected to the process of falsification) by appeal to "basic" or "singular" statements (which describe specific empirical occurrences), and it is falsified "only if we have accepted basic statements which contradict it" (66–68). Popper offers a simple case, a piece of thread with a tensile strength of one pound that breaks when a weight of two pounds is placed on it (38). A hypothesis (called a "universal statement") is advanced that "whenever a thread is loaded with a weight exceeding its tensile strength, it will break." Two "singular statements" are available for testing the hypothesis, "the tensile strength of this thread is one pound," and "the weight put on this thread was two pounds." Since the thread has broken, these singular statements, denoting an experimental test, have failed to falsify the hypothesis, so it is (temporarily) retained, although not positively affirmed. If the weight on the thread were reduced to 1.0372 pounds, and the thread were to hold, the hypothesis would be falsified. But even if the thread were to break, the hypothesis would merely receive additional support because an infinite number of other weights greater than one pound could be tested and because the fact that the thread has broken once at a given weight does not logically demonstrate that it will always break at that weight. The progress of science is not, therefore, according to Popper, a progress built upon empirically confirmed hypotheses, theories, and laws, but rather a progress built upon failure to demonstrate empirically that given universal statements are untrue.

Popper's scientific realism is an immensely influential modern reading of the objectivist argument, but more important, much as it alters the naïve premises of Descartes and Locke, it does not itself avoid the dualism, the subject/object dichotomy, that objectivism introduces into Western epistemology, nor does it eliminate alternative theoretical positions on the dualistic—subjective versus objective—spectrum of possibilities. Popper's appreciation of the fact that "theories are . . . *never* empirically verifiable" (Popper 2007, 18) is a major concession regarding the fallibility of human intellection, one that has been forced upon Western discourse theory with the preference for science over metaphysics. If knowledge is not the original creation of a divine or cosmic intelligence, then it can only be the work of human beings, conceived after Descartes as selves, finite, inquiring subjectivities. And if we have only uncertain knowledge regarding an a priori order of the world, then the existence of that order becomes little more than an act of faith or personal conviction. There are, accordingly at one end of the spectrum, more radically empiricist contemporary arguments than Popper's, notably the work of the logical positivists, including Rudolf Carnap (Carnap 1956, *Meaning and Necessity: A Study in Semantics and Modal Logic*) and the early Ludwig Wittgenstein (Wittgenstein 1968, *Tractatus: Logico-Philosophicus*), who defend induction and the possibility of rigorously concrete empirical propositions. And there are also arguments that move to the other side of Popper toward idealistic theories of scientific knowledge, such as the perspective Popper calls "conventionalism." For conventionalists, among whom Popper includes the French physicist and mathematician Henri Poincare, "natural science is not a picture of nature but merely a logical construction." That is, the scientist composes a simple model that seeks to accommodate the complexities of phenomenal experience. But it is not finally "the complexities of the world which determine this construction." Instead, the construction determines the properties of an "artificial" world, "a world of concepts implicitly defined by the natural laws which we have chosen." Simplicity is the model's primary aspiration. It follows rules of an autonomous human logic, seeks to achieve an ultimate economy of design, and interprets nature through its peculiar lens (Popper 2007, 57–61). For Popper, conventionalism is simply not a true empirical theory because its models lie beyond experimental falsifiability. If a model fails to account for certain features of the external world, then it is adjusted as necessary rather than rejected as false, an arbitrariness that Popper finds unacceptable.

Other modern versions of scientific idealism exist as well, although Popper does not attempt to critique them all, nor indeed would he have been successful in disposing of them had he tried. One example may be found in the celebrated debate between Albert Einstein and Niels Bohr concerning the discomfiting implications of Werner Heisenberg's uncertainty principle in particular and quantum mechanics in general. The debate is recounted in Walter Isaacson's *Einstein, His Life and Universe*, which quotes Einstein's famous rejection of the probabilistic nature of the electron, his complaint that God "does not play dice" (Isaacson 2007, 335). Himself a scientific realist, Einstein prefers the view—let us say the act of faith—that empirical theories accurately correspond with the design of nature. As he wrote to his friend, Banesh Hoffmann, "When I am judging a theory, I ask myself whether, if I were God, I would have arranged the world in such a way" (qtd. in Isaacson 2007, 335). Bohr's response is that "it is wrong to think that the task of physics is to find out how nature *is*." According to the "Copenhagen" interpretation of quantum mechanics, which Bohr and Heisenberg represent, physics only concerns "what we can *say* about nature" (Isaacson 2007, 333). According to the Copenhagen argument, at the quantum level, where researchers are dealing with elementary particles such as the electron and the photon, the process of observing nature directly affects the outcome of the observation. For instance, since we must illuminate an object in order to see it, we can only "see" an electronic particle by means of other electronic particles, specifically the photons that constitute light. But the photons that enable the observation also collide with the particle being observed, affecting its behavior. Since the behavior of what is seen cannot be separated, then, from the process of seeing it, experimental inquiry into quantum phenomena cannot match Einstein's hopeful expectations about a definitive (as opposed to probabilistic) theory of nature at the electronic level. The point here is not to evaluate whether Bohr or Einstein, or Popper or Poincare, is correct, but only to note the persistence of these debates over the nature of scientific truth as testimony to the enduring irony that Cartesian dualism has introduced into objectivist rhetorical theory. The emergence of objectivity as a scientific value has come only and necessarily at the price of the emergence of subjectivity, leaving skepticism, not faith, as the dominant motif of scientific exploration.

STEPHEN TOULMIN

The importance of objectivist rhetoric, its epistemological complexities notwithstanding, is not limited, of course, to scientific inquiry. Indeed, what has made it so important is precisely its broad application even in arenas of public discourse that can never meet the rigorous tests of truth-value that Popper and others have assigned to properly empirical investigation. A good example of objectivism as a pervasive rhetoric outside of science may be found in the work of Stephen Toulmin (1922–2009), whose contributions to logical theory place him in the philosophical tradition of pragmatism, where concessions are made to the limitations of human knowledge and the impossibility of certitude, but where objectivity, the grounding of inquiry in practical theory as a guide to experiential observation, remains feasible in application. The logician, Toulmin (1980, 3) writes in *The Uses of Argument*, "is concerned with the study of proper, rational, normal thinking processes," an assertion that seeks to salvage the possibility of reasoned argument in ordinary human affairs from the quasimathematical, increasingly arcane practices of formal logic, especially as they are defined within the technical confines of logical positivism. In keeping with the objectivist ground of meaningfulness, Toulmin insists that, at the simplest level, argumentative discourse in any domain—politics, law, ethics, or elsewhere—is about the making of what he calls "claims" in the context of overt or potential support for those claims in the form of "backing, data, facts, evidence, considerations, features" (11), or other kinds of experiential information. The best example, he believes, is forensic debate, where claims about guilt and innocence vie with each other by appeal to available supporting evidence. Toulmin declares logic to be nothing more than "generalized jurisprudence" (7), employing overall the same rational processes invoked in the law court for proposing, disputing, and determining law suits. To be sure, "the conclusions we come to, the assertions we put forward, will be of very different kinds," depending on what he calls the "field of argument" (law, medicine, mathematics), and the backing of claims will differ accordingly as one proceeds from the proofs in Euclid's *Elements* to an argument that "Peterson is a Swede, so he is presumably not a Roman Catholic" (12–14). But the essential question for practical or applied logic (i.e., "working logic" as opposed to "idealized logic" [146]) is not "how the standards we employ in criticizing arguments in different fields compare in stringency," but rather "how far there are common standards applicable in the criticism of arguments taken from different fields" (15).

The essence of Toulmin's position lies in a distinction he makes between arguments that are "analytic" and arguments that are "substantive." Aristotle's syllogism is an example of analytic argument, where, since the conclusion is entailed in the premises, the line of reasoning has a formally necessary result. Analytic arguments are tautological because information in the conclusion is already implicitly conveyed in the assertions that support it. Toulmin takes issue with the long tradition, beginning with Aristotle, that privileges analytical argument because, as a practical instrument of public discourse, most arguments are not of this type. The substantive argument depends on assertions that do not logically entail their conclusions. We make claims about the future by citing our experience of the past; we make claims about how people feel by pointing to their speech or gestures; we adopt moral positions, pass aesthetic judgments, and declare support for political causes, "in each case producing as grounds for our conclusion statements of quite other logical types than the conclusion itself" (Toulmin, 1980, 124–25). In effect, Toulmin inverts Aristotle's priority and gives new discursive authority to the enthymeme, which Aristotle justified in practical affairs on the dubious claim that it is a syllogism manqué, in the process expanding to most areas of knowledge a form of reasoning that Aristotle restricted to only a few and establishing forensic rhetoric, one of those few, as the model for all discourse, including science. He contends that Descartes's skepticism about the fallibility of our senses depends finally on the "false expectation" that scientific discourse should take the form of analytic argument, where what we pragmatically demand from science, along with other forms of argument (albeit to a more rigorous standard), is "conclusions for which the presumptions are so strong as to be for practical purposes unrebuttable" (250). Popper takes a similar position, noting that while every empirical statement must be "capable of being tested," we do not require that every statement "must have in fact been tested before it is accepted" (Popper 2007, 26). There is a point at which we are entitled to presume that a statement about the world is satisfactorily verified. Toulmin's response to Descartes's anxiety is, similarly, to eliminate the unreasonable expectation of formal entailment that arises in analytic arguments like the syllogism in favor of a pragmatic question about any line of reasoning, namely, whether or not some "collection of sensory data *justifies* us in claiming knowledge about the world." The practical fact of the matter, he concludes, is that "some things it is more unreasonable to doubt than to believe" (250).

Toulmin's (1980, 97–107) discussion of the organizational structure of an argument in practical discourse is intended not as a recipe for composing texts but rather as a procedure for evaluating them, a "pattern of analysis"—in effect, a protocol for critical reading. The generic strategy of a substantive argument, he says, is to assert a "claim" and to support it with some sort of evidence, a rhetorical structure that can be represented symbolically as "D [data]; So, C [claim]." For example, "Jane was driving at 50 MPH [D] past a sign that said 35 MPH [D] and so has committed a traffic violation [C]." Of course, not just any set of facts can substantiate any claim; there must also be a principle, rule, or other justification that legitimizes the inferences that have been made from facts: given D, we are entitled to conclude C. It is, for example, insufficient to argue that Jane was speeding merely because she was going 50 MPH where a sign happened to say 35 MPH. What is necessary to legitimize the conclusion is what Toulmin calls a "warrant" (W), which is a general proposition asserting the soundness of the argument, in this case, there is a state law that prohibits driving over a posted speed limit." The formula is now "D; So, C; Because W." A warrant applies to all instances of a particular type of argument, identifying the legitimacy of the type, and it is often implicit in a specific instance. But a warrant may or may not necessitate accepting a claim since different warrants may have different force, sometimes unequivocally justifying a conclusion and other times only tentatively justifying it. So, the argumentative formula may at times include either a "qualifier" (Q), or a "rebuttal" (R), or both. Hence, for the warrant to hold in the case of Jane's driving there is a qualifying condition that the traffic sign was clearly visible and its message legible: "D; So, Q, C; Because W." Furthermore, there may be a potential exception to the warrant that may rebut its applicability to the case, as in the circumstance where Jane might have been a police officer racing to the scene of an accident. Now the argument may be written as "D; So, Q, C; Because W; Unless R": Jane was driving at 55 MPH past a sign saying 35 MPH and was therefore speeding (presuming that the sign was visible and legible) because it is against the law to drive over a posted speed limit unless you have a special authorization. One final term completes Toulmin's argumentative structure, and that is the "backing" (B) of a warrant, which he defines as the explanation of its general authority. In an argument involving state law and its possible violations, the backing of the warrant "we are obliged by statute to drive at or below any posted speed limit" would be a specific reference to the appropriate sections of state law pertaining to the traffic code.

The point of this formulaic elaboration is to show how a substantive argument differs from an analytical argument in the limited character of its certitude while nonetheless remaining functionally compelling, even if not formally necessary, in its conclusions. As the argument about Jane's traffic offense proceeds from data to claim, including the various supports and qualifications that legitimize the claim, there is clearly nothing in the structure of the argument that logically requires assent to its conclusion. While in Aristotle's analytic syllogism we are *formally* obligated to conclude that Socrates is rational once we establish that he is a man, there is no similarly formal obligation to conclude that Jane is speeding (which is a substantive argument) because that conclusion, while plausible, is not prewritten in the pattern of the line of reasoning. Yet the argument remains scrupulously devoted to the core propositions of objectivist rhetoric, grounding its meaning in observable experience and factual knowledge, making its claim to authority on the basis of a neutrally analytic rationality. Ultimately, Toulmin's own argument is designed to respond to Descartes's epistemological conundrum that, in the absence of metaphysical necessity, the objective presupposes the subjective so that we can, as a result, achieve no absolutely reliable knowledge on the basis of empirical method. The "proper course for epistemology," he concludes, is "neither to embrace nor armor oneself against skepticism, but to moderate one's ambitions" by requiring of any and all claims to knowledge "not that they shall measure up against analytic standards" but, "more realistically," that they "achieve whatever sort of cogency or well-foundedness" it is relevant to expect in a given field of human inquiry (Toulmin 1980, 48). The compounded ironies that have attended objectivism from its beginnings in the work of Descartes and Locke still plainly reverberate even as this powerful rhetorical perspective continues to exercise its hold on modern European discursive practice. Its central claim to authority is its commitment to "the facts," yet it can never escape, for all its empirical and even mathematical rigor, the human derivation of those facts. Its optimism about the progress of knowledge can never escape its skepticism about the uncertain reliability of its statements. Even its strongest advocates are obliged, on serious inspection, to hedge their confidence in its successes and continuing promise, with a caution echoing from Descartes to Toulmin not that we give up our faith or hope but that we "moderate our ambitions."

MARY BELENKY AND OTHERS, *WOMEN'S WAYS OF KNOWING*

A similar example of pragmatic applications of objectivist rhetoric beyond the rigorous methodology of empirical science may be found in the practices of qualitative research, a form of investigation common to the social or human sciences that relies on narrative representations of experience and their subsequent interpretive analysis. Hermeneutic ethnography, popularized by the anthropologist Clifford Geertz, with its emphasis on "thick description" of cultural phenomena (Geertz 1973), effectively illustrates this approach, applying tools first forged in biblical exegesis and the textual explications of reader-response literary criticism to the study of human social life. Practitioners of qualitative inquiry frankly concede the epistemological challenges of producing objective knowledge and indeed sometimes self-consciously embrace the fictiveness of the fiction of the distanced observer. They insist that the complex, ambiguous, even paradoxical truthfulness available from narrative is especially appropriate for understanding human beings and their textured interactions. But like all objectivist rhetors, they nonetheless ground inquiry in observation rather than, say, the a priori commitments of ontological rhetoric: "real life" provides the material for their analytical fictions. The difference in perspective can be plainly seen in a comparison of the feminist arguments of Cixous, represented as ontological in chapter 3, and the feminist, but in their case objectivist, research of Mary Belenky, Blythe Clinchy, Nancy Goldberger, and Jill Tarule. In *Women's Ways of Knowing: The Development of Self, Voice, and Mind*, Belenky (1986) and her colleagues argue, much as Cixous does, for processes of thinking, forming, and expressing that are distinctive to women, but their strategy for arriving at such a conclusion depends on empirical rather than metaphysical presuppositions. At the same time, the Belenky group also pushes the objectivist envelope, pursuing just as aggressively as Cixous an overtly political investigation that is grounded not in a neutral or distanced "scientific" curiosity but in unapologetic engagement and forthright solidarity with the women they simultaneously observe, champion, and seek to nurture.

Writing as developmental psychologists, Belenky and her colleagues are at pains to make the rhetorical moves expected of a scientific method. Echoing objectivist faith in the gradual, progressive accumulation of knowledge, they review earlier research traditions, pointing out a persistent masculine bias in the literature regarding "modes of learning, knowing, and valuing" that their research is designed to correct. They identify similarly biased earlier models of intellectual development; they frame their own investigations by appeal to precursors like Carol Gilligan (*In a Different Voice: Psychological Theory and Women's Development*) and, especially, William Perry (*Forms of Intellectual and Ethical Development in the College Years*); and they acknowledge their own location in what must inevitably remain an ongoing process of identifying the variety and developmental features of women's perspectives on the world: "We leave it to future work to determine whether these perspectives have any stage-like qualities" (Belenky et al. 1986, 6–17). Echoing objectivist doubt, albeit less formally stringent doubt than Popper's criterion of falsification, they concede the limitations of their work: "There are no agreed-upon techniques for assessing the Perry positions" (10). "These . . . ways of knowing are not necessarily fixed, exhaustive, or universal categories" (15). "Our intention is to share not prove our observations" (16). Most important, emphasizing an observational rather than ideological orientation to their work, they explain, "We proceeded inductively, opening our ears to the voices and perspectives of women so that we might begin to hear the unheard and unimagined" (11). The design of their investigation is case study, featuring interviews of 135 women, 90 of whom were college students from six different academic institutions and 45 of whom were receiving instruction from service agencies supporting women in parenting their children. Questions directing the interview of each participant emphasized "what was important about life and learning from her point of view," questions concerning "self-image, relationships of importance, education and learning, real-life decision-making and moral dilemmas," among others. The interviews, collected over a five-year period, produced more than 5,000 pages of narrative detail, blind-coded so that investigators would be able to conduct their textual analyses unaware of such distinguishing markers as the age, ethnicity, social class, or institutional affiliation of the participants. Belenky and her colleagues insist that they "wanted to hear what the women had to say in their own terms rather than test [the researchers'] own preconceived hypotheses" (11–12).

The authors' interpretation of this body of narrative data, their story about the stories, yields five epistemological positions or conditions representing women's ways of knowing. The first is silence, a condition of passivity, blind obedience, lack of self-image, and powerlessness to mediate the world—in effect an absence of knowing suggestive of deprivation and emotional, if not physical, abuse (Belenky et al. 1986, 23–34). The second is dependency on received knowledge, the opinions of others (most of them male), where accepting authority and listening more than speaking are the behavioral signs of a static self lacking internal resources for growth and capable only of starkly literal, typically dualistic (either/or, true/false) modes of understanding (35–51). The third condition is subjective knowing, which the authors characterize as a "revolutionary step" because it entails the emergence of an autonomous self, an inner voice, able to challenge external authorities and personalize the truth—but which may also entail a rejection of the vehicles of authoritative knowledge, including objectivity, rational analysis, and argumentation in favor of intuition, empathy, and the valorizing of immediate emotional experience (52–86). The fourth condition is procedural knowing, which has two dimensions, "separate" and "connected." In general, procedural knowing is objective, rule governed, and rigorously analytical, the kind of thought associated with logical and scientific method. But the difference between separate and connected procedural knowledge is that the first proceeds from an initial posture of doubt while the second proceeds from an initial posture of belief. Separate knowers are impersonal and skeptical, pursuing their own understanding in dialectical opposition to that of others. Connected knowers are empathic, nonjudgmental, and collaborative, alertly engaging the thought of others, imagining alternative perspectives, conceptual orientations, and patterns of reasoning as a basis for the development of their own (101–30). While these different versions of procedural knowledge both presume a confidently independent self, secure in its values and judgments, and while they are not intrinsically gendered, the authors contend that, for well-recognized cultural reasons, separate knowing is a more familiar posture among men and connected knowing more familiar among women. The fifth condition, implicitly regarded as the most sophisticated or advanced form of knowing, is constructed knowledge, where self and other, subjective and objective, are fully integrated, where "the knower is an intimate part of the known" (137). Constructed knowers, recognizing the complexities of the world and aware of their own participant-observer roles in composing their understanding of it, resist simplifications that lead to artificial compartmentalizing of knowledge, accept diverse points of view, and are able to tolerate ambiguity and uncertainty as features of healthy intellectual relativity.

For the authors, these five epistemological positions map onto life situations—childhood, educational circumstances, family life, mothering—and represent stances from which to confront women's distinctive experiences of the world. The positions blend together cognitive responses to the world with issues of maturation and development in a context of the politics of gender. In this blending, Belenky and her colleagues unhesitatingly leaven their objectivist rhetoric with a conspicuously activist ideological commitment to the rights of women. They aren't first neutral cognition scientists who later apply their findings to everyday life. Rather, in their textual interpretations, they allow a free interplay between a progression from silence to fully realized knower and a parallel progression from domination and repression to freedom and self-determination, describing along the way what the authors clearly regard as the emergence of an ideal woman's subjectivity within ideal social environments that only their developed consciousness can enable them to achieve. To reach the more advanced cognitive conditions, in other words, is to experience not just intellectual growth, but emancipation. The authors' protestations notwithstanding ("We leave it to future work to determine whether these perspectives have any stage-like qualities."), it's impossible to take the five conditions as anything but points along a developmental line and impossible not to hear the authors cheering on the legions of dominated women whose quality of life, both personal and political, stands to rise or fall in proportion as they strive toward the later "stages." The melding begins in the authors' fusion of silence, as an epistemological category, and silenced, as a political category. "In describing their lives, women commonly talked about voice and silence: 'speaking up,' 'speaking out,' 'being silenced,' 'not being heard'. . . . 'feeling deaf and dumb'" (Belenky et al. 1986, 18). Becoming voiced as a knower means asserting oneself as a subjectivity. The second cognitive stage, a dependence on received knowledge, while an advance over silence, still means capitulation to authority and therefore continued social powerlessness. The third stage, subjective knowing is, in the authors' words, a "revolutionary step" precisely because it challenges the tyranny of authority by recourse to the personal voice within, an intellectual but also social progression the authors refer to as "a common path of female development" (56). Procedural knowing, the next plateau, offers women intellectual equality, and perhaps the prospect of social equality, but at the cost of adapting themselves to a male-oriented world that views scientific rationality as more truthful, and more politically powerful, than the intuitive, empathic, relational understanding of women. The final cognitive stage for women, constructive knowing, is not merely the summit of intellectual development but is also the summit of social development, where people listen to each other, value each other's knowledge, respect each other's life experience, and nurture each other in communities of shared, different, and equal subjectivities: "We found that the opening of the mind *and* the heart to embrace the *world* was characteristic only of the women at the position of constructed knowledge" (141).

The methodology of *Women's Ways of Knowing* is as objectivist as that of Popper or Toulmin, but the text's rhetorical genius lies in its appreciation of the cultural status of objectivism, relying on its privilege to leverage the advancement of the authors' social project. Part 2 of the text, "Development in Context: Families and Schools," makes the social project plain in its frank advocacy of liberatory education for women, where teaching and learning "integrate the voices of reason and feeling" (Belenky et al. 1986, 176), mothers developing "the voice of reason" (181) and fathers "the voice of emotions" (182); where "women's mode of talk," namely "question posing" (which the authors assert to be "central to maternal practice in its most evolved form") becomes the model of pedagogy (189); and where ideal teachers are "midwives" who "assist the students in giving birth to their own ideas," "assist in the emergence of consciousness," focus "not on their own knowledge . . . but on the students' knowledge," and "encourage students to use their knowledge in everyday life" (217–219). The purpose of an education framed by these values is women's emancipation, helping them "toward community, power, and integrity," enabling them to achieve a social standing, and a capacity for self-realization, that is denied whenever a combination of oppressive family and oppressive school conditions encourages their retardation at the primitive cognitive levels of silence and dependence on received knowledge (228–29). These conclusions are not "simply" objectivist—that is, verifiably discernible in the data of the collected narratives or otherwise limited to rigorous empirical observation. But neither do the authors aspire to simple objectivism—the procedural knowing that their study in fact aims to critique as one of several less evolved modes of thought. Their work is, like Geertz's, self-consciously an argument for "constructed knowing," for qualitative inquiry. They recognize that stories cannot be falsified, and that one story can't falsify another. Within the epistemological framework of qualitative inquiry, their conclusions represent plausible readings—interpretations—of the stories they have, not so dispassionately, assembled to chronicle women's experience. The authors insist in the last sentence of *Women's Ways of Knowing* that "these are the lessons we have learned in listening to women's voices" (229). No one who accepts as real the experiences of 135 women comprising the narrative universe Belenky and her colleagues have constructed from their interviews can say, objectively, that they are not entitled to derive those lessons.

5
EXPRESSIVIST RHETORIC

THE SOPHISTS

The early Greek sophists, whom Aristophanes called "a ruffianly race of tongue-twisters" (*The Birds* 1694, qtd. in Dillon and Gergel 2003), had the misfortune of dying three times, each time more definitively than before. These itinerant teachers of the arts of discourse, who roamed democratic Athens in the age of Pericles selling their pedagogical services, died first of course in the customary way, generally between the later-fifth and mid-fourth centuries, BCE. But their reputations died as well, primarily at the hands of Plato, who argued successfully that a self-serving, manipulative relativism lay at the black heart of sophistic education, that his own conservative philosophy had greater intellectual integrity, and that, besides, it was unseemly to teach for money. Later, the sophists died a third time, their voices all but wholly effaced as their writings disappeared through lack of the custodial care that saw Plato and Aristotle through the "dark" ages until Arab scholars at Toledo could canonize them for the European Renaissance. All that remains of early sophistic writing, as a result, is some provocative fragments of theory, a few speeches, and some second-hand reconstructions of their thought in the work of other writers, many of whom, like Plato, introduce them mostly for critique or disparagement. The first sophists included such figures as Protagoras of Abdera (490–420 BCE), Gorgias of Leontini (485–380 BCE) (targeted in the Platonic dialogue discussed earlier), Prodicus of Ceos, Antiphon, and Hippias of Elis, among others, and the very unfamiliarity of their names testifies to the thoroughness of their erasure from European history. But had these early rhetoricians died less definitively, they might deserve recognition for composing a story about the meaning of meaning whose dominant themes are far different from the Platonic and Aristotelian certainties of ontological rhetoric, and different also from the word power of magical rhetoric, or the empiricism of objectivist rhetoric. It isn't easy to say what sort of alternative story they might have told simply because it's *too* easy to read

DOI: 10.7330/9780874219364.c005

their pitiful fragments in whichever way one prefers. But putting my own interpretive spin on Protagoras's famous assertion that "man is the measure of all things," I propose that sophistic rhetoric offers an early rendering of the expressivist story, which conveys the view that discursive knowledge is subjective in origin, comprised of verbal and other representations whose meanings derive from autonomous acts of mind and are therefore more responsive to human need and desire than to whatever may lie beyond human consciousness.

Let's pretend, for example, that Protagoras's version of the expressivist story can be found in Plato's *Theaetetus*, which relates a conversation between Socrates and an Athenian mathematician, after whom the dialogue is named, in which the two debate the merits of different views concerning the nature of knowledge. To be sure, whatever the substance of Protagoras's argument may originally have been, it is, in *Theaetetus*, at best a fragmented reconstruction that Socrates relates for his own reasons, shorn of Protagoras's explanatory context. Hence, while Plato and Socrates could be trying their best to represent Protagoras's sophistic point of view, a reader cannot gauge the strength of their determination to speak fairly about a theory with which they strongly disagree. But that said, let's proceed as though Socrates's motives are pure. According to his account, Protagoras claims that man is the measure of all things, "of those which are, that they are, and of those which are not, that they are not." The meaning of this assertion, Socrates says, is that "however each thing appears to me to be, this is how it *is* for me, and likewise, each thing *is* how it appears to you." Hence, in Protagoras's view, the wind is cold for the person who feels chilly but not for another who feels comfortable. The appearance of things, therefore, as perceived, felt, and understood by an individual, constitutes knowledge, "for however each man perceives them to be, it's likely that this *is* the case for him." Socrates immediately objects to Protagoras's contention, protesting the absurdity of a proposition that "nothing is one thing itself in itself," that things can be simultaneously large and small, heavy and light, warm and cold, "that nothing ever is but is always becoming," all according to the perceptions, the subjective interpretations of individuals (Plato 2003b, 10–11). Such a position stands in stark contrast to the ontological reality that is central to Socrates's (and Plato's) metaphysics, and Socrates is plainly uncomfortable with the intellectual obligation to present its claims dispassionately. But to the extent that he succeeds, he has (perhaps) attributed to Protagoras an embryonic statement of the ground of meaningfulness that characterizes expressivist rhetoric, namely the constitutive power of consciousness, or imagination, whose discursive projection of a world outside the mind represents what Samuel Taylor Coleridge will later refer to as a coalescence of subject and object. In expressivist theory, the central question is not whether the flow of an air current has objective reality independent of the perceiving subject, or what that reality might be, but rather what the flow of the air current *means* to the perceiving subject. What is central, in other words, is its symbolic representation, the significance of wind to those who experience it as a natural phenomenon and who capture in their name for it a history of connotative no less than denotative values. The issue is human intelligibility, while the status of objects in themselves is as irrelevant as it is undecidable.

Later in the dialogue, Socrates conjures the ghost of Protagoras to speak in his own voice about how he is able to square this relativism about human knowledge with his claim, as a (paid) teacher of the arts of discourse, that he can offer his students a worthier understanding of things than these students would be able to reach on their own. Protagoras's answer, while in itself unconvincing (perhaps because Plato is not in the habit of putting better lines into the mouths of Socrates's opponents), introduces a distinction, common among the sophists, between nature and convention, where a given state of things, say the priority of man over woman or the existence of the gods, may be understood either as part of the natural order or as a conventional social reality that people have negotiated by comparing more and less useful individual points of view. Protagoras opts for convention, confirming Socrates's summary of his argument, saying that, indeed, "each of us is the measure of the things which are and those which are not." But this individualized awareness can be evaluated by appeal to its practical value and comparative worth in the context of alternative, though also individual, perspectives. He cites an example from medicine, noting that one who is ill may find a certain food to be unappetizing while a healthy person finds it delicious. The sick person is not ignorant about the taste of the food, nor is the healthy person wiser than the invalid. Both have meaningful, albeit opposite, perceptions. But by appeal to standards of comparative worth and utility, where long, shared experience demonstrates, in this instance, that eating is healthier than refusing to eat, the healthy person's perspective has the better claim to social adoption. The point, then, is that while all individual perceptions have value, the normal course of social life involves a process of winnowing the most beneficial or workable perceptions from those that have less promise. People identify the preferable, not by Socrates's intuitive apprehension of the Right or the Good, but by experience, and they seek to persuade those who hold different views that their advantage lies in accommodating conventional agreements about the preferable. The process is both educational and rhetorical, involving just the kinds of public discursive skill that the sophists aimed to teach. As Protagoras says, "In education . . . we must bring about a change from one condition to a better one; and while the doctor makes changes with drugs, the sophist does this with words" (Plato 2003b, 12). Protagoras's argument, detached from the Socratic scorn surrounding it, lays the foundation for the commerce of ordinary life and demonstrates that public discourse, the ceaseless negotiation of conventional rather than absolute realities, is what makes ordinary life possible.

In another dialogue, named *Protagoras*, Plato extends the relativistic argument about social life, conventional reality, and education, although once more straining against his own convictions in representing Protagoras's point of view. In the so-called Great Speech of Protagoras Plato depicts the sophist relating a myth about the origins of society, where the god Prometheus "stole the technical wisdom of Hephaestus and Athena" in order to give human beings "a portion of divinity" and the skill to "articulate speech and words" and invent "dwellings and clothes and beds and food from the earth." Seeking further to protect humans from an isolation and selfishness that would mean their doom, Zeus sends Hermes to "bring shame and justice to men, so that there would be order in the cities and the uniting bonds of friendship" (Plato 2003a, 24–26). The virtues of shame and justice are learned, Plato's Protagoras goes on, in the course of social interaction since they are experiential, not abstract, realities. But these virtues can also be perfected in human beings through instruction, whence both the important role of sophists in educating citizens in their public responsibilities and the propriety of paying them for this public service. He insists that there is "one thing . . . of which it is necessary that all citizens partake, if there is to be a city," and that is "human virtue," specifically "justice and prudence and piety." The teaching of virtue is inseparable from the teaching of discourse since the arts of language enable the transactions of public life while the texts that result from those arts offer rules and examples of proper behavior. Hence, teachers pay attention to the "orderly conduct" of their students, ensuring that after students have "learned their letters and are coming to understand the written word," they are then introduced to "the compositions of good poets" because these contain "many warnings, and many accounts, praises and eulogies of the good men of the past." Once students finish their education, "the city then makes them learn its laws and . . . live in accordance with these" to ensure that they "do nothing arbitrary" and conform to the lawful conventions of civic life. For Plato's Protagoras, "just as the writing teachers trace lines with a stylus and give the tablet to those children who are not yet skilled at writing," so in the same way "the city, having traced its laws, the inventions of the good law-givers of the past, makes them rule and be ruled in accordance with these" (Plato 2003a, 29). Laws are, like the "virtues of justice, prudence, and piety," conventions, not absolutes, "traced" not by the gods but by "law-givers." We conform to them by reconciling our individual preferences and understandings to the contractual agreements of society as a whole, pursuing a public definition of virtuous conduct through willing observance of laws. One may see in this account, notwithstanding significant historical differences between sophistic and Enlightenment philosophy, some parallels that are not far fetched between Athenian and Jeffersonian concepts of democracy.

The arguments of Gorgias and Calicles in Plato's *Gorgias* are similar to those of Protagoras, provided one reads the text against its own grain by offering the sophists in the dialogue opportunity to make their case outside Socrates's skillful manipulation of leading questions. For Gorgias, the practice of rhetoric presumes a sociopolitical context in which the practical realities of competing interests and perceptions, rather than a shared conviction about abstract Truth or Good, serve as the stimulus for debate. The world of politics that Socrates and Plato are determined to renounce in favor of philosophy is precisely the world in which Gorgias plies his practical art. Persuasion does not depend on the timeless rational entailments of dialectic but on a speaker's ability to identify and enunciate, in the social moment, the local and personalized appeals most likely to influence discussion in favor of the speaker's agenda. It's an art of framing issues, managing points of view, and molding opinion, an art of spinning, pitching, hawking, and dealing, based on the realization that truths, beliefs, and preferred courses of action are relative to individuals or interest groups and to the shifting situations in which they find themselves. Gorgias is quite comfortable, therefore, agreeing with Socrates's characterization of rhetoric as "a producer of persuasion for belief, not for instruction in the matter of right and wrong" (Plato 1975, 455a). By representing relative truths from the perspective of motivating interests, the orator is able to "win over the votes of the multitude, practically in any matter he may choose to take up" (457c). But of course the notion of relative truth precisely marks the boundary between Socrates and the sophists. Contrasting philosophy with politics, Socrates insists that the latter is "ever changing [its] views, but philosophy always holds the same," concluding that he would prefer to have his "lyre," or "some chorus that I might provide" for public enjoyment, "out of tune and discordant" rather than "have internal discord and contradiction in my own single self" (482c). Calicles responds that the austere simplicity and naïve inflexibility of metaphysics blind its devotees to the realities of power and interest that shape knowledge and motivate conduct in the real world. He calls philosophy "a charming thing, if a man has to do with it moderately in his younger days," but insists that maturity requires an appreciation of intellectual diversity, competing values, the uncertainties that necessarily attend human affairs, and the social necessity of forging pragmatic agreement out of the welter of individual opinions and prejudices. People who require the childish satisfactions of philosophical absolutism "are shown to be ignorant of the laws of their city, and of the terms which have to be used in negotiating agreements with their fellows in private or in public affairs, and of human pleasures and desires; and, in short, to be utterly inexperienced in men's characters" (485a). In place of Socrates's metaphysical theory of discourse, where the point of words is to declare and teach universal truths, Calicles offers, arguably, the beginnings of an expressivist theory, where local truths, motivated by "human pleasures and desires," formed out of personal interpretations of the world, are represented in language, then exchanged and judged in the give and take of public discussion.

MONTAIGNE

Unfortunately, while these tantalizing fragments of sophistic thought provide traces of a skeptical philosophy of knowledge, a worldly habit of mind, and an understanding of practical oratory as the negotiation of personal interests in the context of public business, they offer little in the way of sustained epistemological argument from which to derive a comprehensive theory of discourse, whether expressivist or otherwise. More recognizable—one might say self-conscious—representations of expressivist rhetoric emerge only centuries later, during and after the European Renaissance, starting with humanist explorations of secular concepts of "man" and the make-up of human consciousness, gathering momentum (as we've seen) in accounts of the new science that featured increasingly skeptical ideas of the relationship between mind and nature, and culminating in nineteenth-century romantic celebrations of the self that emphasized the role of language, or symbolization, in mediating between self and world. Michel de Montaigne (1533–1592), for example, articulates a sixteenth-century expressivism that simultaneously looks back to sophistic themes and forward to romanticism when he makes this announcement, unapologetically, in a note "To the Reader" that prefaces his 1580 collection of *Essays*: "I am myself the matter of my book" (Montaigne 1958). Montaigne echoes Protagoras when he observes, in his essay "Of Democritus and Heraclitus," that while "things in themselves may have their own weights and measures and qualities," the "soul" (i.e., human consciousness) "treats a matter not according to itself, but according to herself" (220). He explains that "once inside, within us," the soul allots [things] their qualities as she sees fit." Hence, death is "frightful" to Cicero, "desirable" to Cato, and "a matter of indifference" to Socrates. Every concept formed in the mind from the ranges of human experience (he cites "health, conscience, authority, knowledge, riches, beauty, and their opposites") is constituted by the mind's autonomous activity: "All are stripped on entry and receive from the soul new clothing, and the coloring that she chooses" (220). But Montaigne differs from Protagoras in turning the ultimately enigmatic "man is the measure of all things" toward an explicit representation of active human consciousness, identifying the mind as the source of meaningfulness. He observes in "Of Pedantry" that "learning," construed as a gathering of information from experience, books, or education, "is not there to give light to the soul that has none, or to make a blind man see." Employing the sense of sight metaphorically to suggest the mind's powers of conception, he says that the value of learning is not to furnish the blind man with sight "but to direct the sight he has" (104). Information lies outside the mind, but vision, the capacity to "see" its value in human terms, lies within. This conviction that the inner light of reflection is the real starting point for knowledge is what turns Montaigne's preoccupation with his personal experiences, feelings, and opinions away from mere self-absorption and toward a theory of human expressivity. As he says in *Of Experience*, "I would rather be an authority on myself than on Cicero. In the experience I have of myself I find enough to make me wise" (822).

In Montaigne, we glimpse, but with reverse emphasis, the same awkward intellectual binary of subject and object that Descartes, Locke, and their descendants have struggled to resolve in articulating an objectivist theory of discourse. As chapter 4 made clear, the price of conjuring a materially concrete, factual domain of the object was to conjure simultaneously its nettlesome other, the interpreting subject, and to initiate a philosophical conundrum, forever undecidable, over how to reconcile the two. Descartes (1960a; 1960b) and Locke (1965) are obliged to acknowledge the mischievous, undisciplined subject as they struggle to form a viable theory of empirical method. They urge skepticism and self-critique in the conduct of scientific inquiry, a care for the denotative power of language and a corresponding diligence in restraining its ulti-mately irrepressible misrepresentations. Expressivism, by contrast, par-ticularly as it develops within the ideological framework of European romanticism, exalts the subject, the power and freedom of the envision-ing imagination, the authenticity of personal insight, and the capacity of language, or symbolization, to constitute the world, not merely as brute (and, in the wake of industrialization, increasingly ugly) factual-ity, but as a richly layered, emotionally responsive montage of fact and human value. Efforts to reconcile subject and object in scientific rheto-ric tend historically toward positivism, as in Locke's privileging of sense data, while the same efforts in expressivist rhetoric tend toward solip-sism, as in Montaigne's skeptical conclusion in "Apology for Raymond Sebond" that, although "all knowledge makes its way into us through the senses," this sensory information is "the greatest foundation and proof of our ignorance" because it is known solely "through the faculty of the knower," who judges of "things" according to his personal "means and will," not according to "the law of their own essence" (Montaigne 1958, 443). The binary is endlessly reinvoked as Renaissance, Enlightenment, and romantic philosophers take turns valorizing one term over, and fre-quently at the expense of, the other. It's an instructive biographical foot-note to Samuel Coleridge's efforts to repair the subject/object divorce that he named his sons Hartley and Berkeley after well-known repre-sentatives of its polarities. David Hartley (2011), an eighteenth-century English psychologist, took Lockean empiricism toward a positivist, behavioral theory of mind, representing cognition as the association of ideas mechanically prompted by the influx of external stimuli. George Berkeley (1982), an eighteenth-century British empiricist philosopher, took the same Lockean starting point toward a radically idealist theory of mind, famously asserting that, with respect to "things" in themselves, "their esse is percipi" (to be is to be perceived), their existence is entirely dependent on cognition, leaving only mind as ultimately real. Coleridge (1965) maps his family history onto the binary as he wends his intellec-tual way toward reconciling its terms in a theory of the creative imagina-tion that is itself based on an earlier effort at resolution proposed by the principal architects of European romanticism, Immanuel Kant and the German transcendental movement.

COLERIDGE

If objectivism is the ideal rhetoric of the scientist, expressivism is the ideal rhetoric of the poet. And no poet more cogently articulates the assumptions of expressivist discourse theory than Coleridge (1772–1834), who is also the philosopher who makes Kantian philosophy accessible to English-speaking audiences at the beginning of the nineteenth century. The centerpiece of Coleridge's theory is the reasoning at the end of chapter XIII of his *Biographia Literaria*, where he distinguishes between primary and secondary imagination, and between imagination and fancy. In the chapters prior to this summary statement, he examines Hartley's associational theory at length, rejecting its depiction of consciousness at the mercy of endless streams of sense data, where "our whole life would be divided between the despotism of outward impressions and that of senseless and passive memory" (Coleridge 1965, 64). The random experiential "despotism" implicit in Hartley's theory is what Laurence Sterne (1940) satirizes in *Tristram Shandy*, whose main character, Tristram, is incapable of writing his autobiography because every recollection of his past life inspires other recollections by arbitrary association, leaving him incapable of organizing the ensemble into coherent narrative. Coleridge strives to identify, in place of Hartley's passive association, an active, formative power capable of rendering "outward impressions" both intelligible and coherent, referring to that power as "esemplastic," a neologism meaning "to shape into one" (Coleridge 1965, 91). The esemplastic power imposes order on the materials of sensory awareness, modifying and synthesizing according to its own judgments of relevance, relationship, priority, and value. Coleridge also rejects, however, Berkeley's idealist conclusion that there is only intelligence and not matter, a view that "removes all reality and immediateness of perception and places us in a dream-world of phantoms and specters, the inexplicable swarm and equivocal generation of motions in our own brains" (77). He seeks instead an "intimate coalition" of "all that is subjective," meaning "the *self* or *intelligence*," and "all that is objective," meaning the phenomena of "*nature*" since "in all acts of positive knowledge there is required a reciprocal concurrence of both" (145). Inspired by Kant's (2008) argument in *Critique of Pure Reason* concerning "transcendental schemata," that is, a priori mental categories or concepts that give shape to experience, Coleridge's theory of imagination is based on this reciprocity, reconciliation, or coalescence, acknowledging the actuality of what lies outside the mind while also establishing the priority of esemplastic governance principles of mind, in terms of which materiality is rendered humanly comprehensible.

The famous definition in chapter XIII begins with the "primary imagination," where Coleridge invokes the ancient authority of Genesis to describe the power of the creative mind. "The primary imagination

I hold to be the living power and prime agent of all human perception, and as a representation in the finite mind of the eternal act of creation in the infinite I Am" (Coleridge 1965, 167). Echoing Kant, Coleridge's definition asserts that perception itself, not just the cognitive activity following a prior influx of sensory information, is creative work that translates mere physical stimuli into meaningful "experience." "We learn all things," he writes, "by occasion of experience; but the very facts so learnt force us inward on the antecedents, that must be pre-supposed in order to render experience itself possible" (79). "Sensation," he explains elsewhere, "is but vision nascent, not the cause of intelligence but intelligence itself revealed as an earlier power in the process of self-construction" (155). Coleridge's response, then, to Locke's tyranny of sensation is to argue that even our earliest awareness of the external "Other" comes preshaped by the primary imagination, which organizes sensory information by its own principles in order to constitute, as a coherent world of meanings, our ordinary, everyday experience, including the familiar physical world—rocks, rainbows, chrysanthemums—as well as the world of human life and institutions—pocket books, stop signs, strip malls, bicycles, sirloin steaks. In effect, by the agency of imagination, we create these worlds in a way that parallels God's creative activity: we think them into existence, not in the sense that we create materiality by our thought but in the sense that we reconstitute materiality as a human artifact, responsive to human requirements and recognizable as such. As in Genesis, the instrumentality by which we accomplish our construction of the world is language or, more generally (although Coleridge never quite explicitly enlarges the concept to this extent), the production of symbols. "An idea," he insists, cannot be conveyed but by a symbol" (85). The meaning of any word includes "not only its correspondent object, but likewise all the associations which it recalls." That is, language is the mediator between mind and external sensation, the means by which imagination constitutes its objects: "For language is framed to convey not the object alone, but likewise the character, mood, and intentions of the person who is representing it" (263).

Secondary imagination is the domain of self-conscious discursive practice, where the objects presented to us by experience and ordinary language are reflectively reconstituted in descriptive, analytic, argumentative, poetic, and other expressive modes. Coleridge (1965, 167) describes it as an "echo" of the primary imagination, "co-existing with the conscious will, yet still as identical with the primary in the kind of its agency, and differing only in degree, and in the mode of its operation." In great poetry, the preeminent example for Coleridge of the power of secondary imagination, the unconscious production of metaphor common to all language (since all verbal conceptualization entails analogy) becomes a conscious and willful act. Through the poet's creative re-perception, love is a "red, red rose," time "like a running grave, tracks me down," the evening is "spread out against the sky, like a patient etherized upon a table," and the ocean is not merely wet, large, cold, and salty, but is also turbulent, majestic, angry, melancholy, and mysterious, the magical environment of Odysseus or the malignant environment of Ahab. A poem "dissolves, diffuses, dissipates, in order to recreate." What is dissolved is the routinized understanding of ordinary life; for instance, according to one of Coleridge's examples, our ordinary experience of trees on a sea coast, as we watch them bend in the night wind, is a scene constructed in the primary imagination. The conscious "recreating" of this scene in poetry gives rise to an image of "Yon row of bleak and visionary pines, / By twilight-glimpse discerned, mark! how they flee / From the fierce sea-blast, all their tresses wild / Streaming before them" (178). In principle, the most original scientific thought is similarly the work of secondary imagination, such as the conscious reconception of the sea in its chemical configuration, in the biology of its life forms, and in the physics of its wave motions. Whether by means of poetic, mathematical, philosophical, technological, or some other symbolic mode, the commonplace is dissolved, concretized, generalized, reordered, and differently understood—as metaphor, as electromagnetic particles, as genera and species, as chemical compounds, as equations or geometric shapes. Ordinary language offers us the world of the everyday, while conscious, reflective discourse, when composed by superior minds, offers us new knowledge through figurative re-perception.

Of course, while all discourse, poetic and otherwise, is conscious, not all minds are superior. The third mental operation that Coleridge identifies is "fancy," his version of Locke's reactive mind, not a transformative faculty but a capacity by which we supplement, evaluate, manage, and superficially rearrange the store of what is already known. Fancy has "no other counters to play with but fixities and definites," receiving its materials "ready made from the law of association." It is nothing more than a "mode of memory emancipated from the order of time and space" and "modified by that empirical phaenomenon [*sic*] of the will which we express by the word choice" (Coleridge 1965, 167). Like secondary imagination, the fancy involves conscious composition, but unlike the truly creative faculty, it falls short of fundamentally altered insight. The lines of poetry cited above, employing personification and other metaphorical devices to depict the trees bending in the wind, exemplify imaginative perception. In the hands of a lesser poet, lines portraying the same natural scene (but in a way, Coleridge says, that might be equally appropriate in a descriptive poem or a "book of topography") would be merely fanciful: "Behold yon row of pines, that shorn and bow'd / Bend from the sea-blast, seen at twilight eve" (178). The poet works in this case, consciously but not imaginatively, with conventional references to pines, wind, and early evening, preserved in memory as images from countless discrete but associated sensory experiences, to organize a familiar picture of the sea coast. Elsewhere, Coleridge further illustrates the point by arguing that Milton is imaginative while Cowley is only fanciful (50–51). Milton's "genius" enables him to compose vivid depictions of earth, chaos, and hell, as well as Satan, Adam, and Eve, all from the creative resources of his own mind, while Cowley (and the other "metaphysical" poets that Coleridge generally disparages) is limited to "wit," consisting of inventive but emotionally unexciting intellectual comparisons and clever plays on words. John Donne's (1612)Valediction: Forbidding Mourning" would exemplify merely fanciful perception where two lovers are likened to the twin points of a drafting compass, one fixed and the other orbiting around it. The simile is labored, lacking passion, and limited in its capacity to elicit insights beyond the superficial similarities of mechanical and human dependency. Extrapolating from Coleridge's distinction, it could be argued that, while Einstein's articulation of the influence of gravity on the propagation of light is an achievement of the secondary imagination, the experiment by which Arthur Eddington demonstrated the curvature of light during a solar eclipse is an achievement of the fancy. Einstein makes new knowledge through a fundamental reformulation of Newtonian assumptions about space, time, light, and the cosmos, while Eddington works within the assertions of Einstein's reformulation (as "fixities and definites") to reveal a set of empirical facts organized just as Einstein had predicted.

SUSANNE LANGER

Coleridge's definition of the creative imagination remains a classic example of the emphasis on personalized human agency, the sovereign subject (in his case, the "genius" of the great poet) that typifies expressivist rhetoric. And his depiction of the mediating role of language, specifically the metaphorical language of poetry, anticipates later expressivist discussions of symbolic action that range far beyond the world of literature and even beyond linguistic forms of signifying. Susanne Langer

(1895–1985), a colleague of the neo-Kantian Ernst Cassirer, and an intellectual kindred spirit, invokes Coleridge in *Philosophy in a New Key*, her study of "the symbolism of reason, rite, and art," taking his lead in situating the forms of knowledge in the transformative action of mind upon materiality through symbols. "Our merest sense-experience," she writes, "is a process of formulation." Out of the materials of sensation, the mind "must select certain predominant forms" if it is to "make report of *things* and not of mere dissolving sensa." Eyes and ears "must have their logic," either "categories of understanding," if we "like the Kantian idiom," or "'primary imagination,' in Coleridge's version of the same concept" (Langer 1973, 89). For Langer, the modern philosophic era is distinguished by one particular "generative idea," a "new key" for our discussions of the forms of human knowledge, that she identifies as "symbolic transformation," the distinctively human practice of composing meaning. Symbolization is "one of man's primary activities, like eating, looking, or moving about," the "fundamental process of his mind." Unlike philosophers of the rationalist and Enlightenment eras, Langer does not associate "mind" with "soul" or "supernatural essence." She insists that human beings are organisms, that "mind," or "consciousness," is not a spiritual or mystical entity separate from body, and that symbolic behavior is grounded in evolved human biology. As such, the media of expressivity, including ritual, myth, language, music, art, and other modes, are susceptible to psychological and anthropological analysis. Symbolization is a biological urge, a yearning, which "actuates" all of the human being's "apparently unzoological aims, his wistful fantasies, his consciousness of value, his utterly impractical enthusiasms, and his awareness of a 'Beyond' filled with holiness" (40–41). It can be rational, pragmatic, and consciously motivated, but it is not essentially any of these, manifesting itself in dreams no less than in mathematical equations, in sacramental rites no less than in philosophical analysis, and in reveries no less than purposeful behavior. It is "the starting point of all intellection . . . and is more general than thinking, fancying, or taking action." It is the forming principle of ideation, understood as "*the sheer expression of ideas*" (43, author's emphasis).

Like Coleridge, and in the way that is characteristic of expressivist rhetoric, Langer focuses on the wellsprings of human creativity, a mapping of the complexities of the self. But unlike him, she does not privilege the poetic, or even the discursive, over other modes of symbolic transformation. Discursivity, she contends, is simply the principle of temporal order, or consecutiveness, featured in certain forms of symbolic activity, chief among them the practices of language. Langer distinguishes between "discursive" forms, like natural language, mathematics, or music, and "presentational" forms, like paintings and photographs, artistic or religious icons, and the imagistic thinking associated with memories and dreams. The former displays meanings successively, relying on syntactic rules that govern temporal arrangement, while the latter displays them simultaneously (Langer 1973, 93). A picture, for example, "is composed of elements that represent various respective constituents in the object; but these elements are not units with independent meanings" (94). Discursive symbols are intrinsically analytic, composing the world according to the logic of grammar, a dispersion of objects, qualities, and actions arranged in patterns of attribution and predication. Even the action of verbal metaphor depends on an evaluation of distributed elements (the grammatical conjunction of *love* and *rose*). Presentational symbols, by contrast, are intrinsically holistic, so that in the case of a painting, the meanings of constituent elements—light and shade, combinations of colors, brush strokes, textures, hues, forms, and figures—"are understood only through the meaning of the whole, through their relations within the total structure" (97). The value of Langer's distinction lies in the range of symbolic mediations that can be incorporated into her theory of rationality and knowledge, allowing her to add to such historically privileged forms as science and philosophy, which valorize fact and discursive argument, the forms of myth, ritual, and dream along with the visual and plastic arts, all of which valorize image and intuition. Resituating language and discourse within a more comprehensive theory of symbolic action fills in the expressivist portrait of the subject as consciousness self-articulated by means of layer upon layer of mediated experiential transformations—rational, emotional, intuitive—each enriching the world picture presented to and by human apprehension with its own distinctive contributions. Feelings, too, Langer observes, "have definite forms, which become progressively articulated," forms that supplement language, "a very poor medium for expressing our emotional nature," with additional powers of representation. The resituating also provides expressivist theories of language and discourse with enhanced access to affective and prelogical forms of meaning making that operate "far below the level of speech" (144). "The fact is," Langer insists, "our primary world of reality *is* a verbal one" (126). But it is a reality informed by greater intellective resources than those of logic, denotation, and dialectic.

Symbolic modes, in their diversity, produce what Langer calls the "fabric of meaning," a multifaceted "complex of impressions and transformations." The "warp" of the fabric "consists of what we call data, the *signs* to which experience has conditioned us to attend and upon which we act often without any conscious ideation." The "woof" of the fabric is symbolism. "Out of signs and symbols we weave our tissue of reality" (Langer 1973, 280). While language stands out against this backdrop, a dominant motif in the fabric, it owes its origins and its distinctiveness to the interplay of symbolic transformations that characterizes, more generally than language, the nature of the organically evolved human mind. She cites the linguist Edward Sapir in support of the contention that "language is primarily a vocal actualization of the tendency to see reality symbolically, that it is precisely this quality which renders it a fit instrument for communication" (109). The capacity to symbolize precedes the development of language as a discursive mode and accounts for its salient properties, namely, its ability to form concepts, which enables "naming, fixating, conceiving objects," and its dependence upon metaphor, "which cannot be properly understood without a symbolistic rather than signalistic view of language" (132). The sign, as Langer defines it, does not entail conceptualization but simply stands in place of something else, in a fixed, one-to-one, paired correlation, directly invoking its object (57). The interpretation of signs is the basis of animal, including human, intelligence. "We answer bells, watch the clock, obey warning signals, follow arrows, take off the kettle when it whistles, come at the baby's cry, close the windows when we hear thunder" (59). But the symbols that distinctively comprise human language go beyond signaling. They "are not proxy for their objects, but are *vehicles for the conception of objects*" (author's emphasis), denoting (which has to do with reference) but also connoting (which has to do with meaning), and through these reciprocal operations reconciling (in Coleridge's terms) the object and the subject (57–67). For Langer, "a concept is all that a symbol really conveys" (71). Animals other than human beings communicate, to be sure, using signs, but according to Langer they do not conceptualize. Dogs may whine, growl, and bark to signify feelings—hostility or fear, danger or alarm, happiness or affection, hunger or pain, all instinctive and immediate responses to situations. But "true language" begins "only when a sound keeps its reference beyond the situation of its instinctive utterance" (105). For human beings, conceptualizing— the making of meaning through symbols—does not depend on immediate need, nor do the resulting concepts lose their meaning apart from a specific occasion of use. Symbolizing does not arise out of pragmatic necessity but from the continuing desire to construct an intelligible world responsive to human requirements, a desire that manifests itself even in language play, like the babbling of infants, without the stimulus of any conscious purpose.

Langer speculates that language could only have arisen "in a race in which the lower forms of symbolistic thinking—dream, ritual, superstitious fancy—were already highly developed." Human language, she hypothesizes, may have built, then, on a substratum of simpler, presentational symbolic behaviors "characterized by vigorous indulgence in purely expressive acts," including "play-forms" such as pantomime, ritual gesture, and dance (Langer 1973, 127). Ritual is "the cradle of language," and metaphor is "the law of its life" (146). Ritual (as chapter 2 discussed) is ceremonial activity for solemn, often religious, ends, involving a prescribed repetition of steps or moves the performance of which is understood to possess a magical or spiritual efficacy. Its purposes are dramatic rather than functional, an affirmation of the bond between the human and the natural (as in a dance commemorating seasonal change) or between the human and the divine (as in a religious rite). As such, it constitutes the essence of symbolic transformation, an affective response to experience that transcends, in its repetition, any specific circumstance of its application, having generalized a relationship, a unity, between an organized pattern of gestures and movements, perhaps including manipulations of objects, and a perceived exteriority. Ritual is the cradle of language because it prefigures in a presentational symbol the analogizing and generalizing features of metaphor, anticipating the discursive metaphorical thinking characteristic of language. Central to any metaphoric reasoning is the perception that X is like Y—the logic of analogy. The physical movements of the ritual invoke and fuse with the experience of the "Other" in an identity of meaning. Moreover, the movements repeated over multiple occasions evolve into an "abstractable form" (141), a conceptual linking across instances, the meaning and value of which are no longer tied to any specific occasion or idiosyncratic feature—the logic of generalization. Langer hypothesizes that the ritual behavior of early human beings, their dancing for example, might have led, in its pleasurable exuberance, its "play-excitement," to shouts and other voiced expression, which over time would have become associated with particular movements and conventionalized in the ritual. Initially, she supposes, these organized sounds would have been purely connotative, like the dance itself, but once conventionalized and freed from instinctive utterance, the voiced symbol could readily have assumed a deliberate use (pointing, naming), occasioning a gradual identification of name and thing that would mark the beginning of words. Upon the discrimination of words, coined and proliferated by the same metaphorical processes, the same analogizing and generalizing that characterized preverbal symbols, a system for associating discrete names—a grammar—could then have developed to connect the primary verbal elements in a "relational structure, a logical edifice," thereby expanding the flexibility of language from simple naming to predicating, attributing, and affirming (130–35).

Of interest, throughout this exhaustive theorizing about the origins and practice of language, Langer maintains such a steady focus on the nature of symbolic behavior that she virtually ignores the communicative aspects of discourse. Indeed, she makes a point of insisting that "the transformation of experience into concepts," and *not* communication, "is the motive of language" (Langer 1973, 126). The human need to articulate exists independent of the usefulness of speech for public transaction, and any attempt to trace language "back entirely to the need of communication, neglecting the formulative, abstractive experience at the root of it" makes it impossible to account for how and why human language could have evolved in its distinctive symbolic form when language has emerged nowhere else in the animal world except as instinctive sign behavior related to natural wants (127). Ignoring the circularity of this argument, what it highlights is a peculiar, not to say paradoxical, feature of expressivism conceived as a *rhetorical* theory, namely its tendency to emphasize articulation at cost to any elaborated, let alone robust, conception of the social. The exalting of the personal over the social does not deny the importance of the social dimension of language, but it emphasizes, as we saw as early as the sophists, that individualized identity precedes social organization and occasions the need to negotiate community life. Protagoras understood the importance of rhetorical training, and education generally, in terms of the need to reconcile personal interest with the public good. For Langer, similarly, the emergence of self as the locus of human symbolic behavior precedes the emergence of society and enables social intercourse in and through the distinctive agency of self-expression. In the other rhetorical perspectives so far depicted, the social is understood to be more important than the individual, a network of compelling moral, legal, intellectual, or other constraints imposed on individuals by appeal to some transcendent collective truth, whether religious, metaphysical, or scientific. Sophistic and romantic ideologies are, by contrast, intrinsically iconoclastic, relativizing truth and thereby rendering the social as a patchwork of competing claims for sovereignty while exalting values of personal expression, freedom of thought, individual autonomy, and the authenticity of personal voice. These values are apparent in Coleridge's privileging of the true poet as exemplar of the workings of creative imagination. Exceptional minds, represented for Coleridge by imaginative as opposed to merely fanciful poets, have authority to advance knowledge, not by adding mundanely to what is already known but by heroically reconstituting the known through the power of personal insight. Such minds even have authority to alter the social order—as Coleridge implies in his early support for the heroes of the French Revolution—because of the strength of their superior re-perceptions. Langer likewise proposes such heroes, "persons of some imagination and effective intelligence," who are drawn to a "realm of reality" that contains "their ultimate life symbols" and whose lives, therefore, are characterized by passion, commitment, and the assertion of personal will even in the face of social opposition. She identifies, among others, "the scholar who will defy the world in order to write or speak what he knows as 'scientific truth'" and "the feminists to whom woman-suffrage was a 'cause' for which they accepted ridicule as well as punishment" (288–89). In the expressivist tradition, the individual mind is the beginning of social organization while the heroic mind is the key to intellectual and social change.

Both Coleridge and Langer derive these familiar themes of the expressivist story—the priority of the self and the symbolic compositions of the natural and social orders—from the inherited narratives of seventeenth-century rationalism, eighteenth-century Enlightenment philosophy, and nineteenth-century romanticism. They presume, in keeping with those traditions, the dependable reality of the concepts on which their reasoning depends, in particular the concepts of self and mind. For Coleridge, the mind is where imagining happens, God's gift of a power paralleling his own, while for Langer, mind, as psychophysical consciousness, is where symbolizing happens. Mind is a "place," therefore, but one whose place-ness remains obscure in their accounts, mostly stipulated rather than explored, the site of faculties (like reason, imagination, and memory) that govern operations (like thinking, creating, and recalling) carried out by instrumentalities (like language). Self meanwhile is the intuition of a substantial, unified, personal identity, the place where me-ness resides, the mind's most important production. Mind, self, and symbolization are understood to be the essence of what it is to be human. What is ironic about this romantic position, however, is that, however relativistic its story might be regarding the nature of the world outside mind and self, it relies on notions of the subject that are anything but relativistic, that are indeed metaphysical and, as such, quite congruent with Platonic Forms or Aristotelian categories. Rationalist philosophers had understood that all metaphysical terms are effectively nouns mistaken for things, a perception that had led Descartes, Arnauld, and Locke, among others, to critique classical metaphysics by reversing

the Aristotelian relationship between logical and grammatical categories. But in the process, these philosophers had created some metaphysical terms of their own, most notoriously *subject* and *object*. Coleridge and
Langer effectively critique the second of these terms, *object*, by reversing
the rationalist priority between the mind and the physical world, arguing that materiality has no intrinsic organization for science to reveal,
whatever the sophistication of its data-driven analysis. But they leave the
metaphysical subject in place, comprised of the mind and the unified
self, understood as the seat of expressivity. They reconcile the terms of
the binary merely by folding one term into the other.

RICHARD RORTY

The contemporary American philosopher Richard Rorty (1931–2007)
challenges this last bastion of expressivist metaphysics by mounting a
critique of the sovereign subject, but he does so without rejecting the
primary theme of the expressivist story itself, namely, the creativity of
individual human beings. His rhetorical twist on that creativity, echoing
Friedrich Nietzsche, is that our most important creation is our selves.
Rorty rejects all metaphysical absolutes and makes a case, turning away
from Kant and toward the arguments of Nietzsche and Sigmund Freud,
for the constructedness of mind and identity. The subject isn't the site
of language, he argues, but rather, no less than the object, a construction of language. It isn't mind that governs language, but language that
effects the composing of mind—a noun, not a place—with a meaning
that merely allows us to imagine a place. Hence, language is not a mediator between mind and materiality but rather the source of the very
terms that had been supposed to require mediation. Rorty's approach
to the subject/object binary, then, is not to resolve it but to ignore it as a
metaphysical pseudoproblem. If language is responsible for composing
the sentence *subject and object are opposed*, then the simple way to eliminate the philosophical difficulty that such a verbal construction introduces is to erase the sentence. In *Contingency, Irony, and Solidarity*, Rorty
(1989) dedicates himself to a revised version of the expressivist narrative, seeking to compose a viable story about the self, and the relationship between self and society, that avoids the essentialism, foundationalism, and universalism that are always the mischievous by-products of
metaphysical thinking. Reversing the terms in Coleridge's and Langer's
accounts, he aims to depict a self that arises out of expression rather
than an expressiveness that arises out of the falsely objectified self. He
begins by asserting the "contingency" of the central concepts of the

narrative, including language, selfhood, and community. Contingency is the opposite of necessity, and Rorty uses the distinction variously to oppose the relative and accidental to the essential, the historical to the foundational, and the local to the universal. He then proceeds to explore a relationship between self and community, the private and the public, that avoids the erroneous assumptions of traditional liberalism about how the pursuit of self-creation parallels and anticipates the development of human solidarity. He challenges, in other words, the incongruous belief at the heart of Enlightenment and Romantic social narratives that selfishness is the wellspring of altruism. Finally, he shows how alternative discourses, specifically the theoretical and the literary, can provide models, respectively, for acquiring "private irony," the reflectiveness that enables self-redescription, and "liberal hope," the empathy for others necessary to achieve human solidarity.

All healthy human beings have identities in progress and are selves in progress, but just in the sense that they are composing autobiographies—self-representations made out of words—that are continually under construction. Rorty refers to the individual's autobiography as a "final vocabulary," a "set of words" used to describe the meaningfulness of the person's life, encompassing upbringing and history, feelings and beliefs, commitments, values, actions, in essence a summary of the self. The vocabulary is "final" only in the sense that, at a specific moment in a person's life, these words "are as far as he can go with language" to explain the self-reference and self-worth that constitute identity (Rorty 1989, 73). Rorty finds support for his story in the work of Freud, who, in Rorty's words, "eschewed the very idea of a paradigm human being," and who, in challenging the idea of the "truly human," challenged also "the attempt to divinize the self as a replacement for a divinized world" (35). Freud rejects the classical story that reason is the deep core of the soul, identical in all human beings, the faculty that enables us to discern the paths to truth and righteousness amidst the emotional and material clutter of our lives. In place of a central faculty of mind or personality, where local actions are subsumed under general principles in the pursuit of a "moral" life, Freud identifies the deployment of "unconscious" as well as rational "strategies" by which human beings adapt to their distinctive environments, "adjusting contingencies to other contingencies." He urges people, says Rorty, to "return to the particular," rather than to moral universals, recognizing relationships of similarity or difference between present and past behaviors. If we can learn to interpret what we are doing today, or thinking about doing, by reference, for instance, to "our past reaction to particular authority figures" or "constellations of

behavior which were forced upon us in infancy," we can adjust contingencies to contingencies in order to "make something worthwhile out
of ourselves, to create present selves whom we can respect" (32–33). In
effect, as Rorty reads Freud, we are the presentations of our case histories, products of the accidental, historical flux of our experience, "weaving idiosyncratic narratives . . . of our success in self-creation, our ability
to break free from an idiosyncratic past" (33). All the minutiae of daily
life, from womb to grave, serve "to dramatize and crystallize a human
being's sense of self-identity." We are webs of the relationships created
by these accrued experiences, and "any seemingly random constellation
of such things can set the tone of a life" (37). We occupy our time from
birth to death weaving those webs in and through the autobiographical
narratives endlessly under construction in our memories. The narratives
are never finished "because there is nothing to complete" but are cease-
lessly rewoven until death forces their abandonment (42–43).

All human beings compose "final vocabularies," but the majority do
so, not only un-self-consciously but under the debilitating illusion that
there is really only "one true description of the human situation, one
universal context of our lives." Failing to understand their contingency,
they are "doomed to spend [their] conscious lives trying to escape" into
some certainty, usually someone else's certainty, rather than embracing
the opportunity that an awareness of contingency represents. Reflective
human beings, by contrast, are "ironists" in their understanding of their
autobiographies: that is, they recognize the contingency of the story (it
is relative, historical, and local); they understand that nothing expressed
within the narrative can resolve their doubts about it; and they do "not
think that [their] vocabulary is closer to reality than others, that it is
in touch with a power not [themselves]" (Rorty 1989, 73). Ironists are
aware of themselves creating themselves and are, to that extent, liberated from the illusion that, as fixed identities, they have neither written
their stories nor have power to "redescribe" them. Reflective human
beings, Rorty's ironists, can recompose themselves by conscious acts of
will, can become "strong" rather than a weak "writers." Rorty invokes
Coleridge's prototype of the writer-hero, the imaginative as opposed to
merely fanciful poet. The ironist's task, he says, "is the one Coleridge
recommended to the great and original poet: to create the taste by
which he will be judged," understanding that "the judge the ironist has
in mind is himself," a hero who "wants to be able to sum up his life in
his own terms" (97). Echoing Harold Bloom's similar characterization
in *Anxiety of Influence*, Rorty identifies the "strong poet" as a "person who
uses words as they have never before been used" to tell the story of their

self-production instead of accepting the descriptions of others (28). More than to Coleridge or Bloom, however, Rorty looks to Nietzsche for the explicit rejection of Plato's illusion of "knowing the truth," recalling Nietzsche's definition of truth as "a mobile army of metaphors." Once we abandon the idea that words mirror a transcendent reality, we can also escape the "idea of finding a single context for all human lives," the belief in an *ur*-biography to which we are all condemned to aspire but without hope of success. While all human beings assuredly die, each finds consolation at death, according to Rorty's reading of Nietzsche, "in being that peculiar sort of dying animal who, by describing himself in his own terms, had created himself. More exactly, he would have created the only part of himself that mattered by constructing his own mind" (27).

Given Rorty's model of the energetic, not to say arrogant, Nietzschean hero preoccupied with self-creation, the question of the relationship between self and society that lurks rather benignly in the expressivism of Coleridge and Langer assumes a decidedly greater complexity in his version of the story. Enlightenment philosophy had presumed a rational parallel between the twin pursuits of striving for self-perfection, which entails the satisfaction of personal needs, and striving for human solidarity, which entails the making of a community based on fairness, consideration of others, and "liberality," a value, prerequisite for social justice, that Rorty defines as the avoidance of cruelty. It is not intellectually accidental, for example, that the writer of the Declaration of Independence, Thomas Jefferson, is also the founder of the University of Virginia. Jefferson, very much a product of the Enlightenment, presumed that the "enlightened" self-interest of the free, educated, rationally astute individual is entirely congenial with, and indeed precursor to, the well-ordered state. But Rorty sees an unbridgeable difference between the imperative of self-creation and the imperative of solidarity because "I-consciousness" and "we-consciousness" entail radically distinct, if mutually important, ambitions. The first involves pursuit of personal identity in the face of death, a compelling need to challenge the extinction that comes equally from actual death and the living death of being "described" by others or by one's own no-longer-sufficient final vocabulary. Only through the poetic achievement of "redescription" can the individual continue to live as an autobiography in progress and thwart extinction, the co-opting or termination of the narrative. But the second involves the self-restraint necessary to avoid cruelty and injustice at the point where one's personal construction of a final vocabulary meets the public need to recognize the alternative final vocabularies of others, and therefore the need to be "aware of all the various ways in which other human beings whom I might act upon can be humiliated" (Rorty 1989, 92). For Rorty, the centuries-old effort to theorize a relationship between the public and the private, an effort that has virtually always subordinated the demands of self to the demands of society, not only to avoid cruelty but to fulfill the mandates of metaphysical abstractions like truth, conscience, morality, and law, has been philosophically futile from the start: "There is no way to bring self-creation together with justice at the level of theory" (xiv). Rorty's resolution of the incompatibility of these ambitions is to propose their coexistence, but not their fusion, in a culture "which has given up the attempt to unite one's private ways of dealing with one's finitude and one's sense of obligation to other human beings" (68), treating "the demands of self-creation and of human solidarity as equally valid, yet forever incommensurable" (xv).

This intellectual coexistence demands, however, that the traditional narrative of democratic society, deploying the language of Enlightenment essentialism, foundationalism, and universalism, must be rewritten in the language of contingency, emphasizing the relative, historical, and local. "Liberal culture needs an improved self-description rather than a set of foundations" (Rorty 1989, 52); in particular, this new description must involve the displacement of religious, philosophical, and suprahistorical accounts by "an historical narrative about the rise of liberal institutions and customs . . . which were designed to diminish cruelty, make possible government by the consent of the governed, and permit as much domination-free communication as possible to take place" (68). In short, an appreciation of the contingency of the individual must be matched in a liberal society by an equal appreciation of the contingency of community. The ironic recognition of strong autobiographers that they are free from the illusion of "an antecedent truth about" themselves, a real essence which others might have detected" (103), must be matched by an equivalently ironic understanding among the citizens of a liberal state that they are free of the illusion of the state's "foundation" in the will of God, the nature of the world, the commandments of an ahistorical morality, or the dictates of a universal conscience. The citizens of Rorty's "liberal utopia" would be people "who had a sense of the contingency of their language of moral deliberation, and thus of their consciences, and thus of their community." As "liberal ironists," they would recognize that "the demands of a morality are the demands of a language, and if languages are historical contingencies, rather than attempts to capture the true shape of the world or the self," then owning one's moral convictions, specifically the conviction opposing cruelty and enabling social justice, "is a matter of identifying oneself with such a contingency" (60). Rorty cites John Stuart Mill in describing the primary function of such ironically conceived liberal communities, those in which "governments devote themselves to optimizing the balance between leaving people's private lives alone and preventing suffering" (63). Their function is to enable productive "encounters" among citizens, honoring the range of personal needs and visions in a pluralist, postmetaphysical world while also recognizing the obligation to negotiate the terms of fair communal living, insuring that the ideals of liberal society "can be fulfilled by persuasion rather than force, by reform rather than revolution, by the free and open encounters of present linguistic and other practices with suggestions for new practices" (60). The truly liberal society is "one which is content to call 'true' whatever the upshot of such encounters turns out to be" (52).

Rorty's definition of liberal society makes clear that his expressivist priority remains the privileging of self-construction in a community dedicated to safeguarding, for all its members, the pursuit of personal identity in the face of death. He is by turns protective of the fragile right to identity and aggressive about the prerogatives of the strong autobiographer. For the private ironist, he writes, "human solidarity is not a matter of sharing a common truth or a common goal but of sharing a common selfish hope, the hope that one's world—the little things around which one has woven into one's final vocabulary—will not be destroyed." The key to realizing this "liberal hope" is the cultivation of empathy, the capacity to sympathize with needs of others that are so akin to one's own, the ability to understand that our social bond "is not a common language but *just* susceptibility to pain" (Rorty 1989, 92). At the same time, throughout his play with the opposition of private irony and liberal hope, his preferred culture hero remains "Bloom's 'strong poet' rather than the warrior, the priest, the sage, or the truth-seeking, 'logical,' 'objective' scientist" (53). Poets are the creative artists whose pursuit of truth, understood in the sense of Nietzsche's "mobile army of metaphors," most powerfully redescribe not merely themselves but the world they construct for themselves and others. The strong poet is the life-affirming personality who rewrites the social narrative, that is, provokes social change by offering a vocabulary that seizes the public imagination at a crucial historical moment. Change is not progressive or evolutionary, according to Rorty, but rather the contingent meeting of a powerful mind and a fortuitous circumstance. He notes that "poetic, artistic, philosophical, scientific, or political progress results from the accidental coincidence of a private obsession with a public need" (37). The heroes of liberal society, "obsessed" with their self-creation, are "the strong poet and the utopian revolutionary," who challenge whatever status quo interferes with their rewriting and who protest "in the name of the society itself against those aspects of the society which are unfaithful to its own self-image" (60). Liberal society, he declares, "has no purpose except to make life easier for poets and revolutionaries while seeing to it that they make life harder for others only by words, and not deeds." Liberal society particularly values these individuals because it understands that "it is what it is, has the morality it has, speaks the language it does, not because it approximates the will of God or the nature of man but because certain poets and revolutionaries of the past spoke as they did" (60–61).

The final issue in Rorty's project is to identify the discursive means by which citizens may educate themselves in the practices of private irony and liberal hope. In the culture of Enlightenment liberalism, he notes, the stories entrusted with articulating the social bonds holding a community together belonged to the disciplines of theology, philosophy, and science, whose theoretical formulations could penetrate "behind the many private appearances to the one general common reality," while literature responded to the particularized needs of the self (Rorty 1989, 94–95). Hence, Coleridge suggests that "the main fundamental distinction" between "philosophy and works of fiction" is that the former "proposes truth for its immediate object instead of pleasure" (Coleridge 1965, 254). But Rorty's culture of ironic liberalism reverses this traditional division of intellectual labor. It relies on theoretical discourse, the final vocabularies of strong figures like Nietzsche, Heidegger, and Derrida, to describe the lay of the conceptual landscape—the scrutiny of metaphysical conceits, the ironic estrangement from other people's descriptions, the inquiry into modes of self-creation—that provides the enabling language of redescription. And it relies on literary discourse, the novel in particular, along with inquiries like ethnography that offer "thick description of the private and idiosyncratic" to stimulate and promote empathy, the sensitivity of liberal society to the pain or humiliation "of those who do not speak our language" (Rorty 1989, 94). Ironic theorists work to ensure that all theoretical formulations, including their own, remain ironic and do not erode into new formalisms which undercut the very freedom to redescribe that ironism posits as the motivating premise of self-construction. The central problem of ironist theory, Rorty says, is "how to overcome authority without claiming authority" (105). Liberal social discourse, by contrast, "would do well to remain as untheoretical and simpleminded as it looks . . . no matter how sophisticated the discourse of self-creation becomes" (121). The imperative at

the heart of public communication is empathy, an "imaginative identification with the details of others' lives" that can lead us to a "loathing
for cruelty" (190). Sympathetic imagination is best stimulated through
concrete depictions of human life, including human beings experiencing pain or humiliation, that help us "notice the effects of our actions
on other people." Texts that achieve this stimulation include novels and
other narratives that allow us to experience either the "effects of social
practices and institutions on others" (like *Uncle Tom's Cabin*) or the
"effects of our private idiosyncrasies on others" (like *Bleak House*).

Rorty's own professional odyssey from philosopher to literary critic in
recent years plainly hints at his identification with the theme of "liberal
hope," the construction of humane, democratic communities based on
citizens' respect for each other's autobiographies-in-progress. But the
authenticity of his moral convictions notwithstanding, there seems little
doubt about where his sympathies lie. They lie where the allegiances of
literary critics virtually always lie, with the writer-hero in search of the
next horizon of self-description, not with the educable reader who may
experience, as a result of literary reading, an "imaginative identification
with the details of others' lives"(Rorty 1989, 190). The critic understands
that writer-heroes achieve more than just marketable portraits of human
sympathy. They also make themselves into models of self-creation, overcoming Bloom's "anxiety of influence," writing against the grain of settled public expectation, and escaping death by redescribing their autobiographies through the mediation of their fictions. It does not diminish Rorty's regard for the imperative of social solidarity to acknowledge
his appreciation of the fact that escaping death must rate higher in the
scheme of things than sympathizing with others, if only because we have
so little to offer others if we are profoundly dissatisfied with ourselves.
Rorty's individualism requires a concept of liberal solidarity that aims
primarily to protect the idiosyncratic creativity necessary for personal
satisfaction, insisting that a community built on the thwarting of diver-
gent personal stories cannot be liberal, while avoiding what Nietzsche's
philosophy fails to discourage, namely, a social order at the mercy of all-
consuming egotists, like Ahab, or Heathcliff and Catherine Earnshaw.
Rorty's urging of a balance of private and public interest is a consistent
theme, but finally, if his sympathies might not quite extend to the libidi-
nal Heathcliff, they certainly would not center on the repressed Edgar
Linton. His preference for the iconoclast is nowhere clearer than at the
end of his account, where in the midst of a final comment on solidarity, he reminds us, again, that "our responsibilities to others constitute
only the public side of our lives, a side which competes with our private

affections and our private attempts at self-creation, and which has no *automatic* priority over such private motives" (194). The hallmark of the expressivist story of the meaning of meaning at least since Kant, and arguably since the sophists, has been the privileging of the subject. Rorty does not deviate from that focus. He deconstructs the transcendental subject, to be sure, but he champions to the end his writer-hero as an archetype of ironic subjectivity.

6

SOCIOLOGICAL RHETORIC

Since rhetoric is always, in some sense, about people communicating, any story about rhetoric, including those discussed in preceding chapters, incorporates an idea of the social. Magical rhetoric ascribes to language the power of communicating with God and depends on the community of believers for its efficacy. Hence, Jesus says in the Gospel according to Matthew (18:20), "Where two or three are gathered in my name, there am I in the midst of them." In *Politics*, Aristotle writes that "since the individual is not self-sufficient when separated," the community or state is "by nature prior to the household or to the individual human being; for the whole must be prior to the part" (Aristotle 2009, Book I, Part 2). Aristotle's description of the occasions for oratory, including the political assembly, the law court, and the public ceremony, makes clear that the purposes of discourse in ontological rhetoric are fundamentally social. In *Discourse on Method*, Descartes (1960a) underscores the importance of community in science, each individual scientist incapable of sustaining empirical inquiry alone and relying instead on the collective effort of colleagues, including future generations of scientists, for the progress of knowledge. In expressivist rhetoric, the social exists as a voluntary incorporation of sovereign individuals, beneficial where harmonious relations ensure safety, strength, and productivity, or a challenge to overcome whenever the collectivity exerts an overbearing will on the individual to the detriment of personal freedom and creativity. Even deconstructive rhetoric, though representing discourse as a textual more than a materially social world, presents that world as a distribution of subject and object positions, power arrangements, hierarchies, I/thou binaries, and other figurations of sociopolitical interchange.

The distinguishing theme of the sociological story about the meaning of meaning is not its recognition of the importance of the social, which is common to all rhetorical perspectives, but rather its privileging of the social as the conceptual starting point for our understanding of discursive practice and the making of knowledge, the starting point for what

DOI: 10.7330/9780874219364.c006

sociological theorists like Peter Berger and Thomas Luckmann (1967) call "the construction of reality" in *The Social Construction of Reality: A Treatise in the Sociology of Knowledge*. This privileging is a dramatic, perhaps counterintuitive, reversal of the relationship between individual and society that typifies our four previous accounts of rhetoric, where the personalized human being constitutes the site of knowing and speaking, and where social interaction is presumed to be subsequent to individuated perception, conception, and verbalization. God gives speech first to Adam, and writing first to Moses; Plato's Philosopher-Ruler teaches and governs society by virtue of his developed capacity to apprehend metaphysical Truth; the Cartesian scientist constructs hypotheses and objectively tests them against experience before submitting the results to the scientific community for confirmation; Coleridge's poet manifests the power of imagination through the insight and authenticity of personal voice. In each of these perspectives, society is simply the assemblage of independently conscious individuals—perceivers who amass composite perceptions, thinkers who share their knowledge, speakers who join in conversation. The sociological account of meaningfulness, by contrast, valorizes interhuman, communal consciousness (collective knowledge or ideological awareness), which human beings produce through their engagement in shared practices of signification—making the world through signs. Society in this view is not an aggregate of independent identities; instead, it is the network of human interrelationships from which identity is derived. Society constitutes individuals, not the reverse, since the modes of signification by which persons individuate themselves, most significantly the practices of language, are a priori social practices defining the very possibility of individuation.

According to sociological rhetoric, human persons, material beings, form their subjectivities out of a dialectic between physical needs, which they project into the world, and preexisting social affiliations, including gender, ethnicity, class identification, family, religion, country, and other ideological values, along with the means of signifying those affiliations, which they internalize from the world. Social reality envelops individual consciousness, the sense of one's distinctiveness, because the self depends for its objectification on the articulating of its needs, and the modes of articulation, language preeminently, are social in nature and as such prior to the individual user. To be an individual, for example, one needs a self-reference, a name like *I* or *Wilhelmina*, and an autobiography relating one's place in the world. These words and narrative representations, together with the affiliations they describe, don't originate with the individual but are borrowed from the inheritance of language and social consciousness for purposes of self-composition. Any knowledge, whether the understanding of self and everyday life or the more specialized understanding available from scientific and other formal discourses, arises out of a dialectic between the perceiving, learning human person and the already constructed, shared objectivity preceding the learner—the broad social agreement, materialized in signs, that things are as they are. Knowledge becomes knowledge—as opposed to error, personal opinion, and idiosyncratic or hallucinatory experience—only upon social ratification, the collective understanding that something is true. Language, finally, or any signifying practice, incorporates and constrains individual speakers, equally defining the social and the personal. Language is, to be sure, spoken by individuals, yet it cannot be understood as speech unless a community recognizes its signs and shares its conventions. Signification is the architect of the human world, the means of its construction and the source of all its objectifications, including institutions, histories, knowledges, laws, rituals, legitimations, hegemonies, and public as well as private selves. As Berger and Luckmann (1967, 185) conclude, "The sociology of knowledge presupposes a sociology of language." Accordingly, the ground of meaningfulness in sociological rhetoric is what I will call intersubjectivity, the social consciousness that groups of people compose through verbal and other signs in the ceaseless production of human reality.

THOMAS KUHN

Berger and Luckmann (1967, 5–6) identify three intellectual antecedents of the sociology of knowledge, the most important of which is the work of Karl Marx, who offers the "root proposition" that "man's consciousness is determined by his social being." A second antecedent is the work of Friedrich Nietzsche, whose brash skepticism about rationalist notions of knowledge and truth provides intellectual background relevant to expressivist, sociological, and deconstructive rhetoric alike. And a third is the work of Wilhelm Dilthey, whose contributions to hermeneutics and historicism establish the theme of "the relativity of all perspectives on human events" and "the inevitable historicity of human thought" (7). While there is little doubt that Marxian and subsequent Marxist arguments are the most broadly recognized forms of the sociological narrative (and will occupy the larger part of this chapter), it's important to recognize that they do not exhaust the story line and that there are versions of the story that have little to do with the overarching economic and political themes that dominate Marxism. A good example of the hermeneutic and historicist rendering is Thomas Kuhn's (1922–1996) *The Structure of Scientific Revolutions,* an influential contribution to the philosophy and history of science that, while claiming no explicit debt to Dilthey, nonetheless pursues parallel emphases related to the sociohistorical evolution of scientific thought through the production of alternative "paradigms" or "world views." Kuhn's position, contrary to that of classical objectivism, is that science does not develop historically by "the accumulation of individual discoveries and inventions," as though progress were a single, unbroken arc of intellectual achievement comprised of universal assumptions about the facts and theories that are to be counted as "scientific" and timeless commitments to fixed methods of investigation (Kuhn 1970, 2). Scientific development is, instead, a history of constructions, disruptions, and reconstructions of the paradigms of "normal science," understood as "research firmly based upon one or more past scientific achievements . . . that some particular scientific community acknowledges for a time as supplying the foundation for its further practice" (10). Normal science is, according to Kuhn, socially composed, the intersubjective practice of a "community" sharing specific ideas about the "what" and "how" of investigation, the founding traditions and milestones of achievement, and the legitimacy of established belief. Furthermore, it is historically situated, not only specific to a time and place but also continually subject to stress as a result of conceptual antagonisms or research anomalies, inevitable within current scientific knowledge or practice, that force conditions of crisis upon the community. The consequence of significant stress is "paradigm shift," the emergence of a new set of intellectual and methodological assumptions fundamentally altering the social composition of "normal" scientific endeavor.

Fundamental to Kuhn's sociological view of science is a reciprocity or dialectic between what he calls a "paradigm," a particular model of scientific knowledge and practice (cell biology, Newtonian mechanics, superstring theory) and the scientific community whose collective labor has produced the paradigm. "The emergence of a paradigm," Kuhn explains, "affects the structure of the group that practices the field" by constituting, among other elements, its focuses of attention, forms of necessary expertise, instrumentation requirements, procedural rules—and its very understanding of the nature of nature. The community constructs the paradigm through its research and legitimizes it in the academic journals, textbooks, and research funding networks that define a scientific field's agendas, accomplishments, history, heroes, and traditions (Kuhn 1970, 18–19). Individual scientists have no status as scientists outside a context of social relations, including disciplinary identification, educational credentials, shared research assumptions, collaborative achievements, and peer validation, that establishes their orthodoxy—that is, paradigm allegiance—and hence the authority of their research. Independent scientists don't aggregate as scientific communities; rather, scientific communities establish the identity of the individual scientist. What identifies the community meanwhile is its collective agreement about the substance and form of its paradigm, a network of laws, theories, hypotheses, operating procedures, and modes of instrumentation, the appropriate understanding or manipulation of which is critical to the comprehensibility and acceptance of additional theoretical ideas or experimental results. Those independent ideas and results don't aggregate on their own as laws, theories, or other new knowledge; rather, existing normal science constitutes their validity as contributions to an already paradigmatic body of knowledge. "The study of paradigms," Kuhn says, "is what mainly prepares the student for membership in the particular scientific community with which he will later practice" (11). Once accepted to that community, the individual scientist takes the paradigm for granted: "He need no longer, in his major works, attempt to build his field anew, starting from first principles and justifying the use of each concept introduced" (19–20). Indeed, under the conditions of "normal science," the paradigm, "like an accepted judicial decision in the common law," becomes "an object for further articulation and specification under new or more stringent conditions" (23).

Paradigmatic scientific research, the substance of normal science, does not, according to Kuhn, seek to "produce major novelties, conceptual or phenomenal" (Kuhn 1970, 35). Instead, its emphasis is on what Kuhn calls "puzzle solving," the effort to resolve problems whose solutions are predictable according to the paradigm but whose complexity requires the overcoming of conceptual, mathematical, instrumental, and other challenges (36). Normal science is a "cumulative enterprise" (52), a steady pursuit of the details of a paradigm, where the scientific community progressively elaborates the paradigm even as the paradigm defines the identity of the community. But normal science, essentially a project of saying more and more about less and less through puzzle solving, is not what accounts for the really striking developments in scientific inquiry. The historical disruptions that lead to scientific "revolutions," which entail the dialectical reconstruction of paradigms and scientific communities alike, are not the result of merely intractable puzzles but the result of an inadvertent discovery of irreconcilable novelty or a newly foregrounded awareness of latent paradigmatic dissonance. "Discovery commences," Kuhn writes, "with the awareness of anomaly," a realization that nature "has somehow violated the paradigm-induced expectations that govern normal science" (52–53). One example is Renaissance astronomy's dissatisfaction with the imprecise match between the observed orbits of planets in the solar system and the orbital representations of Ptolemaic cosmology. Another is the nineteenth-century recognition that the speed of light remains constant regardless of the position or motion of an observer. Anomalies only stand out, only become anomalous, against the backdrop of a particular paradigm, but once they are recognized as novel, they begin to put pressure on the social edifice of scientific knowledge. New theories must emerge to resolve unexplained discord, and if none prove accommodating, the result can be "a period of pronounced professional insecurity . . . generated by the persistent failure of the puzzles of normal science to come out as they should." As crisis deepens, the "failure of existing rules" becomes "the prelude to a search for new ones," leading to scientific revolutions like the Copernican overthrow of Ptolemy or the modifications of Newtonian mechanics in relativity theory (67–68).

The scientific response to the crisis of anomaly is what most clearly demonstrates the social and contextual nature of scientific knowledge. A paradigm exists because a scientific community has reached consensus about the substance of its theory and practice, while a community exists because it has been constituted through the collective research effort to produce the paradigm. Kuhn (1970, 111–35) likens the community paradigm to a world view, not merely an organized collection of ideas and facts but a way of seeing things, a dispersion of values, a strategy of interpretation. As such, the world view is what makes orderly investigation of nature, the construction of ideas and facts, possible in the first place. "There is no such thing as research in the absence of any paradigm," Kuhn writes. "To reject one paradigm without simultaneously substituting another is to reject science itself" (79). Given that a theoretical or observational anomaly exists outside the pervasive social agreement represented by a prevailing paradigm, it's a challenge to the coherence of the world view, and the community initially resists its implicit threat to coherence either by ignoring it as inconsequential or by trying to incorporate it into the paradigm through puzzle solving. Only at the extreme does its persistence lead to paradigm shift. More important, its very status as an anomaly depends on the social consensus it violates. That is, in the absence of paradigmatic agreement, the anomaly could not be perceived as anomalous and may not be regarded as noteworthy given that scientific investigation routinely dismisses findings outside of its range of predictable results. The perception of anomaly is often the achievement of a struggle over years of dismissal to come to terms with the persistence of a novelty: "Initially, only the anticipated and usual are experienced even under circumstances where anomaly is later to be observed" (64). But if the anomaly focuses community attention, the only possible remaining response is paradigm reconstruction because the anomaly cannot be independently meaningful outside all world views. The very concept of scientific progress, then, is synonymous with paradigm replacement, understood as a struggle inside the scientific community, not to add the latest new discovery to universal knowledge but to reconstruct its internal, historical consensus about how to see the world: "The act of judgment that leads scientists to reject a previously accepted theory is always based upon more than a comparison of that theory with the world"; it is based ultimately on a comparison of competing paradigms "with nature *and* with each other" (77). The process of comparison and substitution is typically lengthy, and it can also be turbulent as supporters of the accepted paradigm struggle for authority with supporters of a proposed alternative, as textbooks vie with textbooks, as "normal" and "revolutionary" scientists compete for research funding. There are no one-person world views, and the solitary scientist, Copernicus or Newton, who overthrows a paradigm single-handedly, is a mythic construction of the romantic age. "Copernicanism made few converts for almost a century after Copernicus's death," Kuhn notes, and "Newton's work was not generally accepted, particularly on the continent, for more than half a century after the Principia appeared" (150–51). The construction of new knowledge in the discourse of science, as Kuhn portrays it, may occasionally be initiated by heroes, but it is achieved only by communities.

KENNETH BURKE

Early in *A Grammar of Motives*, Kenneth Burke (1897–1993) is at pains to insist that it's not the purpose of his "dramatistic" method "to abide strictly by any one system of philosophic terms." He is "more concerned to illustrate" the five conceptual points of the "pentad" than to "select one particular casuistry as our choice among them" (Burke 1969a, 67) Taking him at his word leaves me with no explicit authorization to identify him with the tradition of sociological rhetoric. The central premise operating across all of Burke's work, that human beings are symbol-making and symbol-using animals, could arguably situate him, on the contrary, in expressivist rhetoric, squarely in the tradition of Kant, Coleridge, Cassirer, and other neo-Kantians. Alternatively, his yearning—which is plain enough in the later chapters of *A Rhetoric of Motives*—for a transcendent human condition characterized by universal order and justice beyond the strife of war and the agonistic "scramble" of rhetoric ("insult and injury, bickering, squabbling, malice and the lie, cloaked malice and the subsidized lie" [Burke 1969b, 19]) can only be regarded as Platonic, while any hope he may actually have held out for the achievability of such transcendence might suggest the magical tradition, invoking Teresa of Avila's mystical union with the infinite as the "ultimate identification" (328–33). Then again, his more earthly (but not strictly materialist) concern for ideologies, hierarchies, and the struggles of opposing interests, not to mention his alarm at class bias and global capitalist profiteering, show the influence of Marx and Marxism. Burke is a polymath who takes the conceptual support he needs from whatever philosophical tradition may offer it. But Burke, too, has his motives, and the concept of "identification," which is at the heart of his rhetorical theory, encourages his intellectual location according to the "attitude" (another important Burkean idea), or perspective, of the history that seeks to include him. My reading of his story of the meaning of meaning leads me to "identify" him with sociological rhetoric because of his emphasis on the drama of human relations, the web of motives, and the social structures within which individuals forge (and are forged by) relationships through shared engagement in discursive practice. Burke's rhetor is not conceived as an autonomous, self-conscious wielder of language—Coleridge's supremely imaginative poet, or Rorty's heroic autobiographer in liberal solidary with, yet ironically detached from, other subjectivities. His rhetor is socially enveloped within the "scene" of language (symbolic action), and socially positioned by means of myriad identifications, differentiated interests, and hierarchical orders. The actions of his rhetor, an actor among actors in the drama of interpersonal relations, are influenced by an infinitely complex dispersion of motives, conscious and unconscious, discordant no less than harmonious, from sexual to supernatural—his own motives, those of others, and also those implicit (such as the pursuit of privilege or influence) in the social structure itself. Burke's theory, then, in his own "dramatistic" terms, privileges the "scene/agent ratio." Like the dancer and the dance in William Butler Yeats's (1928) *Among School Children*, the players aren't distinguishable from the play.

As a literary critic, Burke is less concerned with the production of texts than with rhetorical criticism, the close reading of literary as well as other documents in order to understand, through parsing the subtleties of their language, the complex of motives that drive interpersonal conduct (including the production of texts). Taking his lead from dramatic literature, the action of a play, he articulates the hermeneutic of "dramatism," a practice that "treats language and thought primarily as modes of action" (Burke 1969a, xxii). Dramatistic method features an interplay of five interdependent and overlapping terms, or points of reference, the variable arrangement of which enables the making of statements designed to identify and analyze motive—"what is involved, when we say what people are doing and why they are doing it" (xv). Referred to as the "pentad," these points of reference are "act," "scene," "agent," "agency," and "purpose," each term enabling the framing of a question: "what was done (act), when or where it was done (scene), who did it (agent), how he did it (agency), and why (purpose)" (xv). Burke offers an initially simple example of how the terms can be deployed to provide the basis for analyzing motive: "The hero (agent) with the help of a friend (co-agent) outwits the villain (counter-agent) by using a file (agency) that enables him to break his bonds (act) in order to escape (purpose) from the room where he has been confined (scene)" (xx). It is possible to locate motive by appeal to any of the five points of reference or any combination of points (which Burke calls a "ratio"—such as "scene/agent" or "scene/act"). Hence, one could look for motive in the agent, a love of freedom that moves the hero to escape; or in the scene because the room represents a condition of imprisonment; or the agency, where the hero's practical inventiveness and skill result in the use of the file; and so on (xx–xxi). The terms as such are "grammatical" in the sense that they comprise a structure—the pentad—out of which explanatory statements regarding motives can be made. They are the generative forms of a language of rhetorical critique. As such, they can produce analyses at variable levels of generality, from the concrete, narrative example of the hero breaking bonds to broader, more abstract statements about the rhetoric of a political philosophy or a cultural institution. Hence, "a legal constitution is an *act* or body of acts (or enactments), done by *agents* (such as rulers, magistrates, or other representative persons), and designed (*purpose*) to serve as a motivational ground (*scene*) of subsequent actions, it being thus an instrument (*agency*) for the shaping of human relations" (341). The language of critique can be adapted therefore across genres of discourse, from poems to product advertisements to political manifestos and texts of all sorts. It remains, of course, language about language, for the terms of the pentad are not "necessary 'forms of experience'"; they are rather "necessary 'forms of *talk about*' experience." Burke's concern "is primarily with the analysis of language rather than with the analysis of '*reality*'" (317) but with the understanding that modes of symbolic representation serve as the means by which the world of practical experience is formed and, through action, negotiated.

If the grammar produces its analytical statements across all forms of discourse, it can also produce them from various ideological perspectives depending on which terms in the pentad are assigned priority. While, theoretically, the terms interanimate, each intrinsically ambiguous, each inferring the others in an endless dialectic (Burke 1969a, 402), because dramatistic method is itself a symbolic practice, it is also in itself rhetorical and therefore subject to adaptation according to the assertion of some privilege among the terms. The assertion of privilege is an expression of "attitude" (443) or stance related to philosophical predisposition: "Dramatistically, the different philosophic schools are to be distinguished by the fact that each school features a different one of the five terms, in developing a vocabulary designed to allow this one term full expression" (127). Hence, where scene is the governing perspective, the philosophical school is materialism; where agent governs, the school is idealism; where agency governs, the school is pragmatism; where act is emphasized, the school is realism; and where purpose is primary, the school is mysticism. In practice, the complex arguments of particular philosophers are more readily identified by appeal to Burkean ratios. Marx, for example, is not a "vulgar" materialist but rather a dialectical materialist, where the dialectic is explicitly object/subject or matter and consciousness (200). Marxist philosophy begins by "grounding *agent* in *scene*," that is, subjectivity in materiality, and then proceeds to "the systematic featuring of *act*," namely class struggle in pursuit of an ethical imperative of social justice (210). If we were similarly to apply a Burkean ratio to Thomas Kuhn's arguments for the sociology of science, the dominant perspective would also be scene/agent, where the historically situated community of scientists or the paradigm of "normal science" constitutes the scene, the normal scientist and the revolutionary scientist constitute the agent and counteragent respectively, the agency is puzzle solving for the former and the tracking of paradigmatic dissonance for the latter, the act is experimentation, and the purpose is to add to the accumulation of scientific knowledge. Motives may, of course, be assigned and analyzed from any of the five perspectives (from agency, pride in research virtuosity; from purpose, a desire to contribute to the work of a scientific community; from agent, self-promotion), but given Kuhn's "attitude," or philosophical predisposition, the scene/agent ratio will dominate with particular emphasis on the desire to affirm membership in the community by acting to validate the paradigm or else standing heroically outside it by drawing attention to its anomalies.

Dramatistic method is evidently grounded in dialectic, the give and take of opposing views, a circumstance that, according to Burke, carries beyond the rhetoric of critique and into all domains of practical human relations, which are "at every turn affected by the nature of verbal dialectic" (Burke 1969a, 338). Dialectic underlies at once the (inter)actions of a play and the (inter)actions of the pentad, while both serve as representative anecdotes (partial illustrations) of actual social intercourse. This insight moves Burke from grammar to rhetoric, the application of the pentad to the investigation of motive in situations that are explicitly suasory. It also moves him, through the mediation of yet another representative anecdote, toward the investigation of human conflict—the condition that is most unhappily represented by the scourge of war. The epigraph on the title page of *A Grammar of Motives*, "*Ad bellum purificandum*"—literally, "toward the purification of war," arguably "toward the purification of those human impulses that lead to war"—reveals the extent to which Burke understands his project in the context of social responsibility and the pursuit of justice. "The world as we know it," he insists, "the world in history, cannot be described in its particularities by an idiom of peace. . . . The representative anecdote must contain militaristic ingredients" (337). Rhetoric then, to continue the chain of representations, is understood, perhaps at its worst, to be a form of ritual combat, the clash of irreconcilable positions, where division, not to say divisiveness, is emphasized and legitimized in the very structures of discursive formulation (thesis/antithesis, pro/con, attack/defense). But the aim of Burke's project is to reclaim rhetoric at its *best*, partly through a contrivance of redefinition, as a vehicle of symbolic action equally effective for asserting and maintaining bonds of interrelationship so that warfare might become "an admonitory anecdote" less for "stating what mankind *substantially is* as for emphatically pointing out what mankind is *in danger of becoming*"—so that "when there is much preparation being made *for* war, we might at least aim to prepare with equal zest *against* it" (330).

The concept to which Burke turns in *A Rhetoric of Motives* for reunderstanding the nature of rhetoric is identification. Traditionally, persuasion has served as the distinguishing motive of rhetorical discourse, a term that necessarily implies moving one person or group to the position of another across some ground of division—in deliberative oratory agreement or dissent, in forensic oratory innocence or guilt, in epideictic oratory praise or blame. Moreover, the divisions of views among speakers

and hearers are complicated by divisions in the social order itself, hierarchies of position and status—familial, political, religious, economic,
educational—resulting inevitably from the pursuit of advancement and
the attendant search for advantage. Burke does not argue that rhetoric
is not about persuasion, but he argues that persuasion can be situated
within a larger framework that accommodates, in true dialectical fashion, the opposites of division and "consubstantiality," where in any social
intercourse people "have common sensations, concepts, images, ideas,
attitudes," where "a way of life is an *acting-together*" (Burke 1969b, 21).
He argues that "the classical notion of clear persuasive intent is not an
accurate fit for describing the ways in which the members of a group
promote social cohesion by acting rhetorically upon themselves and one
another" (xiv). To the extent that "the basic function of rhetoric" is "the
use of words by human agents to form attitudes or to induce actions in
other human agents" (41), a better "fit" lies in the idea of identification,
where the critical move in a persuasive appeal is the representation of
shared social location (we're all Americans), shared history (I was once
a farm boy myself), shared values (we're all after justice), and therefore mutual interests. Identification is a necessary beginning "precisely
because there is division. Identification is compensatory to division. If
men were not apart from one another, there would be no need for the
rhetorician to proclaim their unity" (22). The achievement of successful
rhetorical appeal lies in the establishing of "a wider context of motives"
than those peculiar to individuals in specialized isolation, such as atomic
experts whose moral environment, as applied scientists, may be limited
to their technical proficiency but whose views of atomic bombs may be
liberalized by appeal to their identification as parents or citizens (30–
31). Rhetoric, by this change of emphasis, becomes a medium for socialization "considered as a moralizing process," where the individual person seeks "to form himself in accordance with the communicative norms
that match the cooperative ways of his society" (39). Putting it succinctly:
"Belonging . . . is rhetorical" (28). Indeed, Burke points to "the principle
of courtship" as "the use of suasive devices for the transcending of social
estrangement" (208).

Burke's elevating of identification as a strategy of social cohesion
explains why his theory, in his own terms, is plausibly viewed, as is
Kuhn's, from the perspective of the scene/agent ratio—the sociological
perspective. The rhetor (agent) performs, in the dramatic sense, within
the scene of human relations, which is virtually coterminous with the
scene of language or symbolic action, persuading audiences of their collective and mutual interests (act) by means of suasory appeals (agency)

in order to maintain the social fabric (purpose). "Audience" in this view takes on features that distinguish it from the classical concept, where it is taken as "something *given*," a stock character already and ontologically divided from the rhetor as a fixed set of differences. According to Burke, the "heterogeneity of modern life" together with the emergence of modern media make it more appropriate to consider the constructed nature of an audience, a group "carved out" of the social fabric, as market analysts contrive the groups that are most likely to desire commercial products. While such an understanding reminds us that rhetoric has a manipulative dimension—that identification is motivated and strategic, hence deserving of cautious inspection—it usefully opens up the double meaning of the term *identification* as a process of distinguishing, or naming, no less than a process of interrelating. An audience is identified, hence divided, from the social collective as the very means of articulating a new mutuality of interests. It's in the nature of communication, and in the nature of language itself (Burke 1969b, 43), to sustain just this duality, carving out the world grammatically and lexically in order to recompose it in new configurations, new sentences and paragraphs. In the same way, the rhetor and the audience, from the communicative (not the biological) point of view, are carved out of the rhetorical situation, suggesting the dialectic in the scene/agent ratio. "In its essence," Burke explains, communication involves the use of verbal symbols for purposes of appeal. Thus, it splits formally into the three elements of speaker, speech, and spoken-to." The separateness is a precondition for any appeal, "for if union is complete, what incentive can there be for appeal?" Rhetorically, he concludes, there can be courtship only insofar as there is division" (271). But the reverse is true as well: since there is always division, because it's intrinsic to language and communication, there is always rhetoric. "Wherever there is persuasion there is rhetoric," he says, "and wherever there is 'meaning,' there is 'persuasion' (172). By that logic there are no unrhetorical uses of language.

Burke draws two conclusions, one in the *Grammar*, the other—a progression from the first—in the *Rhetoric*, concerning the ultimate aims of his dramatistic inquiry. His purpose in the *Grammar*, he says, is "to express toward language an *attitude* embodied in a *method*." The attitude is one of "linguistic skepticism" about the communicative practices of the "Human Barnyard" with its "addiction to the Scramble." But it's a skepticism matched by "linguistic appreciation" of the scope of human verbal "resourcefulness." His project has been directed "'towards the purification of war,'" understood in its literal meaning as well as in its adapted reference to the verbal combat of the Barnyard, grounded in the hope that "the *Grammar* should assist to this end through encouraging tolerance by speculation." Looking toward the *Rhetoric*, he proposes to study the "competitive use of the cooperative" in order to find delight in the Barnyard by displaying the inventiveness of rhetorical artifice through the application of his method. He calls his stance "neo-Stoic resignation," likening it to "the attitude of a patient who makes peace with his symptoms by becoming interested in them." The moral imperative beneath the resignation is to use rhetorical criticism to help steer a course between "dissipation" and "fanaticism" in a "global situation" characterized by industrial expansion and vast political as well as commercial bureaucracies. "Linguistic skepticism, in being quizzical," that is, in its application as a mode of cultural critique, "supplies the surest ground for the discernment and appreciation of linguistic resources" (Burke 1969a, 441–43). While the *Grammar* concludes in resignation, the *Rhetoric* moves modestly and cautiously toward a hope of transcendence, which Burke suggests lies implicit in the concept of identification. "Since the individual is to some extent distinct from his group, an identifying of him with the group is by the same token a transcending of his distinctness." Identification, he goes on, "attains its ultimate expression in mysticism" (which is the philosophic school associated with "purpose" in the pentad), a losing of the self in commitment to some godlike power (Burke 1969b, 326). To be sure, an "ultimate identification" with human "fragments" of the mystical is as likely to entail the demonic as the divine: Burke lists the mysticism of war, of sex, of money, of drugs, among others. Mysticism is "no rare thing" among human beings who, through their actions, beliefs, and symbols, are eager to find their transcendence in "hierarchies" (structured gradations of achievement and status) both social and spiritual. Many find solace in "the thought of the great holocaust"—political and military officials, journalistic hacks— "their motives hierarchically amplified, and empowered, with the great new weapons" (331–32). But Burke closes with a last, hopeful challenge to "students of rhetoric": since, "for better or worse, the mystery of the hierarchic [the peculiarly human striving for perfection and status] is forever with us, let us. . . . scrutinize its range of enhancements, both with dismay and in delight." And at the same time, "let us observe, all about us, forever goading us. . . . the motive that attains its ultimate identification in the thought, not of the universal holocaust, but of the universal order," where "all classes of beings are hierarchically arranged in a ladder . . . of mounting worth, each kind striving toward the *perfection* of its kind, and so towards the kind next above it," the whole aspiring to God, "the end of all desire" (333).

MARX

Paradoxically, unlike Kuhn or Burke, the most broadly influential narrator of the story of sociological rhetoric, the economic and political
philosopher Karl Marx (1818–1883), has virtually nothing to say about
language, discourse, or the materialization of intersubjectivity through
signs. Perhaps his most suggestive statement about language occurs in
The German Ideology, written in collaboration with Friedrich Engels, when
he and Engels observe, tantalizingly, that "language is practical consciousness" (Marx and Engels 1978, 158), going on to define consciousness not as Mind, Spirit, or Self in the idealist terms of Kant or Hegel but
as human beings' collective awareness of the nature of their participation in the material world. "Thinking," for Marx, is not a disembodied
phenomenon but a form of physical labor, the production of a certain
kind of work amidst the network of social relations that any labor entails.
Language practice, the use of signs, understood as articulate consciousness, is the manifest work of thinking, important for the construction of
the material world in much the same way that using a shovel or cooking
with a wok is important. But Marx does not elaborate on his provocative observation about language, leaving it to be pursued later by various neo-Marxist literary critics and philosophers of language, among
them Mikhail Bakhtin, Valentin Volosinov, and Raymond Williams. What
he does address, however, albeit in the context of an economic rather
than linguistic or rhetorical narrative, is a set of preparatory themes on
which the story of sociological rhetoric will later depend. They include
the materiality of human beings and the human world (representing
Marx's rejection of idealist, private consciousness), the priority of the
social over the individual (representing his rejection of private property
along with privatized consciousness), and the historical constructedness
of everyday life (representing his rejection of essentialism and universalism). An extended discussion of these themes occurs in the *Economic
and Philosophic Manuscripts of 1844*, where Marx explores the material,
social, and historical dimensions of human life and consciousness by
particular reference to capitalist and communist economic practices.
He seeks there to define the human by appeal to the concept of material labor situated amidst the social relations that derive from and condition labor. He critiques capitalism (an emblem of individuality and
self-ishness) because it alienates workers from their work and from the
social relations that constitute their humanity. He praises communism
(an emblem of community and altruism) because it renounces private
property, represented as a dispersion of hoarded, fetishized objects produced by workers who have been estranged from their natural social

being in order to support an imperative of profit rather than communal need. And he identifies the process of historical change that has led to, and will lead away from, the socioeconomic condition of alienated labor. While his contrast of economic philosophies is not directly germane to a story about discourse, the conceptual touchstones that underlie it, his renderings of our now familiar themes of subject and object, self and society, metaphysical necessity versus historical contingency, anticipate the ways in which neo-Marxist rhetoricians will tell the sociological version of that story.

Naturalism, or historical materialism, is Marx's response to Hegel's idealist resolution of the subject/object binary. Marx regards the binary as a metaphysical opposition that has served historically to support the condition of human alienation by legitimizing European capitalism. The concept of disembodied, spiritualized mind alienates people from their reality as physical beings, estranging them from their participation in the material world, while the concept of unmediated objectivity alienates them from the products of their labor, the forged substance of their material lives. The human being is, first and foremost, an "active natural being," intimately part of the physical world, not a spirit separate from it, "real, corporeal *man*, man with his feet firmly on the solid ground, man exhaling and inhaling all the forces of nature" (Marx 1978b, 114). The human being is also, by nature, a producer, a worker, whose "productive life is the life of the species," a "life-engendering life." Like all animals, human beings must work in order to live, but the human species differentiates itself from other animals through the character of its work, which is not merely instinctual but is conscious and motivated: "Man makes his life-activity itself the object of his will and of his consciousness." While other animals produce "only under the dominion of immediate physical need," the human being "produces even when he is free from physical need and only truly produces in freedom therefrom." The human being "proves himself a conscious species-being" (i.e., demonstrates the biological distinctiveness of the human species) "in creating an *objective world* by his practical activity" (76). Although, as a worker, the human being "can create nothing without nature, without the sensuous external world" (72), and although a man depends upon the substance of material nature as it appears "in the form of food, heating, clothes, a dwelling," his work puts a human stamp on the rest of nature, "which makes all nature his *inorganic* body" (75), producing a humanly constructed world in which "nature appears as his work and his reality" (76). The end of his labor, in short, is *"the objectification of man's species life,"* the composing of his collective humanity in the process of composing a life-world responsive to his species needs. By imposing their will on the rest of nature through work, human beings' first and most important production is their humanity, nature "linked to itself, for [humans are] a part of nature," but linked self-consciously and collectively, both aware of their work and also aware of themselves as "universal and therefore . . . free being[s]" (75). The resolution of the subject/object binary, in other words, is to be found, according to Marx, not in Hegel's spiritualism but in the material productivity of the human being, by means of which "he contemplates himself in a world that he has created" (76). Human beings know their world in the same way that a shoemaker knows a shoe: as the intimate product of their own labor.

For Marx, "man's species life," or existence as a "universal" being, refers, not to our personal or singular reality, but to our collective reality, our condition as social beings. Other animals, in his view, live life individually in the sense that they feel hunger or pain or instinctual urges entirely as independent organisms. But human beings are conscious of themselves as a species and hence a collectivity so that, for them, human life and social life are effectively one and the same. "What is to be avoided above all," Marx writes, in his definition of communism, "is the re-establishing of 'Society' as an abstraction *vis-à-vis* the individual. The individual *is the social being*" (86). In his *Grundrisse: Foundations of the Critique of Political Economy*, Marx explains that "society does not consist of individuals, but expresses the sum of interrelations, the relations within which these individuals stand" (Marx 1978c, 247). The human being is "not merely a gregarious animal, but an animal which can individuate itself only in the midst of society. Production by an isolated individual outside society . . . is as much of an absurdity as is the development of language without individuals living *together* and talking to each other" (223). As human beings, then, we do not join together to form societies but instead derive our individuality from the social realities in which we already and necessarily participate. Our labor exists within a network of productive relations. Our cultural, religious, family, political, and other self-identifications are possible only by reference to those categories of social life. Even our most intimate thoughts are thinkable only because of the language inheritance that allows us to think them. "Not only is the material of my activity given to me as a social product (as is even the language in which the thinker is active): my *own* existence *is* social activity, and therefore that which I make of myself, I make of myself for society and with the consciousness of myself as a social being" (Marx 1978b, 86). The relationship between individual and society is, to be sure, dialectical: "Just as society itself produces man as man, so is society produced by him." But the individual exists—as *human*, not just physical, being—in and for other individuals, "his existence for the other and the other's existence for him," because the social is "the life element of the human world" (85).

For Marx, then, the human life-world, subjectivity as well as objectivity, is "material"—meaning concrete, sensuous, physical as opposed to abstract or spiritual, and also "social"—meaning intrinsically collective as opposed to personal or private. It has one more attribute as well: it is "historical"—meaning changeable, indeed in his view evolutionary, as opposed to fixed or eternal. The life-world is better understood as a process than as a condition, the continuous reconstruction of social reality as humanity applies its labor to the satisfaction of its needs. Human beings bring material, temporally situated modes and practices of production, to the making of all facets of the human world— ways to build houses, ways to grow cotton, ways to make shirts, ways to transport goods, ways to write books, ways to govern a population, ways to bring up children, ways to treat the sick, ways to wage war. Specific social relations (divisions of labor) surround these modes and practices and differ historically according to differences in the productive forces themselves. As Marx (1978a) explains in his preface to *A Contribution to the Critique of Political Economy*, people "enter into definite relations . . . of production which correspond to a definite stage of development of their material productive forces"—exemplified, for instance, by the class distinctions and labor relations that existed among landowners, overseers, paid workers, and slaves in the nineteenth-century American South as technological advances in the harvesting of cotton increased and centralized production capabilities while sparking demand for cheap labor. Productive forces and relations constitute, in their totality, "the economic structure of society," a foundation on which rises "a legal and political superstructure" along with "definite forms of social consciousness" (4). The modes of production (for instance, the cotton gin and the steam engine) and the productive relationships surrounding them (the plantation system) constitute the economic "base" of a given social reality, while a network of political, legal, religious, ethical, intellectual, artistic and other cultural forms constitute the ideological "superstructure" that legitimizes it, including laws validating the status of slaves as property, scientists "discovering" the subhuman characteristics of slaves, churches preaching against miscegenation, and literature portraying a genteel, harmonious, and paternalistic Southern culture. Human beings, however, are agents of their history, conscious of their relations to their environments and motivated, as their needs require, to change the conditions of their life-worlds. "As everything natural has to have its beginning," Marx writes, "man too has his act of coming-to-be—history—which, however, is for him a known history, and hence as an act of coming-to-be it is a conscious self-transcending act" (Marx 1978b, 116). Social change originates from circumstances of oppression, dissatisfaction, and conflict when "at a certain stage of their development, the material productive forces of society" clash with "the existing relations of production" so that "from forms of development of the productive forces these relations turn into their fetters," creating conditions of "social revolution" (Marx 1978a, 4–5). Hence, by the time of the civil war, critics of slavery, including many slaves themselves, dissatisfied with their experience of the life-conditions of the plantation economy, contest the exploitation as well as the dehumanization of African workers and agitate for socioeconomic change.

What is significant here is Marx's emphasis on "self-transcendence," his contention that human (meaning social) life and consciousness are ever under construction, ever historically situated and subject to change. Human progress unfolds historically as a dialectic between existence—how human beings actually live in the temporal moment—and essence—what they endlessly aspire to make of themselves. Change, however, lies in material work, not in abstract thought. As he says in the preface to the *Contribution to the Critique of Political Economy*, "The mode of production of material life conditions the general process of social, political, and intellectual life. It is not the consciousness of men that determines their existence, but their social existence that determines their consciousness" (Marx 1978a, 4). In the *Economic and Philosophic Manuscripts*, Marx exemplifies the idea of history viewed as "conscious self-transcending" by reference to the progression from capitalism, the dominant form of nineteenth-century European economic life, to communism, emphasizing the particular dissatisfactions in the capitalist configuration of human labor that motivate the resolve to "transcend." Briefly put, he tells a story about the inevitability of socioeconomic change as human beings experience the degeneration of their work from collectively producing their life-world to producing "property" for the benefit of others in exchange for wages. Under capitalism, human beings are alienated from their labor and from each other, their essential nature as producers at odds with the circumstances of their social and economic reality. The alienation derives from a malignant form of objectification, where workers are rendered as mere wage earners, hence dehumanized objects in the self-ish capitalist production system, and where goods are objectified as commodities, which are "fetishized" (i.e., worshipped as idols of personal consumption), vested with artificial "surplus" value in order to enhance their price and the capitalist's wealth. Communism represents, for Marx, an inevitable historical evolution, the next (but not necessarily the last) step in the emergence of social consciousness, a progression born of human discontent, where, through the "positive transcendence of private property," the worker is reunited with other workers in the truly "human, i.e., social mode of existence" while the products of collective work are revalued according to their importance for satisfying truly human, that is communal, needs (Marx 1978b, 85). But its inevitability consists, not in the power of intellectual appeals to reason or righteousness, but in the power of work. It will take "actual communist action to abolish actual private property," and the struggle will be "in actual fact a very severe and protracted process" (99). Marx's story, then, beyond the local theme of communism versus capitalism, is finally about the historical achievement of our humanity through collective work, a struggle for transcendence that identifies change rather than stasis as the natural human condition and that locates the processes of change not in abstract thought or in the rare actions of heroic individuals—the scientist, the poet—but in the material, collective labor of ordinary people.

VALENTIN VOLOSINOV

The narrative of sociological rhetoric builds upon these Marxian themes (the materiality of consciousness and the life-world, the priority of the social over the individual, and the historical constructedness of human life) as it explores the roles of language in constituting the human community. One influential version of the sociological story is that composed by Mikhail Bakhtin (1895–1975) and the members of the Bakhtin circle, in particular Valentin Volosinov's (1895–1936) account in *Marxism and the Philosophy of Language*, which stands as the primary contribution of the circle to linguistic and rhetorical thought. (I'll follow the conventional practice of invoking Volosinov's signature and leave open the extraneous question of Bakhtin's contribution to the text.) Volosinov's explicit purposes in turning to semiotic and discursive issues that Marx himself had barely suggested are to "bring out the position that the philosophy of language occupies in the Marxist worldview," and to concretize "the productive role and social nature of the utterance" (Volosinov 1973, xv). In the context of Marx's dialectical opposition of base, the economic production of a specific social reality, and superstructure, the ideological representation of that reality, Volosinov says conclusively that "the domain of ideology coincides with the domain of signs" (10), and that "without signs there is no ideology" (9). Hence, the "productive role" of ideological signs is to constitute the socioeconomic superstructure, the world of political, ethical, legal, religious, artistic, literary, and other ideas, values, and institutions that provide the cultural substance of a materially and historically specific social reality. Actual existence, embodied in modes of production and social relations (the base), gives rise, through the mediation of signs, to the ideological contents of the superstructure, which comprise social consciousness and which, in turn, enable the production of individual consciousness, or what Volosinov calls "inner speech," the subjectivizing of the objective content of verbal signs. The role of signs, in other words, is to construct consciousness itself, understood both objectively as a society's understanding of the nature of its involvement in the life-world that its own labor has constructed, and also subjectively as a person's experience of (no less ideologically constructed) individuality within that life-world. Consciousness can only arise, and "become a viable fact," according to Volosinov, "in the material embodiment of signs" (11). As for "individual consciousness," the formerly sovereign "subject" of idealist speculation, it is, for Volosinov, "not the architect of the ideological superstructure, but only a tenant lodging in the social edifice of ideological signs" (13).

Signs themselves, like the ideological consciousness that they produce, are (to reiterate the Marxian themes) material, social, and historical. Signs are "particular, material things," in the case of language the products of sounds and sound combinations, the phonic substance of speech, but also made up of other materials insofar as nonverbal signs may be derived from "nature, technology or consumption." What makes a natural or manufactured object into a sign is the fact that it "does not simply exist as a part of a reality" (a tree in nature or a tool of production) but also "reflects and refracts another reality," specifically, the substance of ideology. A hammer as tool is not a sign, he says, but the hammer and sickle emblem of the former Soviet Union constitutes a sign because it has ideological content: "Everything ideological possesses semiotic value" (Volosinov 1973, 10). A sign of whatever type or composition is "a phenomenon of the external world," featuring "some kind of material embodiment, whether in sound, physical mass, color, movements of the body, or the like." It is therefore "fully objective," not (as in idealism) merely "a coating" for conceptual content residing in the ethereal "mind." Volosinov's sign differs from Langer's symbol precisely in its depiction as a material rather than a psychic object, an occurrence in "outer experience," namely "the surrounding social milieu" rather than inner experience, the disembodied world of the self (11). Language, as the primary form of signification, is not, then, to be located anywhere except in the concrete practice of actual speech, what Volosinov calls the "stream of verbal communication" (81). He critiques two alternative understandings of verbal signification, one proceeding from what he calls "individualistic subjectivism," the neo-Kantian view of language activity as "an unceasing process of creation realized in individual speech acts" (48), and the other proceeding from "abstract objectivism," the structuralist (Saussurean) view of language as a "stable, immutable system of normatively identical linguistic forms which the individual consciousness finds ready-made" (57). Both views locate language practice in the rational Cartesian subject, the first emphasizing privatized utterance outside the social world, the second emphasizing theoretical "structures" that lie outside of material history and lived human experience. Volosinov's "stream of speech" metaphor rejects the sovereignty of the isolated statement as well as that of the grammatical form by representing language as the concretely physical domain of "dialogue," which is at once material rather than abstract, grounded in human interaction, and ever changing through time.

For Volosinov (1973, 94), "verbal interaction is the basic reality of language." Language is the lived social experience of signifying, "not the abstract system of linguistic forms, not the isolated monologic utterance, and not the psychophysiological act of its implementation." Signifying, as a conventional activity, can only occur in settings where people share communal awareness of the conventions. Every sign is "a construct between socially organized persons in the process of their interaction." The forms of signifying, which are historically as well as communally situated, "are conditioned above all by the social organization of the participants involved and also by the immediate conditions of their interaction" (21). One can readily comprehend (though not necessarily explain) language emerging historically as a product of shared human work, developing out of the imperative of social cooperation (rather like producing the two-handle saw). But one cannot so readily comprehend language emerging out of individual consciousness (Langer's accretion of ritual grunts and shouts), its meanings communally unavailable until subsequently negotiated, or still less language prefabricated as a rational edifice to be only subsequently filled in by actual speech. For Volosinov, what refutes "individualistic subjectivism" is the fact that language always preexists the specific user and is only meaningful because its meanings are already collectively shared. Any utterance, he writes, "is a borrowing on the speaker's part from the social stock of available signs." We create the illusion of personal ownership, including the sense of distinctive voice or style, by isolating our own speech from the social repository of formal, lexical, and stylistic usage, failing to hear our utterances as echoes of the speech practices existing everywhere around us. Meanwhile, what refutes "abstract objectivism" is the fact that language changes over time, not just its vocabulary but also its forms, however impervious to change it may appear at a given historical moment. The problem with a grammatical theory of language (proposing structural stability at a given moment in time) is that it cannot account for ceaseless and far-reaching alterations, such as the Great Vowel Shift in Indo-European languages or the evolved preference for weak over strong verbs in English. A synchronic system, Volosinov writes, "does not correspond to any real moment in the historical process of becoming"; hence, to the historian of language, "a synchronic system is not a real entity." Such a system exists, if at all, only "in the subjective consciousness of an individual speaker belonging to some particular language group at some particular moment of historical time" (66). Indeed, it exists chiefly in the retrospective distillations of scholarly analysis (transformational-generative linguistics, tagmemics, stratificational grammar, prescriptive grammar, among others), which create illusions of structural stability by abstracting grammar from the lived experience of speech. Given these social and historical facts, Volosinov's conclusion is that language "acquires life and historically evolves . . . in concrete verbal communication, and not in the abstract linguistic system of language forms, nor in the individual psyche of speakers" (95).

The verbal sign, for Volosinov, has one additional, and critical, feature beyond its material, social, and historical character, and that is its transitivity, its functional mediation between the social and the psychological worlds. "The ideological sign," he writes, "is made viable by its psychic implementation just as much as psychic implementation is made viable by its ideological impletion" (i.e., its filling up with ideological content). In other words, the sign cannot function as a sign, is not "made viable," unless and until it has meaning for the individual speaker: "There is no outer sign without an inner sign." It is through the transitivity of the sign that social and individual consciousness are dialectically related. Subjectivity is derived from the ideological substance of social consciousness, but the perceived reality and "truthfulness" of the linguistic and other significations that constitute the "outer" domain of ideology depend on the speaker's "inner" recognition of their value *as* significations. "The ideological sign must immerse itself in the element of inner, subjective signs; it must ring with subjective tones in order to remain a living sign" (Volosinov 1973, 39). Language presents itself to individual speakers as an intimate voice in their heads, or rather an intimate dialogue among voices—"inner speech." It feels personal and private, seemingly dwelling within, much as Coleridge or Langer had suggested, as the capacity for self-expression. Personal voice is, effectively, the essence of language in expressivist rhetoric. But in sociological rhetoric it is only the psychic manifestation of language, speech lodged, transitively, in the individual. Inner speech, then, *is* subjectivity, "the semiotic material of the psyche" (29), the self composed of the applied meanings of ideological signs. Those signs comprise a fundamentally social and historical reality, independent of individual speakers, but their capacity to signify, their continuing value, depends on the validation they receive as users exchange them in the give and take of actual speech. Signs emerge "only in the process of interaction between one individual consciousness and another." Speakers participating in the stream of speech create a "chain of ideological creativity and understanding," mutually reinforcing, and also historically modifying, both the form and the content of signs (11). They do not merely borrow ideological signs, then, from a language impervious to the idiosyncratic utterance, but instead they perpetually renovate those signs through individual use, a process that manifests itself as the historical changes so evident to diachronic (historical) linguistics.

The "chain of ideological creativity" is embodied in what Volosinov (1973, 118) calls "dialogue," characterized as "the real unit of language that is implemented in speech." Dialogue is a meeting of subjectivities, inner speech interacting with inner speech. "The context of this inner speech," he says, "is the locale in which another's utterance is received, comprehended, and evaluated." Since dialogue entails both speaking and understanding, ideological signs are at once produced, recognized, construed, confirmed, critiqued, and otherwise acted upon through tacit, "interior" moves on the part of individual participants. Meaning in dialogue cannot reside, therefore, in the words themselves, or in "the soul of the speaker," or in "the soul of the hearer." Meaning can only be "the effect of interaction between speaker and hearer," realizable as such "only in the process of active, responsive understanding" (102). Challenging questions arise, of course, concerning how one speaker receives the speech of another, what the "mode of existence of another's utterance" is in the "actual, inner-speech consciousness of the recipient," and how the utterance is "manipulated" in that other consciousness, as well as what "process of orientation" it necessitates for the recipient's subsequent speech (117). Volosinov responds by proposing

that dialogue entails pragmatic (rather than abstractly formulaic) codi-
fications, a discursive praxis distinct from the grammar of the utterance,
reflecting "not subjective, psychological vacillations, but stable social
interrelationships among speakers," and enabling mutual orientations
(118). Grammar participates in these orientations since the "individual
motives and intentions of a speaker" can only be realized "within limits
imposed by current grammatical possibilities." But dialogic praxis takes
speakers and hearers beyond the boundaries of the individual utterance
and into the interactions of authentic speech, where motives and intentions are pursued "within limits of the conditions of socioverbal intercourse," specifically some range of discursive and textual conventions.
The conditions and possibilities of dialogue, both grammatical and discursive, "are given quantities" that "circumscribe the speaker's linguistic
purview," and "it is beyond the speaker's individual power to force that
purview open" (143). At the same time, however, these grammatical
and discursive conventions, although imposing in the moment, remain
socially and historically situated. Discourse always simultaneously constrains speakers and also changes through their material speech.

RAYMOND WILLIAMS

While Volosinov works to integrate an explicitly sociological account
of language and discourse into the Marxist worldview, recognizing the
central role of signifying in the production of ideology and practical
consciousness, Raymond Williams (1921–1988), similarly alert to the
social importance of language, seeks to map the conceptual terrain on
which Marxist discourse theory might be applied to a general theory
of culture. He describes his critical vantage point as "cultural materialism," which he characterizes as "a theory of the specificities of material
cultural and literary production within historical materialism" (Williams
1985, 5). As a literary as well as a cultural critic, his focus is specifically
on how written discourse, including literature, participates in the construction of culture, and his approach, in *Marxism and Literature* and
Keywords, among other works, is to examine the meanings of particular
Marxian and/or neo-Marxist "keywords" that he regards as essential to
his inquiry. Williams's principal keyword, "culture," is understood as the
material, historically situated construction, and ever-changing record, of
meanings, ideas, values, and institutions that a society produces through
practices of signification. "Literature," another keyword, is understood
both in the narrow sense of culturally privileged texts and also in the
larger sense of "writing," a signifying process that encompasses the many

forms of memorialized language. In Williams's lexicon, both "culture" and "literature" lose their traditional associations with "civilization," "intellectual life," and "the arts," ideas inherited from the abstract, foundational, universalized thinking of the Enlightenment, which presumed the power of an evolved rationality to create "higher forms of social and natural order" (16–17). For Williams, citing Marx, culture is "man making his own history" (19), the production of the human in all its historical variety. Many animals are "social" in the limited sense that they cooperate, instinctively, in their self-preservation. The human being alone, Marx had insisted in the *Manuscripts of 1844*, "makes his life-activity . . . the object of his will and of his consciousness" (Marx 1978b, 76). Human beings, Williams (1985, 19) agrees, are social beings whose culture is the material product of their collective labor, "a constitutive social process, creating specific and different 'ways of life.'" Language, and more generally the production of signs, is the embodiment of that constitutive process, while writing, both a producer and a product of culture, is the inscription of practical consciousness in graphically objective forms.

Marxism and Literature identifies and explores three conceptual tiers of cultural and literary analysis, beginning with what Williams regards as the four major ideas of his critical project, "culture," "literature," "language," and "ideology," then proceeding to familiar notions in Marxist cultural theory, like "base/superstructure," "determination," "reflection," and "hegemony," and concluding with the praxis of writing, including "conventions," "genres," "forms," "authors," and "alignment." He offers historical interpretations of these and other keywords, showing the range of meanings for each in Marx's own work as well as that of his commentators and intellectual successors. The result is an examination of the potential for cultural analysis available from the Marxist critical vocabulary as it has evolved through philosophical debate over more than a century. Williams's choices and definitions of keywords, the privileging of language and culture over traditional emphases on "productive forces," determination, and the base/superstructure formula, are significant in their fundamental reorientation of classical Marxist thought, which had come to rely on the conceptual model of a determining base and a determined superstructure as the starting point for cultural analysis (Williams 1985, 75). As a political economist, Marx himself is preoccupied with the modes and relations of production by means of which human beings construct everyday life, and neither he nor Engels ever adequately theorizes the domain of thought, feeling, and ideology, which is effectively the world of culture. Classical Marxism, according to Williams, exaggerates and mechanizes the separation between base and superstructure, artificially distinguishing material "being," in the sense of action in the world, from "consciousness," or thinking about the world. Williams revalues the traditional Marxist understanding of base/superstructure by recognizing only its metaphorical, not its conceptual, significance and by insisting on the dialectical interaction of its terms. The trouble with the classical model is its spatialized evocation of a socioeconomic structure, which implies distinct, prioritized categories of social relations, including hierarchical connections between what is "basic," namely, human work, and what is understood to be a derivative overlay, namely, human thought. The classical Marxist formulation that "social being determines consciousness" (83) not only separates material production from consciousness but also fixes the relation of the two as reductively causal rather than dialectical. Given that formulation, the relationship between society and art, for example, can only be seen as deterministic: literature passively "reflects" or "mediates" social reality but has no active role to play in its reproduction (95–100). The heart of Williams's project is to invigorate the concept of culture by understanding in a dialectical way "the indissoluble connections between material production, political and cultural institutions and activity, and consciousness" (80). Cultural work and activity, in his view, do not comprise a superstructure erected over the social formation but are "among the basic processes of the formation itself" (111).

An important example of Williams's rewriting of traditional Marxist understandings is his treatment of the concept of ideology, which has accumulated an array of negative and positive significations through its uses both within and outside of Marxist social theory. Marx's belief that the conscious social narrative derives from, and is determined by, human beings' material positions in the life-world, the concrete modes and relations of production, leads to a necessarily skeptical reading of ideology as the self-interested story told by the ruling classes, those in control of production, in order to legitimize their power. The issue for the critic, then, is to read "through" the mystifications of this narrative to the objective socioeconomic realities it conceals, recognizing ideology as either "a system of beliefs characteristic of a certain class" or as "a system of illusory beliefs—false ideas or false consciousness—which can be contrasted with true or scientific knowledge" (Williams 1985, 66). Williams wants to resist both the doctrinaire objectivist prejudice of this view of ideology and also the restriction of the concept to illusory beliefs at cost to any richer analysis of the role of signification in generating all forms of social consciousness, including even revolutionary forms.

The restriction to false knowledge prevents "the more specific analysis of operative distinctions of 'true' and 'false' consciousness at the practical level, which is always that of social relationships, and of the part played in these relationships by 'conceptions,' 'thoughts,' ideas'" (68). In the end, while retaining a localized meaning of ideology as the formal thought of a particular class, Williams also provisionally commends Volosinov's broader reading of the term as "the general process of the production of meanings and ideas" (55), noting that "there is an obvious need for a general term to describe not only the products but the processes of all signification" if Marxist analysis is to offer a sufficient understanding of how signs constitute the many forms of practical consciousness (70–71). Williams's semantic evaluation of ideology, like that of his other keywords, is principally a search for those meanings that will enable a comprehensive, rather than reductive, examination of cultural life against the current of a traditional Marxism all too prone to doctrinaire scientific positivism.

Williams takes a similar tack in revisiting the classical Marxist idea of determination, a mechanistic understanding of which can lead to the view that "no cultural activity is allowed to be real and significant in itself, but is always reduced to a direct or indirect expression of some preceding and controlling economic content, or of a political content determined by an economic position or situation" (Williams 1985, 83). Williams's analysis intends to move beyond a reductive view of determination that stresses "the 'iron laws' of . . . . an objective external system of economy," which then places the social formation beyond the influence of human desire or will, to a more flexible understanding of the concept as both "the experience of 'objective limits'" and also "the exertion of pressures" against those limits, including "pressures exerted by new formations with their as yet unrealized intentions and demands" (86–87). Williams's dialectic of "limits and pressures" allows for the role of cultural processes (including art and literature) in the active production rather than passive "reflection" of social reality (95–100), ensuring that "society" is not understood in abstract structuralist terms as merely a "'dead husk' which limits social and individual fulfillment," but is recognized as a "constitutive process with very powerful pressures which are both expressed in political, economic, and cultural formations" and also internalized to "become 'individual wills'" (87). Clearly, Williams's general intention in expanding the concepts of ideology and determination is to insist that the production of cultural meanings and values is far from a rigidly constrained, uniform, or one-directional social process leading to or supporting monolithic ideological formations. Were that

the case, there could have been no *Uncle Tom's Cabin* to contest the rationales of the plantation system. Culture, he insists, is better understood
as a dynamic process than as an achieved reality, and as a heterogeneous
rather than homogeneous work in progress. Culture is both limits and
pressures, "dominant" formations that exert a normative influence on
social life, "residual" formations that preserve the influence of earlier
institutions and practices, and "emergent" formations that challenge
the dominant culture (121–27). It is not sufficient, therefore, to define
ideology as "the general process of the production of meanings and
ideas" without adding ideas of difference and contestation, denoting
the stresses that arise as practices of signifying, and the results of those
practices, vie for authority in the construction of culture at any historical
moment. Ideology is better understood as a plural than a singular term.

    The keyword to which Williams turns in order to explore the con-
testatory aspect of cultural production is "hegemony," an idea he bor-
rows from the work of Antonio Gramsci (1971) which discriminates
the collective creation of social reality by appeal to historically specific
"distributions of power and influence" among groups or classes competing for the protection of their interests. Relations of domination and
subordination are natural features of all social organization, and in a
class-based society they take the form of class hierarchy and struggle.
The dominant class produces dominant ideology, "a relatively formal
and articulated system of meanings, values, and beliefs, of a kind that
can be abstracted as a 'worldview' or a 'class outlook.'" According to
Williams, Gramsci distinguishes usefully between ideology and practical
consciousness, regarding the first as the "articulate upper level" of the
second, part of consciousness but not coterminous with it. The idea of
hegemony explains how dominant ideology, which always includes the
legitimizing of its domination, is internalized in social consciousness as
a "saturation of the whole process of living, . . . the whole substance of
lived identities and relationships," to such an extent that "the pressures
and limits of . . . a specific economic, political, and cultural system seem
to most of us the pressures and limits of simple experience." In short,
hegemony explains how ideology becomes "common sense," no longer articulate but pervasive in social consciousness. Once established
as common sense, dominant ideology sustains itself through the willing
self-identification of individuals with its beliefs and need not be crudely
enforced through manipulation, indoctrination, or other forms of overt
control. It has become "the sense of reality for most people in the society," manifested as traditions, institutions, and other cultural formations, a reality that incorporates and rationalizes "the lived dominance

and subordination of particular classes" (Williams 1985, 109–10). At the same time, however, hegemony is never singular, total, or exclusive. On the contrary, not only must it be continually "renewed, recreated, defended, and modified," but it is also "continually resisted, limited, altered, [and] challenged by pressures not at all its own." Inevitably, "forms of alternative or directly oppositional politics and culture exist as significant elements in the society" (112–13). To challenge hegemonic social relations is necessarily to challenge the dominant ideology, first by revealing it as an ideology, not "common sense" but the "articulate upper level" of consciousness, an array of ideas and beliefs serving the interests of the dominant class. Once rendered visible and articulate, it may be contested by means of similarly articulate alternatives. Culture, then, is not a smooth, comprehensive structure or system, irresistibly "adaptive, extensive, and incorporative." It is instead an endless competition of meanings and values, replete with "authentic breaks within and beyond it," which includes not merely ostracized outsiders but "pre-revolutionary breakdowns and actual revolutionary activity" (124).

At the center of this cauldron of cultural activity and process is language, together with other forms of signification. Williams's account of language closely follows that of Volosinov, similarly critiquing the view of European rationalism that language is merely "an instrument or medium taken up by individuals when they had something to communicate" (Williams 1985, 32), similarly agreeing with Marx that language, on the contrary, constitutes the material substance of practical consciousness, "an indissoluble element of human self-creation" (29). Verbal and other signs are "living evidence of a continuing social process, into which individuals are born and within which they are shaped, but to which they then also actively contribute," achieving "at once their socialization and their individuation" (37). Language is "the active creation of meanings," not a "simple 'reflection' or 'expression' of 'material reality,'" but the articulation of this active and changing experience; a dynamic and articulated social presence in the world" (37–38). It is a mode of production, not a mere "superstructural by-product of collective labour" (44). As the embodiment of ideology and practical consciousness, it is also, of course, fully implicated in the differential and contestatory material practice of forming the life-world, including the production of hegemonic relations. Volosinov had noted that "each period and each social group has had and has its own repertoire of speech forms for ideological communication" and that these forms "are conditioned above all by the social organization of the participants involved and also by the immediate conditions of their interaction"

(Volosinov 1973, 20–21). Those forms include dialect variations, distributed as standard and nonstandard, specialized vocabularies, the regulations of public grammar, and specific styles and usages approved as educated or polite speech. He alludes to the contestatory nature of signifying practices—to culture, that is, as a clash of opposing rather than complementary interests—when he acknowledges that signs constitute "an arena of the class struggle" and observes that "the ruling class strives to impart a supraclass, eternal character to the ideological sign, to extinguish or drive inward the struggle between social value judgments which occurs in it, to make the sign uniaccentual" (23). Williams follows Volosinov, taking up these and other issues of language and class struggle, not through analysis of speech, however, but with respect to writing and literature since they represent, respectively, the mode and object of production that Williams is most intent to explore in developing his general theory of culture.

Predictably, Williams's sociological account of written discourse, especially the privileged category of literature, pointedly challenges expressivist concepts of authorship and creativity that valorize the seemingly personal and private nature of writing as well as the individualized genius of the imaginative writer. He approaches these concerns directly through analysis of the keywords "author" and "creative practice." Williams's writer, no less than Volosinov's speaker, is socially constructed from the start, not the producer but a product of the conventions, genres, and forms of written language. As a "social individual," the writer is, of course, specific, "but within the social forms of his time and place," most notably the historical moment of the written language (Williams 1985, 193). Writing is "trans-individual" (195–96), an act saturated in discursive relations and therefore always public, not private. Engaging in the practices of writing is what constitutes the writer as a writer, whose development, activity, and finished products "can be grasped as a complex of active relations, within which the emergence of an individual project, and the real history of other contemporary projects and of the developing forms and structures, are continuously and substantially interactive" (196). Actual writers, however physically secluded, are always surrounded by voices, the voices they hear in their heads from the recollected speaking and writing of others that form their consciousness. Their "own" voices are not the origin of their writing but something crafted in its sentences, available as voices only in and through the verbal and discursive forms with which they work. The writer, including the literary artist, exhibits "creativity," not in "the ideological sense of 'new vision,'" but in "the material social sense of a specific practice of self-making" or "self-composition" (210). Working within the social relations of written discourse, themselves woven into the fabric of consciousness and ideological hegemony, writers individuate themselves by an act of will, compose voices, reproduce or critique everyday life, make fictions intended to show "that people are 'like this' and their relations 'like this,'" and in the rarest and best instances, those of "literary" art, engage in an "active struggle for new consciousness." Literary creativity is always the expression of practical consciousness, but it can become "the long and difficult remaking of an inherited (determined) practical consciousness," not "casting off an ideology" but "confronting a hegemony in the fibres of the self," a struggle that takes place "at the roots of the mind." It can entail "the reproduction and illustration of hitherto excluded and subordinated models," or "the embodiment and performance of known but excluded experiences and relationships," or even "the articulation and formation of latent, momentary, and newly possible consciousness" (212).

In other words, writing actively constitutes and reconstitutes culture by embodying social relations, including emergent, counterhegemonic relations, in objective graphemic forms, which are themselves the products of those relations. Immersed in the historically specific social realities that produce not only genres, conventions, and forms, but also constraints regarding appropriate subject matter, presentation of material, and modes of composition, the writer's process of self-creation as writer entails acts of what Williams calls "alignment and commitment" with respect to the ideological and hegemonic conditions that determine the writer's practice. Alignment refers to the fact that writing always "expresses, explicitly or implicitly, specifically selected experience from a specific point of view" (Williams 1985, 199), while "commitment" refers to the "conscious, active, and open" choice of an alignment, whether cooperative or contestatory (200). Williams is plainly invoking here the dialectic of "limits and pressures" he had explored earlier in his reading of the keyword determination. Writers and writing are indeed determined by social, including discursive, limits "within which the scope of commitment as individual action and gesture must be defined" (204). But just as speakers, according to Volosinov, modify the stream of speech through material acts of speaking, in the process altering the substance of practical consciousness, so, for Williams, the deliberate practices of writers may exert pressures against both discursive limits and (other) hegemonic realities. "Social relations are not only received; they are also made and can be transformed" (204). Williams offers a sociological account of discourse, then, that depends on a creative tension between the intersubjective constraints of writing and the individuated conscious alignment of writers. More generally, he offers a dynamic theory of culture centered on writing as a form of labor through which human beings produce, and reproduce, their world. Not content to leave cultural production to the classical Marxist domain of the superstructure, he finds a place for writing and rhetoric, and literature as well, in the world of work, that is, among the basic activities to which Marx points in elaborating his concept of human self-transcendence through the ceaseless production of ordinary life. "To write in different ways," Williams says, "is to live in different ways" (205).

7
DECONSTRUCTIVE RHETORIC

In the world of deconstructive rhetoric, a text is not a mirror held up to nature, as it was in the ontological tradition; it's a mirror held up to other mirrors. Discourse is a house of such mirrors, texts facing other texts, words reflecting and refracting other words. Terry Eagleton illustrates the nature of language from the vantage point of deconstructive rhetoric by pointing to the peculiar character of the dictionary as a closed, self-referential network of endlessly interrelating signifiers and signifieds (Eagleton 1983, 128). When we want to know the definition of a word, we don't rummage around in "the world" for a suitable experiential reference. Instead, we turn to the dictionary, where, upon looking up the word, we encounter nothing but other words. When we seek information about these words, we find still more words, some of them looping back to the first word, others extending the network of signification outward to additional possibilities of meaning—synonyms, antonyms, homonyms, homophones, analogues, archaisms, synecdoches, metonymies, metaphors, etymological predecessors, alternate forms, variable usages, a glittering array of signs each, always, directing us somewhere else, never stopping at itself as the sign behind all signs, the transcendental sign. The network only continues to expand as we pursue the meanings of sentences, paragraphs, essays, books, collections of books, alternative discourses (literature, science, law), and multiple languages. The process of signifying has no starting point, no termination, no textual boundaries, and most important, no exit from the network of significations that sprawls from any and every point. There is always and only more language, endlessly commenting on itself, explaining itself only to itself. In a memorable postmodern short story, John Barth (1969) likens this endless reflexivity to being "lost in the funhouse." The story's teenage protagonist, Ambrose, wanders amidst the mirrors of an amusement park funhouse, which is located in a larger funhouse called Ocean City, Maryland, which is located in the funhouse of World War II America, each place a hall of mirrors, reflecting and refracting its own

DOI: 10.7330/9780874219364.c007

misshapen images, each contributing to Ambrose's fractured impressions of yet another funhouse—himself. Of course there is no Ambrose really, for he and his mirrors, his places, are all effects of language, fictions in the encompassing story of "Lost in the Funhouse," which, as its own narrator laments, refuses to follow the form of a "conventional dramatic narrative," with a predictable rising/falling plot line, and so creates, enfolds, and loses Ambrose along the path of a disjointed action in search of its denouement.

The principal theme of the deconstructive story about the meaning of meaning, its ground of meaningfulness, is the intertextuality of discourse. To understand the concept, consider the intertextuality of the current chapter, where I intend, momentarily, to undertake the composing of a text, in English, that is based on the reading of another text, first written in French, named (by its English translator) *Of Grammatology*, on which the signature, Jacques Derrida, is inscribed. "Derrida's" text has itself composed readings of still others, all translated (hence rewritten) from French to English by writers other than those already mentioned, and these texts are named *Essay on the Origin of Languages*, *General Course in Linguistics*, and *Tristes Tropiques*, on which the signatures Rousseau, Saussure, and Lévi-Strauss are inscribed respectively. "I" am about to write, then, "my" reading of a written reading of several other written readings, composed by multiple writers in two languages. Furthermore, "my" reading of "Derrida" is filtered through, or influenced by, "my" readings of many other texts besides, some of which have also read Derrida in pursuing their motives, needs, or desires, and all of which "I" have read, perversely as it were, in a way that satisfies me in pursuing mine. Derrida has filtered his readings in the same perversely motivated ways, while Rousseau, Saussure, and Lévi-Strauss have done so also. Meanwhile, I speak conventionally of "I," but my "I" is of no more determinate significance than the other "I"s in this verbal funhouse, merely a pronominal reference to the signature on the cover of the current text. That text conventionally "belongs" to me, as the copyright page insists without a trace of irony, but it "really" belongs only to the English language (as do "I"), since, plainly, the language I employ for its writing is not my own creation, and my reading is borrowed from other readings. The "I" that names this borrower merely marks a subject position, "the writer," in the text. "You," another pronoun marking another subject position, read the writing of my reading of "Derrida" in ways that are conditioned by "your" history of readings and by the motives that "you" bring to this text. That reading is yours to compose, not mine to compel. But "you," the reader, have just as indeterminate a status as "I" have, since the rhetorical choices that have positioned me in textual history have also positioned you. Your reader's privilege does not constitute "control" of the text but only the substitution of your reading history for mine. We all reside, like Ambrose, in the intertextual hall of mirrors— Derrida, Saussure, Rousseau, Lévi-Strauss, "you," the reader, and "I," the writer. There is no outside, no extraverbal, transcendent source for our images. "We" are all endlessly constructed as images by the textual mirrors themselves.

SAUSSURE AND DERRIDA

In a series of interviews published together in a text called *Positions,* Jacques Derrida (1930–2004) identifies the intellectual provocations that have led to poststructuralism (and the emergence of what he and others sometimes call deconstruction) in the structural linguistics of Ferdinand de Saussure (1857–1913), specifically his *Course in General Linguistics.* Ironically, Saussure's (1959) *Course* is well suited to the funhouse of deconstruction because it was in fact not written by Saussure but only compiled by editors working from the unpublished lecture notes of his students, a text at two removes from the signature on its title page. In the *Course,* "Saussure" explores the general principles of semiology, offering an account of the features of verbal signs in particular, the structural characteristics of language, and the synchronic and diachronic perspectives from which language may be studied. Saussure proposes structuralism as an objective science of linguistic description in which local verbal phenomena are incorporated under general rules or laws: phonology, morphology, and syntax, the rules of the language game. These structural rules represent the underpinnings of actual speech and specify the coherent cultural reality of language, much the way that the rules of chess define the game and organize its play. Chess is a world of its own; it does not derive from or comment on other worlds. The pieces on the chess board have no meaning outside the game, and—more important—their meaning inside the game is entirely a function of their differential values within the structure of play. That is, a rook is not identified by the material from which it's made, or by some particular shape or color, or by anything peculiar to itself. Its value as a piece is understood entirely by reference to its functional difference from a bishop, just as the bishop is understood only by reference to the knight, and so on. The game is a coherent system of interrelated positions and moves, values that regulate the details of play. Saussure's method typically entails the construction and contrastive analysis of binary oppositions—signifier/signified, speech/writing, langue/parole, syntagmatic/associative, synchronic/diachronic, static/evolutionary— so that the result of analysis is an elaborated structure of opposed formal entities, well illustrated by the branching tree diagrams of Noam Chomsky's transformational-generative grammar. Structuralism after Saussure becomes an intellectual vantage point that dominates twentieth-century inquiry, not just in linguistics but across the humanities and social sciences as these disciplines seek to identify the underpinnings of cultural phenomena of all sorts, from kinship systems to literary narratives to forms of dress.

Saussure's principal concepts are well known and can be readily summarized in anticipation of explaining the *post* in poststructuralism as well as the Derridean neologism that is *deconstruction*. "Langue" refers to the system of signs and grammatical structures that constitutes the primary object of linguistic inquiry, while "parole" refers to the individual speech act (a secondary object of linguistic inquiry) and "langage" refers to the social and historical materiality of speech (Saussure 1959, 9–13). Writing is derivative from speech, the signifier of a signifier. "Linguistics," the study of langue as the system of verbal signs, can be either synchronic, where language is studied as it exists in a single historical moment, or diachronic, where it is studied as it changes over time (79–100). "Semiology," which includes linguistics, is the general science that studies the life of signs within society (16). The verbal sign is a unit of language (langue) comprised of an arbitrary, dialectical relationship between what Saussure calls a "signifier" (a sound image) and a "signified" (an idea), two terms that may be conceptually distinguished but that are in fact simply two perspectives on the same entity, like the two sides of a sheet of paper (113). The sign is arbitrary in the sense that its signifier has no natural or necessary relationship with its signified (69), making language a game, therefore, that plays by its own conventional rules. Verbal signs are complexly linked through both semantic and structural (including phonological, morphological, and syntactic) relations. The first linkage is evident in the "associative" relations of the dictionary, where any word is defined by, compared to, and contrasted with other words, while the second linkage is evident in the "syntagmatic" relations of temporally successive units in an English sentence: article+adjective+noun, or subject+verb (122–27). All linguistic signs are distinguished by their "value," that is, their structural and semantic differences from other signs (111–22). As Saussure explains, "Just as the game of chess is entirely in the combination of the different chess pieces, language is characterized as a system based entirely on the opposition of its concrete units" (107). Hence, we know the meaning of *bat* by virtue of knowing that it is structurally different from *mat* and *hat* as well as semantically different from *squirrel* and *pigeon*. Arguably, the most provocative observation in Saussure's linguistic theory relates to this differential value of the sign: "Everything that has been said up to this point boils down to this: in language there are only differences" (120).

In a conversation with Julia Kristeva in *Positions*, Derrida identifies points of departure in his writing that lie implicit in the structuralist concepts of Saussurean linguistics, beginning with the rich ambiguities in Saussure's account of the sign. In two respects, Saussure "powerfully contributed to turning against the metaphysical tradition the concept of the sign that he borrowed from it": first by proposing an inseparable relationship between signifier and signified, and second by emphasizing "the differential and formal characteristics of semiological functioning" (Derrida 1981, 18). By installing the signified inside the sign, he identifies reference as a feature within language, not a connection between language and something beyond it, some realm of pure thought free of the play of signification. The system of signs articulates a world peculiar to itself, like the chess game, and does not derive from or correspond to a world outside the language game. Moreover, by insisting on the formal dimension of language, he detaches the sign, as a pure value, from any material manifestation, specifically its historical connection to speech, showing that the sign "is no longer in a privileged or exclusive way phonic." The concept of langue, the set of rules, the structural underpinning, frees our understanding of language from misleading associations with the human voice, regarded historically as the site of consciousness, or as consciousness itself, the place where thought is immediately and familiarly present. Recall Plato's confidence in spoken discourse (which Derrida calls "phonocentrism") and his anxiety about the muteness of writing, its inability to explain itself. Finally, Saussure's depiction of language as a system of pure differences eliminates the self-identity of the sign, its independence from other signs as a fixed location of meaning. Instead, each sign within the system, like the pieces of the chess game, is comprehensible only in its differential relationships, creating the unstable effect of the dictionary, where meaning is always elsewhere in the system rather than present in the discrete sign. Intertextuality, the endless dependency of meaning upon other meaning across all boundaries of signification, from the word to the book, the phoneme to the discourse, begins from Saussure's assertion about language as a system of differences.

The problem with Saussure, however, as Derrida goes on to explain, is that he fails to appreciate the implications of his account. First, his maintenance of a rigorous distinction between signifier and signified, and his association of the signified with a mental correlative, "leaves open the possibility of . . . a concept simply present for thought, independent of a relationship to language," which Derrida (1981, 19–20) calls the "transcendental signified." Belief in the transcendental signified as a meaning that lives beyond the games of language is "logocentrism," a Derridean term that recalls the earlier discussion of ontological rhetoric with its belief in determinate relationships among rationality, language, and truth. Second, although Saussure eliminates the necessity to privilege speech in the study of langue, he nonetheless capitulates to tradition in continuing an emphasis on speech consistent with the objectivist, empirical aspirations of structural linguistics. Hence, he speaks of the signifier as a "sound-image," contradicting his own view that what is essential to language is not "langage," material speech, but the system of signs (21). Third, by retaining the prejudice in favor of speech, he allows the continuing identification of voice, consciousness, and the intimate "presence" of ideas before the mind, reinforcing rather than repudiating Plato's phonocentrism (21–22). Fourth, by allowing consciousness and the possibility of the transcendental signified to remain in his account, he falls back on the psychologism (22–24) discussed earlier in expressivist rhetoric. Derrida adds that the very idea of structure, the dominant term in the argument for structuralism, "can simultaneously confirm and shake logocentric and ethnocentric assuredness," depending on how it is understood and used (24). Saussure introduces, but then evades, a fundamental question concerning the structural propensities of language, namely the nature of the coherences that language produces through its construction of texts (including the texts of linguistic science), the nature of the truth-claims implicit in the grammatical and logical orderings within and among texts.

Poststructuralism refers to the critiques that Derrida, Michel Foucault, Julia Kristeva, and others bring to bear regarding the supposed rationality of discursive representation, a rationality that is both argued in structural analyses of culture and implied in the structural integrity of texts. It is not an organized body of ideas and methods in the way structuralism has been, and none of the critics who have been called poststructuralists have been willing to accept the label. Given their skepticism about the funhouse of language, this reluctance is hardly surprising: poststructural writing features an extreme terminological self-consciousness, where the words chosen to mark its insights are frequently bracketed, placed under erasure, or otherwise highlighted to insist on their tentativeness and insufficiency—the absence of their seeming presence. Typically, poststructural critiques emphasize the instability, indeed the fictiveness, of textual arrangements of all sorts, their contrived structures of belief, value, oppositional argument, judgment, and conclusion. If language is a system of pure differences, and meaning is always elsewhere, forever deferred to the next value in the system, then both the individual sign and the system of signs constituting text are impossible to characterize as fixed identities. Those critiques pay particular attention, however, to texts that seek to insist on the special authority of their achieved coherences, master narratives that claim to have named the transcendental signified, totalizing and reductive discourses that claim to have encompassed all possible significance and resolved all complexity. Such texts imagine that they reside outside the funhouse, that their references lie beyond language, that their coherence, completeness, and certitude are achievements of rational thought rather than rhetorical illusions enabled by the structuring characteristics of language. Poststructural critiques are politically engaged, revealing the instability of texts despite their designs to appear otherwise, reading their tactics for concealing the contingencies of their own production, the artistry of their storytelling, as power moves. They take special exception to the reductive, and worse the hierarchical, arrangements implicit in such classical European binaries as man/woman, sacred/profane, nature/culture, and white/black, understanding the power of these starkly simple (albeit fictive and unstable) oppositions to structure a world of privilege, discrimination, and disenfranchisement. Derrida's *deconstruction* is one word, though not the only word, with which to name the inherent instabilities of all rhetorical construction, while also naming those politically self-conscious reading practices that reveal the structural illusions enabling texts to announce themselves as Texts. Deconstruction, Derrida writes in a letter to Jean-Louis Houdebine, "is not *neutral*. It *intervenes*" (Derrida 1981, 93).

OF GRAMMATOLOGY

The particular binary that preoccupies Derrida in *Of Grammatology* is the ancient European priority of speech over writing, a priority fraught with epistemological, cultural, and political implications for the West. His deconstruction of speech/writing anticipates his proposal of a history of writing not as that concept has been conventionally understood from Plato to Saussure—a derivative, graphic representation of speech—but as a more general concept provisionally called "arche-writing" (*arche* is the Greek root for "beginning") that encompasses all manifestations of the linguistic sign. Grammatology is the analytic, historical study of arche-writing and deconstruction is its method. In her preface to *Of Grammatology*, Gayatri Spivak describes deconstruction as the revealing and opening up of a binary, in this instance speech/writing, through hermeneutic practices of reversal and displacement (Spivak 1974, lxxvi-lxxvii). Reversal subverts the hierarchical arrangement of the terms: hence, the customary priority of speech in Western rhetorical theory, including the attendant secondariness of writing as mere signifier of a signifier, is critically destabilized in order to challenge the misleading and oppressive logic that sustains it. But the reversal is also displaced, denying the metaphysical claim of binariness itself as the meanings of the two opposing terms are shown to leak into each other, each a "supplement" filling the insufficiencies of the other. Derrida does not valorize writing simply as a flamboyant rhetorical trick, turning Plato on his head in order to drag additional meanings from the ancient polarity. He is not arguing the supremacy of writing but rather exploring the nature of verbal signification in general through the concept of arche-writing— the linguistic sign understood as a structure of "differance," where the play of the trace, the written mark, entails always the evoking of what is not present, yet also, because of the existence of the mark, not absent, a dispersion of supplements through which "a necessity is announced: that of an infinite chain [the dictionary paradox], ineluctably multiplying the supplementary mediations that produce the sense of the very thing they defer: the mirage of the thing itself, of immediate presence, of originary perception" (Derrida 1974, 157).

Divided into two essays, the first part, "Writing Before the Letter," sketches the theoretical matrix of (provisional) concepts—presence, trace, differance, arche-writing—that constitute grammatology as a "positive science." It interrogates the privileging of speech in order to open up the complicity of speech *and* phonetic writing, historically intertwined, in maintaining the "metaphysics of presence" (the view of meaning as transcendental signified). The second part, "Nature, Culture, Writing," is an illustrative grammatological inquiry critiquing the texts of two reluctant representatives of the logocentric tradition, the structural anthropologist Claude Lévi-Strauss and the philosopher Jean-Jacques Rousseau, who join Saussure as foils for Derrida's deconstruction of the speech/writing binary and his elaboration of arche-writing. Lévi-Strauss is critiqued for his "liberal" reverse-ethnocentric assumption of the existence of "natural" or "innocent" societies, declared to be innocent because they lack phonetic writing and therefore avoid the inherently violent hierarchical organizations of social order that written discourse (theology, history, ethics, law) produces. Rousseau is identified as Lévi-Strauss's genealogical precursor, depicting similarly idealized images of the authenticity of nature while maintaining the speech/writing binary as a quasiethical distinction between purity (access to presence) and corruption (the fall into absence). By showing that Lévi-Strauss's depiction of the nonliterate culture of the Brazilian Nambikwara Indians, despite its nostalgic privileging of speech, nonetheless (resistantly) incorporates a concept of arche-writing, Derrida suggests simultaneously the necessity of writing, in this generalized sense, to all human culture; the complex consequences of writing as the source of justice and injustice, social cohesiveness and violence, alike; and Lévi-Strauss's own gestures toward deconstructing the binary. Then, by showing that Rousseau's account of supplementarity, the "dangerous" perversity of the nonnatural (including writing), nonetheless both "condemns and rehabilitates" the nonnatural even while privileging what is original and pure (including speech), Derrida further amplifies the scope and significance of writing in general while also revealing Rousseau's ambivalent and contradictory attitudes toward both his privileged terms and supplementarity itself. In other words, consistent with his contention that deconstruction is a move within texts, not a forced critical intervention from without, Derrida shows Rousseau and Lévi-Strauss to be equally reluctant in their complicity in logocentrism, their reluctance marked—as it is in Saussure—by movements in their texts that subvert the very concepts on which they rely.

In part 1 Derrida explains that the Western metaphysics of presence "begins" in the human voice, where language is mistakenly supposed to originate. Logocentrism is "the exigent, powerful, systematic, and irrepressible desire for . . . the transcendental signified" (Derrida 1974, 49), the presence of the "thing-in-itself" or the presence of the idea of that thing as the mind presents it. Plato's phonocentrism naturalizes logocentrism by proposing that the voice "has a relationship of essential and immediate proximity with the mind." When Aristotle characterizes spoken words as symbols of mental experience, he is proposing, similarly, that "the voice is closest to the signified, whether it is determined strictly as sense (thought or lived) or more loosely as thing." All subsequent forms of signifying, including writing, "are derivative with regard to what would wed the voice indissolubly to the mind." Phonocentrism, the priority of speech, presumes "the absolute proximity of voice and being, of voice and the meaning of being, of voice and the ideality of meaning" (11–12). Through the voice, we hear ourselves thinking, we conceive the interiority of the things our speech seemingly enables us to call forth; the closeness of the heard voice to the self, the domain of consciousness, enables an illusion of "the effacement of the signifier," thereby creating an intimate experience of "the signified producing itself spontaneously, from within the self." For Derrida, this illusion is "the history of truth" because language, in the enclosure of speech, "is lived as the elementary and undecomposable unity of the signified and the voice, of the concept and a transparent substance of expression" (20). In the medium of voiced language, "the formal essence of the signified is *presence*, and the privilege of its proximity to the logos as *phone* is the privilege of presence" (18).

Writing, meanwhile, throughout the European "epoch of the logos," serves as the subordinate term in the binary, in its silence a debasement of the spoken word, "the mediation of a mediation," an exteriorization of, and to that extent an estrangement from, the experience of truth as (vocal) presence. Derrida's strategy for recuperating this subordinate concept (both reversing and displacing the binary) is to open up the semiotic logic on which the priority depends, specifically the immanent truthfulness of the sign. Writing is actually "older" than speaking if one thinks of the relative antiquity of magical as opposed to ontological rhetoric. Derrida notes an historical ambiguity in the valuation of writing, distinguishing between the "fallen writing" represented in the *Phaedrus* and a "natural, divine, and living writing" metaphorically invoked within the Judeo-Christian tradition as the sacred book, or the book of nature and natural law, understood as unmediated presence, "a meaning already constituted by and within the element of the logos" (Derrida 1974, 14–15). The Word of God refers equally to God's *speaking* the world into existence and God's *writing* the Ten Commandments, both manifestations of divine truthfulness; the Word of God is equally the "voice" and the "book" of nature. Writing becomes debased within this situated semiotic logic only when it is reduced to copying, as in Aristotle, when the *voice* of God is no longer "heard" in the *word* of God—or when, recalling the arguments of previous chapters, ontological rhetoric displaces magical rhetoric. Recuperating writing necessitates liberating it from its historical subordination not merely to speaking but to the logos, including "the idea of the book," an idea that is, according to Derrida, "profoundly alien to the sense of writing" because it invokes "a totality, finite or infinite, of the signifier" and serves as "the encyclopedic protection of theology and of logocentrism against the disruption of writing, against its aphoristic energy" (18).

Derrida's alternative logic would recover writing as an "enlarged and radicalized" concept that "no longer issues from a logos" and that entails "the de-construction of all the significations that have their source in that of the logos. Particularly the signification of *truth*" (Derrida 1974, 10). Writing, he argues, broadly "encompasses" all structures of human signification, including speech, phonetic inscription, modern forms of information processing (cybernetics and electronic media), mathematics, choreography, music, cinematography, sculpture, and other "languages," none of which depend, as speech does, on phonation. "The concept of writing," he says, "exceeds and comprehends that of language," designating not only the "outside" of signifying—"physical gestures of literal pictographic or ideographic transcription"—but also the "inside"—"the totality of what makes it possible" (8–9). The history of writing, in this sense, incorporates the more local history of the book—that is, linear writing, whose "death" is at hand in the age of hypertext and other modes of intertextuality. Indeed, it incorporates even the history of speech in the sense of that "fully present speech" that Plato announces and then exalts over writing as its mere translator (8). Writing, by Derrida's (indeed even Saussure's) alternative logic, cannot be a secondary sign system, subordinate to speech, because all signs are conventional and therefore none can be more "natural," or closer to some exteriority, than another. It's in the nature of signs to refer only and always to other signs: presence is not less elusive in one than in another. "Writing is not a sign of a sign, except if one says it of all signs, which would be more profoundly true" (43). The absence of the voice in this more generalized idea of writing dispels the illusion of "presence" in signs, constituting itself then as the demystified linguistic sign and "the common root of speech and writing" (74). Phonetic writing is a "supplement" of speech—a plenitude added to a plenitude. The overabundance of significance in each term, along with the terms' mutual dependence, collapses both the hierarchy of speech over writing and ultimately the binary itself. Derrida explains that "the movements of deconstruction do not destroy structures from the outside." Instead, they "inhabit" the structures, "operating necessarily from the inside, borrowing all the strategic and economic resources of subversion from the old structure" (24). The ancient priority of speech over writing contains the seeds of its own destruction.

Out of that destruction (deconstruction) emerges arche-writing, which in its liberation both from the voice and from the illusory totality of the book depicts a condition of the linguistic sign as no longer implicated in the metaphysics of presence. Stitching together the ensemble of provisional and bracketed concepts comprising the "theoretical matrix" of part 1, the Derridean logic (albeit unacceptably definitive in such a formulation) works like this: (1) The linguistic sign marks the site of a *trace*—notation of absent presence, the fleeting impression we have when we speak or write, listen or read, that words convey determinate meanings. (2) Recalling the endless postponement of signification in dictionary entries, where the "location" of meaning in the sign is always elsewhere, and always different from itself, what the *trace* momentarily fixes is the play of *differance* that is fundamental to signifying: "The (pure) trace is differance" (62). Derrida coins the word *differance* in order to capture at once these two related features of signification—"differing and deferring" (23)—the impossibility of a sign's self-identity and the subsequent inevitability of its deferral of meaning. (3) *Arche-writing*, then, as Spivak (1974, xxxix) explains, "is the name of the structure always already inhabited by the trace," the play of differance that is the sign. And (4) *grammatology* is "the science of 'the arbitrariness of the sign,'" the "science of writing before speech and in speech" (Derrida 1974, 51).

The second part of *Grammatology* introduces the "age of Rousseau," proposing—in terms of the discursive perspectives introduced in earlier chapters—a shift of historical European logocentrism away from the metaphysics of ontological rhetoric to the preoccupation with consciousness, the sovereign subject, characteristic of expressivism. Rousseau "repeats the inaugural movement of the *Phaedrus* and *De Interpretatione* but starts from a new model of presence; the subject's self-presence within *consciousness* or *feeling*" (Derrida 1974, 98). The prior "threat" of writing, which the West routinely frames in ethical terms—Plato's "bad" (phonetic) writing—had been the loss of presence resulting from the divorce of language from speakers who intend their signifieds and assure transmission to identifiable hearers. The new threat of writing, no less ethical in character, for the age of Rousseau lies in a loss of the pure and natural, the authentic and unmediated truth of human consciousness articulated in oral societies and corrupted with the development of literacy—phonetic writing. Derrida settles on Rousseau and Lévi-Strauss as the signatures of this resituating of the threat of writing because Rousseau is "the only one or the first one [between Descartes and Hegel] to make a theme or a system of the reduction of writing profoundly implied by the entire age" (98), while Lévi-Strauss acknowledges Rousseau as the founder of anthropology and declares himself Rousseau's disciple. According to Lévi-Strauss, Rousseau introduces the central problem of anthropology, the distinction between nature and

culture, the first associated with a native sincerity and authenticity of consciousness born of the unmediated meaningfulness of self-presence, the
second with corruption and violence born of the distancing (absence)
and subsequent alienation of individuals. The turn from nature to culture is represented, then, as a fall from innocence into the experience
of social hierarchy, bureaucratic differentiation, and injustice—features
of "civilization" authorized by the power of writing to facilitate distancing while producing history and the rationales of social organization
that history provides. The "natural" condition entails, for Rousseau, "the
image of a community immediately present to itself, without difference,
a community of speech where all the members are within earshot," while
the "cultural" condition entails "social distance, the dispersion of the
neighborhood," which enables the emergence of "oppression, arbitrariness, and vice," a breaking up of the "co-presence of citizens" (136–37).
While the speech/writing binary articulates European epistemological
and metaphysical conditions in part 1 of *Grammatology*, it articulates
sociocultural and political conditions in the discussion of Lévi-Strauss in
part 2, where the speech/writing binary is mapped onto the binary of
nature/culture.

Derrida's deconstructive reading of *Tristes Tropiques* centers on a "writing lesson" that Lévi-Strauss describes during his participant-observer
investigations of the nonliterate Nambikwara Indians when his field
notes inadvertently serve to introduce the chief of the tribe to phonetic writing. The chief, according to Lévi-Strauss, recognizes the power
of writing to assign and enforce social prestige, asks the investigator
for one of his note pads, and traces a series of wavy lines on the page,
regarding them with great seriousness and showing them to Lévi-Strauss
as though engaged with him in a transaction of signifying. Lévi-Strauss
abets the playacting by pretending to decipher the script. Later, when
the tribe assembles for an exchange of gifts, the chief pulls out his script
and pretends to speak from it, using the gesture as a vehicle for assign-
ing different objects to different individuals, thereby equating his political power with the power of the script. According to Derrida, the reader
is encouraged to read this account as a "parable" about the debased and
debasing authority of phonetic writing to produce "hierarchization, the
economic function of mediation and of capitalization, [and] participation in a quasi-religious secret" (Derrida 1974, 126). The parable is
complete when Lévi-Strauss adds at the end of his account that the chief
subsequently falls out of favor with the tribe, leaving open the possibility
that his followers may have associated his mock writing and reading with
deceit. For Lévi-Strauss, the intrusion of literacy, the primary colonizing

agency of Western civilization, into the life of the Nambikwara signifies an act of political violence by concretizing social stratification, power relations, exploitation, and bureaucratization, all understood to be features of societies that have lost a primal innocence associated with oral truthfulness. Faithfully reiterating the speech/writing binary, but now reinscribing it within anthropology's nature/culture binary, Lévi-Strauss concludes the story of the Nambikwara with a generalized reflection on the extent to which writing has been historically implicated in the rise of empires, the creation of castes and classes, and the exploitation and enslavement of the nonliterate by the literate. While writing has also enabled the production and consolidation of scientific and other knowledge, this advantage is, for Lévi-Strauss, only a secondary consequence of its power to regulate, systematize, and control for political advantage. The "authenticity" of natural/ oral tradition, where person is linked to person and generation to generation through speech, is sacrificed, with the arrival of civilization/writing, to an "unauthentic" idea of community where people are bound together at a distance through the administrative machinery that writing and its documents enable (136–37).

Derrida's response to Lévi-Strauss's interrelating of the speech/writing and nature/culture binaries is to counter the "writing lesson" with other portions of the Nambikwara narrative, not only destabilizing the "truths" of the binaries but also showing how Lévi-Strauss's own observations implicitly tend toward the deconstruction. For example, he cites the anthropologist's account of the privileged but also delicate political position of the chief relative to the rest of the people, making it apparent that the social hierarchization represented in the "lesson" as a consequence of writing is in fact already evident in the organization of this nonliterate tribe. More important, Derrida's point here is not that societies without writing also experience the violence of social stratification. It's that the Nambikwara already possess arche-writing, which is indeed a source of violence, just as Lévi-Strauss suggests of phonetic writing, but which is also the source of knowledge, social structure, and other positive cultural effects. Derrida reveals the Nambikwara's arche-writing by inspecting Lévi-Strauss's casual anecdote about the tribe's prohibition of the use of proper names, the making of direct references to each other in social interaction. The anthropologist describes an encounter with Nambikwara children, one of whom, when struck by another at play, runs to him and whispers a secret in retaliation—the name of her assailant. He goes on to describe his encouragement of other children to reveal more names of tribal members, noting however that, once adults discovered what the children were doing, the children were reprimanded (Derrida 1974, 111). Derrida argues in reading this anecdote that "from the moment that the proper name is erased in a system, there is writing" (108). The unnamed name is the presence of absence, the trace of differ*a*nce that is arche-writing. If we understand writing as the play of signification, not merely the phonetic script of Lévi-Strauss's secondary and debauched binary term, "it should be possible to say that all societies capable of producing, that is to say of obliterating, their proper names, and of bringing classificatory difference into play, practice writing in general" (109). To conceive of a society without arche-writing is, for Derrida, profoundly ethnocentric, albeit a reverse ethnocentrism concealing itself as "liberating progressivism," where an ostensibly "innocent" oral culture, free of exploitation and oppression, must be paternalistically defended from "bad writing" as the emblem of exploitative civilization. It is arche-writing, not speech, that enables knowledge and social organization, though it is also arche-writing, not phonetic writing, that enables domination (a condition that hierarchy makes possible but that is not synonymous with hierarchy). "There is no ethics without the presence *of the other* but also, and consequently, without absence, dissimulation, detour, differance, writing. The arche-writing is the origin of morality as of immorality" (140).

Of Grammatology concludes with a lengthy deconstruction of Rousseau's *Essay on the Origin of Languages"* in which Derrida amplifies his analysis of the speech/writing binary during the age of Rousseau while also explicating yet another provisional concept in his "theoretical matrix," the "logic of the 'supplement'" (Derrida 1974, 7). While the binary had been mapped onto the anthropologist's opposition of nature and culture in the discussion of Lévi-Strauss, it is mapped in the Rousseau discussion onto the romantic philosopher's opposition of the normal and the perverse. The phrase from Rousseau that initiates Derrida's deconstruction—"that dangerous supplement"—comes not from the *Essay* but from *Emile*, where it is a reference not to the linguistic sign but to masturbation, the perverse other of "normal" sexual gratification, a matter of considerable moral and medical anxiety for both Rousseau and the Enlightenment at large. The reinscription of speech/writing in the psychic binary of normality and perversion supports Derrida's contention that the ancient ontological model of presence is supplanted in expressivism by the "subject's self-presence within *consciousness* or *feeling.*" The age of Rousseau psychologizes signification, allying it to emotion as well as thought, portraying representation as imaginative projection, a means of articulating needs and desires, longings, hopes, and fears. It's a means also of experiencing pleasure, specifically the pleasure of presence: "Presence is always determined as pleasure by Rousseau . . . pleasure is always a receiving of presence" (280). "Normal" ("natural") sexual experience entails a gratification of the longing for presence, the presence of the desired. Autoeroticism, by contrast, motivated equally by the longing for presence in absence, is a perversion of the natural—dangerous to life in its artificiality and insufficiency, its lack of fulfillment—and its consequence is frustration. Whether speaking of masturbation or of writing, Rousseau uses the same reference to supplementarity: as Derrida quotes him, "Languages are made to be spoken, writing serves only as a supplement to speech" (144). Speech is the possession of presence—"self-presence, transparent proximity in the face-to-face of countenances and the immediate range of the voice" (138). Writing is absence, "dangerous from the moment that representation there claims to be presence and the sign of the thing itself" (144). The parallel for Rousseau between autoeroticism and writing lies in their similar displacement of the real by the illusory, the debased supplement of the real, a corruption that is both psychically and morally damaging. The parallel for Derrida is no less intimate, but it's a parallel between sexuality and signifying, and it is encompassed within the logic of the supplement: "Privation of presence is the condition of experience. . . . In as much as it *puts into play* the presence of the present and the life of the living, the movement of language does not . . . have only an analogical relationship with 'sexual' auto-affection. It is totally indistinguishable from it" (167).

Just as in the deconstruction of *Tristes Tropiques*, Derrida's reading of the *Essay* recuperates Rousseau's notion of a dangerous and sinful writing by the close inspection of Rousseau's own inconsistent and indeed ambivalent representations of the speech/writing binary. While language originated, according to Rousseau, in warm southern climes, where its power lies in the expression of emotion, it developed in northern climes, where its power lies in ideation. Writing arises alongside this increasing (northern) rationality because, as Derrida explains Rousseau, "the more a language is articulated, the more articulation extends its domain, and thus gains in rigor and in vigor, the more it yields to writing" (Derrida 1974, 226). While Rousseau generally valorizes the oral immediacy of early southern language as the "voice," the self-presence, of passion, metaphor, nature, life, and denigrates the rational, developed, and scribal northern language of coldness, inauthenticity, displaced representation, and the death of presence, he does not conclude that one set of values excludes the other, that the development of language is the extinction of passion. For example, Derrida shows, through extensive quotation, that Rousseau readily valorizes the visual sign—the gesture, the picture—(as quoted in Derrida, "one speaks more effectively to the eye than to the ear" [239]), noting that "when the immediacy of presence is *better represented* by the proximity and rapidity of the gesture and the glance, he praises the most savage writing, which does not represent oral representation: the hieroglyph" (237). But instead of acknowledging the visual power of the grapheme, Rousseau simply tolerates the contradiction, revisiting the values of phonetic writing, the supplementary visual sign, "clandestinely as he plays with the different parts of his discourse" (239). This clandestine visitation parallels Rousseau's treatment of autoeroticism in the *Confessions*, repeatedly condemning its sinfulness while returning to it "as an active obsession whose 'present' is constantly reactivated" (153). What he fails to recognize, cannot allow himself to recognize, is that masturbation is what "permits one to be himself affected by providing himself with presences, by summoning absent beauties." Masturbation, in other words, precedes sexual relations by offering an absent/present eroticism that allows "actual" fulfillment to be imagined in the first place. While Rousseau is obliged to regard autoeroticism as a "contingent evil coming from without to affect the integrity of the subject," he cannot give up "what immediately restores to him the other desired presence; no more than one can give up language" (153).

But Derrida's preoccupation with Rousseau's clandestine indulgence of inconsistencies takes him a step beyond the mere opening up of instabilities in Rousseau's speech/writing binary toward a representation of the *Essay* not merely as the depiction but as a dramatization of its theme—the theme of supplementarity. He perceives in Rousseau's writing a tendency to "neutralize . . . oppositions by erasing them; and he erases them by affirming contradictory values at the same time" (Derrida 1974, 189). This erasure is precisely the action of differance that writing necessitates—not phonetic writing but arche-writing, the differing/deferring action of the linguistic sign. "The concept of the supplement," Derrida says, "is a sort of blind spot in Rousseau's text, the not-seen that opens and limits visibility." The text is an acting out of what it cannot self-consciously say, the theme of supplementarity conveying "the being-chain of a textual chain, the structure of substitution, the articulation of desire and of language, the logic of all conceptual oppositions taken over by Rousseau." The *Essay* "tells us in a text what a text is, it tells us in writing what writing is" (163), and it does so by enacting the logic of the supplement: "Writing will appear to us more and more as another name for this structure of supplementarity" (245). What, then, is a supplement? For Derrida, it's "another name for differance" (150). The concept of the supplement contains two interwoven, mutually dependent meanings, accretion and substitution (200), addition and replacement. The supplement is always external to whatever it supplements, always different—as "the sign is always the supplement of the thing itself." As addition, the supplement is a surplus, "a plenitude enriching another plenitude"—in this sense, writing for Rousseau is supplementary as the mediation of a mediation and a negative value, "sinful" like masturbation in the sense that it constitutes an improper addition to the self-sufficiency of nature, conceived as presence. But a supplement may also be compensatory, replacing an insufficiency, repairing a lack. In the case of writing, in Derrida's sense of arche-writing, the sign marks the site of the trace, neither presence nor absence, a nonpresence that neither speech nor phonetic writing repairs (144–45). Rousseau is conscious of the first meaning but not conscious of the second, the *Essay*'s blind spot. Yet in his choice of the concept of supplement to identify the relationship of writing to speech, he "dreams" a writing that he cannot think, "a writing that takes place *before* and *within* speech" (315). He condemns writing as the absence of presence, but he also rehabilitates it "to the extent that it promises the reappropriation of that of which speech allowed itself to be dispossessed" (142), that is, arche-writing.

LYOTARD

Derrida's poststructuralism and the deconstructive hermeneutic that serves as its signature depict but do not exhaust the dispersion of cultural attitudes and practices that have come to be called postmodernism. In terms of the conceptual framework deployed in previous chapters, postmodernism is principally a critique of objectivism, the rhetoric associated with modern science and technology, a belief system valorizing positive knowledge and social progress. But it is also, more comprehensively, a profound skepticism toward all forms of metaphysics, whether the classical ontology of Aristotle, the detached structural empiricism of physical science, or the sovereign subjectivity of romantic expressivism. It challenges all the traditional coherences of the West, the nominalizations that have marked European epistemological self-confidence: faith, truth, permanence, order, unity, definition, identity, authenticity, authority, structure, system, hierarchy, tradition. In their place, it articulates local and provisional meanings, differences, uncertainties, paradoxes, and ambiguities, not to champion reckless incoherences of nihilism and anarchy but to resist the terroristic moves of intellectual or political ideologies that seek to assert hegemony. Postmodernism doesn't valorize meaninglessness; it opens up the abundance of meaning, liberating whatever has been suppressed or repressed in the interest of maintaining arrangements of power. Not all manifestations of postmodern critique display the methodological preoccupation that marks Derrida's relentless pursuit of semiotic binaries in need of dismantling, but they invariably extend the assault on what Derrida has called "regimes of truth," the claims of totalizing stories about the naturalness, the encompassing necessity, of social, intellectual, political, economic, and other structures. The focus of critique is invariably texts, the discourses that produce them, and the knowledges they convey, signifying a recognition that regimes of truth are always compositions—what Foucault calls "the prose of the world"—and as such can be deconstructed, their tactics and power moves revealed, their statements revised, reorganized, or erased. Through practices of irreverent reading, texts are turned against themselves and interrogated for their claims of transcendent coherence, clarity, and sufficiency. Their legitimations are opened to inspection.

The term *postmodernism*, denoting this irreverence both as a cultural attitude and a hermeneutic, is first introduced in Jean-Francois Lyotard's (1984, xxiv) *The Postmodern Condition: A Report on Knowledge*, where it is famously defined as "incredulity toward metanarratives." The central problem that Lyotard (1924–1998) poses is the "condition of knowledge in the most highly developed societies" at the current cultural moment—by which he means scientific and technical knowledge in the postindustrial world of electronic communication. The issue is not the substance of knowledge but its *condition*, the means by which it is authenticated as a social institution, and specifically the implications for its just and democratic use. Any institutional discourse, any public, disciplinary knowledge, requires some form of legitimation, enabling those who practice it, who fund and otherwise support it, or who seek advantage in its applications, to believe in its importance, trust its statements, practice by its principles, and consolidate whatever social importance they derive from it. Historically, legitimation has been achieved through the mediation of overarching and regulating representations called (variously) grand narratives, master narratives, or metanarratives, stories about stories that authenticate the knowledges incorporated within their plots while needing no authentication themselves. A metanarrative tells a story about the nature, power, and authority of texts within a particular discursive field, the heroes who have composed the discourse, its lofty goals (truth, progress, development, wealth, peace, emancipation), the nature of its knowledge and truth claims, the rules of inquiry (methodologies, forms of evidence or proof), governing institutions, historical milestones of achievement, challenges overcome, mountains still to climb. Lyotard uses the word *modern* to identify the condition of knowledge when it legitimates itself by appeal to metanarrative, arguing that the postmodern moment is so-called because it is experiencing a "crisis of narratives," a collapse of confidence in stories about the importance of other stories. The crisis of narratives has in turn produced a crisis of legitimation. His concern, then, is for the implications of incredulity, the available means of legitimation following the loss of faith in grand narratives (xxiii).

According to Lyotard (1984, 3–6), scientific knowledge in the material conditions of the cybernetic age is constituted as prolific quantities of "information," bits of data stored in and retrieved from vast banks (like the Internet), externalized, depersonalized (i.e., divorced from "knowers"), commodified, and globalized. Information circulates within its own economy, in the same way money does, as electronic traces (0/1, +/−, switch on/switch off) flickering across the system. No intimacy exists between signifier and signified, or between producers and consumers; those who purchase and use information are themselves merely data points, IDs rather than identities, fragilely composed (as victims of ID theft can attest) out of birth dates, social security numbers, and credit card accounts. Quaint concepts like "the training of minds," "learning for learning's sake," and "communal inquiry" are losing their claims to public attention (as brick-and-mortar universities are discovering). The traditional conception of knowledge implicit in these formulations, a personal and shared experience of learning, is steadily losing its classical use-value—its capacity to satisfy individual human needs. Instead, information is understood to be a commodity pragmatically exchanged in support of productive capacities that require information-based "expertise." Those who are privileged to produce, store, and trade in informational commodities ensure the control of information for their own economic advantage and enjoy the political power that their control affords. That power is no longer necessarily located in its traditional setting, the nation-state (including educational institutions), a formation that is becoming increasingly outmoded. Lyotard describes an alternative logic: "Society exists and progresses only if the messages circulating within it are rich in information and easy to decode. The ideology of communicational 'transparency,' which goes hand in hand with the commercialization of knowledge, will begin to perceive the State as a factor of opacity and 'noise.'" Models for an alternative circulation of capital, and centering of political power, have long since been available in the military-industrial complex and multinational corporations, which are positioning themselves as the new "decision makers," not only regulating the pursuit of science (by emphasizing the utility of scientific work, as opposed to the "joys of discovery"), but also by controlling the social institutions that support the information economy.

Lyotard (1984) explains that science, both traditionally and in its contemporary transformation, has itself largely occasioned the postmodern skepticism about narrative that has led to the current crisis of legitimation. To explore the implications of the crisis, and to suggest a provisional solution, he turns to the concept of "language games," taken from Ludwig Wittgenstein's *Philosophical Investigations* (1968), where language use is represented as speech acts in which speakers follow overt as well as tacit grammatical and rhetorical codes (the rules of the game) in order to make "moves" toward achieving their communicative ends (winning the game). Any language, understood as practice, is comprised of a multitude of language games. Since societies are configured by means of signs, "language games are the minimum relation required for society to exist. . . . the social bond is itself a language game," played according to rules of communicative interaction that in dialectical fashion govern but also emerge from the myriad other language games that comprise it (Lyotard 1984, 14–17). Most traditional knowledge (including legitimation stories) is in narrative form, representations of cultural values composed as history, literature, philosophy, and other liberal arts. In several crucial respects, scientific knowledge differs in kind from narrative: (1) it emphasizes denotation as the only acceptable language game (i.e., it isn't affective), (2) it distances itself from the social bond (so, it doesn't value public opinion), (3) it relies only on the competence of the knowledge producer, not the knowledge receiver (so, it doesn't invite popular feedback), (4) it regards its statements as in principle provisional and subject to falsification (so, it doesn't settle for belief), and (5) it represents itself as cumulative and corroborative (25–26). Given such fundamental differences, the relation between the two knowledges is "incommensurable" (23), and the incommensurability is what has provoked the crisis of legitimation.

Unlike routine conversations among individuals, institutionalized language games (public discourses) require formalized conventions of interaction, "supplementary constraints" for statements to be declared admissible, constraints that serve to "filter discursive potentials," negotiate the domain of utterable assertions, approve communicative proprieties, and arbitrate the moves of the game (Lyotard 1984, 17). Historically, the conventions of scientific discourse have been woven into metanarratives portraying science as the "unfettered pursuit of knowledge," for example, or "the instrument of social progress," where, as in any game, the rules of play are contextualized within a depiction of the game's ends, aspirations, and importance. Lyotard recognizes that science, no less than any other institutionalized discursive practice, continues to require validation—the explanation of its greater claims to authority and resources than, say, astrology or creationism. And the stakes are high because the regulation of science as a public discourse is linked to the regulation of society at large, such as to governmental institutions (which dispense research funding) as well as schools and universities (which control access to the game, and which increasingly include corporate sponsors like IBM and Bill Gates). Ultimately, the question of legitimation is a question of economic power and political control (8–9): Who decides what will count as knowledge? What decision makers get to make the rules of the game? Lyotard concedes that "it is not inconceivable that the recourse to narrative is inevitable, at least to the extent that the language game of science desires its statements to be true but does not have the resources to legitimate their truth on its own." And as evidence of a continuing odd coupling of narrative and scientific discourse, he points to the fact that "the state spends large amounts of money to enable science to pass itself off as an epic" (28). But the question is painfully clear: how are the language games comprising scientific knowledge to be legitimated in a cultural environment that is skeptical of metanarratives? More important, how is any legitimation that emerges going to serve the interests of a just and democratic society, even as multinational corporations seek to consolidate their information-based wealth and power?

Currently, given the cultural authority of positivist discourse, these questions are being answered by appeal to the concept of "performativity"—"the best possible input/output equation"—where proof of value lies not within the unfolding plot of a grand narrative about the heroic pursuit of truth but instead within a set of "objective" benchmarks, like those of science itself, that include money, technological efficiency, improved performance, and power: "The State and/or company must abandon the idealist and humanist narratives of legitimation in order to justify [a] new goal. . . . Scientists, technicians, and instruments are purchased not to find truth, but to augment power" (Lyotard 1984, 46). Technological "results" in the form of "data storage and accessibility," along with the "operativity of information," are effectively self-legitimating because they display, by the rules of objective proof, "not only good performativity, but also effective verification and good verdicts." They legitimate "on the basis of their efficiency," while their efficiency is reciprocally validated "on the basis of science and law" (46–47). Performativity is, however, a ruthless language game of power moves in which governmental, corporate, and other decision makers focus on maximizing the operational effectiveness of the social system through regulating the processes by which information is constructed, accessed, and deployed, not just in science but in all the domains of a technologically ordered society. For example, the goal of higher education, under such a regime, becomes its "optimal contribution . . . to the best performativity of the social system," specifically the production of skilled workers able to "tackle world competition" and meet the system's technical requirements—so many doctors, engineers, stockbrokers, and managers. The transmission of educational information does not require teachers or traditional forms of instruction; instead, electronic technologies could handle much of the practical work of dispensing knowledge, "linking traditional memory banks (libraries, etc.) and computer data banks to intelligent terminals placed at the students' disposal" (48–53). To the extent that these predictions from 1979 have subsequently become history, Lyotard's portrait of delegitimation and the triumph of performativity is on the mark. But he is far from sanguine about the social and ethical implications of the brave new world emerging as a result. He notes that Wittgenstein's strength is that he did not opt for the prevailing positivism of his era "but outlined in his investigation of language games a kind of legitimation not based on performativity." He concedes that "most people have lost the nostalgia for the lost narrative" but insists it does not follow that "they are reduced to barbarity." There is a way forward that does not depend on governmental or corporate social engineering, a way inspired by Wittgenstein's game theory and grounded in the knowledge that "legitimation can only spring from [people's] own linguistic practice and communicational interaction" (41).

Lyotard's proposal is to ground legitimation in what he calls "paralogy," a practice suited to the postmodern moment because it emphasizes local over global knowledge, discontinuities and anomalies (Thomas Kuhn's word) over smooth consolidations of knowledge, local, provisional rules (i.e., "moves") within the language games of science over systematic, encompassing arguments about the progress of knowledge, and an ongoing, disruptive conversation in which some discursive moves entail changing the rules or even inventing new games (like superstring theory) instead of searching for (let alone claiming) a grand "consensus." Lyotard (1984, 53) takes his lead from what he calls "the pragmatics of scientific research" as Kuhn had described them in *The Structure of Scientific Revolutions*. Science does not proceed from the "positivism of efficiency"—in fact, just the opposite. It entails "looking for a 'paradox' and legitimating it with new rules in the games of reasoning" (54). Local science produces the "little narrative" rather than the grand narrative, with only temporary consistencies of rules, claims, and connections to other knowledges. Science interrogates its language games from within (as Einstein and Bohr contested the epistemological conundrums of quantum mechanics), ensuring the impossibility of any totalizing rationale of investigation. The condition of the most creative science depends on dissent (revolution, in Kuhn's terms) rather than consensus ("normal" science). The language games only multiply instead of resolving toward the plenitude of a positive knowledge. With each change of rules, a new framing of the discourse emerges, including venerable precursors, prior history, methods (the invention of the calculus, or electron microscopy), and applications (fossil or nuclear energy). Discussions of science's denotative statements need to be rule governed, but the rule depictions are "metaprescriptive," not metanarrative, focused on an encouragement to make yet additional statements, with ever-evolving rules. The opposite of paralogy is "innovation," a value driven by the terroristic moves of performativity, where a stabilizing social criterion authenticating science is imposed externally and where the terrorism consists in the willingness of the system to close someone out of the language game by appeal to the needs of an ostensibly common project (say, providing funding only to biological research that guarantees new pharmaceutical products) and to efficiency in the pursuit of that goal (say, sponsoring only researchers with established track records). The outlier is banished for violating the rules of an imperial language game (63). It may be that the future of knowledge legitimation will incorporate all of the current options, local narrative, paralogy, and performativity. But Lyotard's hope is that paralogy, matched to a robust negotiation of metaprescriptives, may constitute "the outline of a politics that would respect both the desire for justice and the desire for the unknown." The prerequisite for this future politics, Lyotard insists, is a level playing field—which means "public free access to the memory and data banks" of scientific knowledge (67)—an Internet model of postmodern democracy.

TRINH MINH-HA

As Lyotard's investigation of metanarratives and performativity makes clear, the irreverent hermeneutic of postmodern rhetoric is well suited to interventions that aim to criticize oppressive intellectual or political regimes. Cultural criticism can hardly proceed from vantage points that are incapable of imagining culture as a work in progress rather than a transcendental signified, nor could it coherently champion the political standing of groups whose stories are either subordinated to or effaced by a dominant discourse. When culture is thought to be constituted within fields of signification and understood as a discontinuous intertextuality, then textual critique provides a strategy for identifying oppressive conditions, explaining inequities, and negotiating ameliorative revisions. Naming oppression is not, to be sure, synonymous with the practical political work of eliminating it, but acquiring "literacy" about the transactions of power and privilege—recognizing them, revealing them, and contesting them within the texts of culture—are preconditions for cultural change. An additional precondition is the capacity of the oppressed to imagine themselves as discursive subjects rather than objects (what Paulo Freire [1969] in *Pedagogy of the Oppressed* speaks of as "conscientization"). This is a familiar line of reasoning among cultural critics since Raymond Williams, and the postmodern feminist and cinematographer Trinh Minh-ha (1952–) provides an effective illustration of how it operates to challenge privileged cultural formations. In *Woman, Native, Other: Writing, Postcoloniality, and Feminism*, Minh-ha offers a critique of totalizing objectivist discourse, exemplified by the discipline of anthropology, together with an oppositional portrait of the local and intimate knowledges available from storytelling, in order to explore writing, women's writing, and the subjectivities of third-world women within the cultural conditions of Western patriarchal rationality. For Minh-ha, virtually the entire European heritage of rhetoric—magical, ontological, objectivist, expressivist, sociological—has been so many chapters of an epic about language as ritual combat, an agonistic male fantasy about supremacy and subordination, where dialectic—argumentation—is the metaphorical weapon of choice. As woman, native, and "Other," as the subaltern, Minh-ha seeks to claim a (decentered) cultural identity on the only ground the Eurocentric epic has left for cultivation, a ground of multiple selves, fragmented voices, and mixed discursive modes—narrative, analytical, poetic, and graphic—the ground of the marginalized.

Minh-ha begins by positioning herself within the two discursive worlds she inhabits, the master's story and the subaltern's story. The master's story is *his*(s)tory, panoramic, encompassing, and insistent, while the subaltern's story is *her* story, a small text enveloped and subordinated in the larger one. The master's story dates to when "a group of mighty men attributed to itself a central, dominating position . . . overvalued its

particularities and achievements . . . wrapped itself up in its own thinking . . . and claim[ed] to speak the minds of both the in-group and the
out-group." This is the story of European rationalism and colonialism,
the voice that drowns out lesser voices. Minh-ha introduces the suppressed opposing story by imagining a remote village (but available,
of course, to the prying eye of the anthropologist) where an important community discussion, say the "problem of survival with this year's
crops," is taking place, a meeting for which all the members of the village—women, men, children—come together, casually and unhurriedly,
as equals. They engage amiably in relaxed conversation while carrying
on the other business of ordinary life. "A mother continues to bathe her
child . . . two men go on playing a game . . . a woman finishes braiding
another woman's hair." The activities don't prevent people from listening and speaking. No one comes "right to the heart of the matter . . . for
the heart of the matter is always somewhere else." There is "no catching, no pushing, no directing, no breaking through, no need for a linear
progression." The meeting "wanders in old sayings and remembrances
of events that occurred long ago." A man "starts singing softly and playing his lute," some women "drowse on a mat they have spread on the
ground," the discussion goes late into the night and when it's over every
member of the village has spoken. The chief is there "to listen and
absorb," not to impose his will, and he does not speak more than others.
This story of the village gathering sets the stage, and the tone, for Minh-
ha's discussion of a series of problems—woman as writer, the positivist
hegemony of the master, the identity of the third-world woman, and, at
the close, the status of storytelling. The story of the gathering "never
stops beginning or ending . . . appears headless and bottomless for it is
built on differences" (Minh-ha 1989, 1–2).

The third-world woman writer must struggle among competing subjectivities—woman, writer of color, woman writer, woman of color—and
therefore competing priorities in a culture that has already encoded
these identities within an ideology of domination, where the position
and definition of writer have been established in Eurocentric and patriarchal terms while race and gender differences mark only derivative
roles, if any roles at all, for the "Other" who writes. The "Other" finds
herself framed as a borrower of language who must respect the rules
of writing if she seeks the privilege of being read. Since the rhetoric of
the West has deemed writing to be the "vehicle of thought," the rules
emphasize clarity and correctness, coherence, linearity, logical entailment, intellectual distance, and voicelessness (the mark of objectivity,
the oracular voice), instrumental values associated with classical functions

of language: "to communicate, express, witness, impose, instruct, redeem, or save"—the obligation to send out "an unambiguous message" (Minh-ha 1989, 16). Writing, and writers, must be "well-behaved," proving their self-discipline and civic responsibility through an obsessive eagerness to "prune, eliminate, forbid, purge, purify" (17). It's not as though these values have no alternatives (the language of Taoism and Zen is "perfectly accessible but rife with paradox"); their election is historical and politically situated, and it has constituted the world of power and privilege that Eurocentric patriarchal writers enjoy. The bind of the third-world woman writer, already designated as an outsider, is how to "borrow" language without appearing to be a thief ("she who, steals language" [15]), how to speak from subjectivities that emerge from her gendered and ethnic difference while not jeopardizing her access to public discourse. Can she speak her truth by following the master's rules without alienating herself from that truth? Can she transgress the rules and still find a publishing outlet and an audience? The bind is more than aesthetic because the third-world woman writer understands the "social function" of writing (10), conceives her task as writing with a social conscience, creating what Sartre called "art engagé" in order to make a space within the dominant discourse for those whom it has rendered as objects. Writing with a conscience means, in part, writing with a *guilty* conscience—because the writer is sensitive to the privilege attending her literacy: "Committed writers are the ones who write both to awaken to the consciousness of their guilt and to give their readers a guilty conscience." The personal guilt derives from her relative proximity to power, her relative access to the "discourse of authority and arrogance," compared to her illiterate sisters who work in fields rather than studies or libraries. Her commitment, driven by that constructive guilt, is the pursuit of freedom from oppression, the reclaiming of subjectivity. "The function of literary art . . . must be to remind us of that freedom and to defend it" (10–11). But the question arises, what then is the nature of the third-world woman writer's subjectivity, writing against oppression from within the discourse of oppression? Minh-ha's text is haunted by Audre Lorde's (2007) famous conclusion about the same bind: "The Master's tools will never dismantle the Master's house."

For Minh-ha, the science of anthropology typifies the dominant, objectivist discourse of the West, and with particular relevance to the "native," the subaltern that it has named, with haughty scientific detachment, as the "Other." "Anthropology as human science is nowadays the foundation of every single discourse pronounced above the native's head" (Minh-ha, 1989, 57). The anthropologist serves as the official marginalizer of non-Western societies, claiming to be "the spokesman for the entire human race—never hesitating to speak about and for a vague entity named *man*" (49). According to Minh-ha, "One of the conceits of anthropology lies in its positivist dream of a neutralized language that strips off all its singularity to become nature's exact, unmisted reflection" (53). Claiming a benign, even well-intentioned, curiosity, the anthropologist inspects the "native," the different and exotic, with a condescending and paternal gaze, observing strange behaviors, "myths," curious social arrangements, love-making rituals, "the skin of native life" (56), his language of scientific truth reinscribing a colonial order even as he asserts the moral imperative (the *noblesse oblige* of the West) to safeguard the diversity of cultures and assist the social progress of "the handicapped who cannot represent themselves." Anthropologists "strip your identity off and paste it back on, calling it your creative aspect of 'revitalization,' a positive affirmation of your own cultural traditions, heritage, and identity, which will also, obviously. . . . be of potential significance for anthropological analysis of culture change" (59). Minh-ha asks how, in the face of this domineering European discourse, the "Other" can write an escape from her "identity enclosure," as "third-world," "minority," "colored," and "woman." Borrowing liberally from the Derridean semiotic of difference, displacement, and undecidability, she pursues her answer through a rhetoric of resistance that challenges the claims to authority in the discourse of the master, recognizing however that resistance doesn't mean aggression (which at best could only offer a new hierarchy for an old one) but rather a steadfast commitment to the freely speaking subject, recognizing everyone but privileging no one. She circulates intertextually both inside and outside the master's house, inside when she turns the language of abstract critical analysis back on the arguments of anthropology or when she articulates theoretical positions regarding women's writing, but also outside when she communicates ethnic and gendered values through storytelling, poems, and photographic as well as cinematic images of women whose lives and circumstances provide the impetus for her work.

Avoiding identity politics, Minh-ha insists that "sexual difference has no absolute value." But avoiding the erasure of difference, she also insists on the gendered and ethnic character of political action, an acknowledgment of "the critical processes by which" she has "come to understand how the personal—the ethnic me, the female me—is political" (Minh-ha, 1989, 102–06). The concept of gender "is pertinent to feminism as far as it denounces certain fundamental attitudes of imperialism and as long as it remains unsettled and unsettling" (113).

Arguments to ignore or transcend gender, like arguments to ignore or transcend ethnicity (as in melting-pot mythology), are either naïve or cynical, the first if they imagine people will forget what they fear merely by putting their hands over their eyes, the second if they contrive hollow platitudes to put a pious face on their prejudice. To "defend a gendered way of living," Minh-ha says, is "to fight for difference, a difference that postpones to infinity and subverts the trend toward unisex behavioral patterns" (116). A gendered way of living includes also a gendered way of writing, not a reified "women's way of writing" but a feminized representation of writing that exhibits a power to change the values and objectives of discourse. For Minh-ha, feminized writing entails rejecting the "Priest-God scheme," the writer as "author," procreator of words and worlds, ruler and pontificator, deliverer of sacred messages. Borrowing (for she is a "borrower of language") from the feminist critic Helene Cixous, among others, Minh-ha agrees that the feminized writer must write her body and write through her body, "rethink the body to reappropriate femininity." The body, unlike the head (the site of cold rationality, distinction making, structures, regulations, codes) values sharing, the warmth of the touch, desire, giving, caring. If the metaphor of patriarchal discourse is the phallus, where texts are formed through egocentric insemination of language by the "creative" mind, the metaphor of feminized discourse is the womb, where texts are the products of gestation and nurturing. Fathering is displaced by mothering. The feminized writer is, in her maternal love, "neither possessed nor possessive, neither binding nor detached nor neutral." She doesn't exert control over language but rather allows language to work through her, a process of birthing the text (36–40). Like the village conversation, feminized writing goes on in the midst of ordinary life, not in heroic solitude, because child bearing and child rearing are social acts characterized by unselfish and patient attentiveness. There are no winners or losers, no one is judged, silenced, or marginalized; there is no subaltern. "Writing the body" is a way of "making theory in gender, of making of theory a politics of everyday life, thereby rewriting the ethnic female subject as site of difference" (44).

Storytelling is, of course, not intrinsically an alternative to egocentrism, rationality, and domination. The story, no less than argument or analysis, can suffer the imposition of a rhetoric of beginning, middle, and end, the teleological structuring of the world according to colonialist or equally presumptuous aspirations: there are Rudyard Kiplings as well as Jamaica Kincaids. But Minh-ha contrasts the corrupted master narratives of European culture with the local narratives of societies satisfied to value story for community rather than conquest—her story versus his(s)tory. And she recognizes a power in narrative that is unavailable to argument—the power to find truth without fact, to reveal order without imposing hierarchical structure, and to save the intimacy of memory from the distance of history, all values that the master, in his disdain, has left behind as scraps for the subaltern. The story that Minh-ha trusts is "Grandma's story," the story that "uncivilized" and "native" mothers have told their children since before writing, before history, and before civilization, a story that has earned our trust because it is as intimately, uncompromisingly honest as nursing. For Minh-ha (1989, 136), "Telling stories and watering morning glories both function to the same effect." The mother's story makes no grand claims and is not burdened by illusions of comprehensiveness, objectivity, or factuality; it isn't argumentative or hortatory; it is unhurried and neither begins nor ends ("it will take a long time for living cannot be told" [119]). It offers mysteries and delights to the child out of the joy and pain of the mother's experience, honoring the obligations common to all nurturing: "The story must be told. There must not be any lies" (143). The archive of mothers' stories is the shared experience of the community (121), an experience whose most public sharing is entrusted in some oral cultures to professional storytellers—diseuses, griottes, fortunetellers, witches—who are also commonly women. These community storytellers, sometimes considered to have magical powers, accept the sacred trust that derives from the experience of nurturing in order to guard and transmit the truths of culture from one generation to the next. "The story depends upon every one of us to come into being. It needs us all, needs our remembering, understanding, and creating what we have heard together to keep on coming into being" (119). By appeal to this representation of the community narrative, its integrity grounded in mothering—the most unselfish of human practices—Minh-ha identifies a space for writing and the writer that European discourse theory has historically neglected. Through Grandma's story, the subaltern speaks, perhaps beginning a new chapter in the story of Western rhetoric.

AFTERWORD
Critical Reflections

Having elaborated a system of conceptual oppositions, grounds of meaningfulness, for understanding European rhetorical theory, let me specify the claims I'm prepared to make for it and also caution against the philosophical hazard of mistaking its limitations for virtues. Chief among the limitations is the tempting reductiveness of its categorical structure. We are quickly lured into reification if the tidy simplicity of this framework of discursive ideologies encourages us to avoid grappling directly with theoretical texts, situated in their own histories, and thereby experiencing the intellectual bazaar to which they belong, a teeming, cacophonous babel of voices. Once reified, the scheme has potential to turn rhetorical theory into a parlor game: Is Aristotle an ontological theorist or *really* a closet objectivist? Is Kenneth Burke a Marxist or an expressivist? Where should we put Nietzsche? I'm a deconstructive rhetorician; what are you? The reduction of rhetorical perspectives legitimizes a reduction of the theorists themselves, pinned and wriggling like insects run afoul of an entomologist: What do we really learn about Teresa of Avila if all we attend to is her exemplification of magical rhetoric? Is the work of Mary Belenky and her colleagues adequately summarized when the authors are cataloged as empiricists, labeled with a Scarlet E? Close behind the danger of reification is the dangerous illusion of comprehensiveness, where my six stories about rhetoric claim a sufficiency, or have a sufficiency thrust upon them, that discourages pursuit of different stories, themes, and organizing principles. Since my decisions about protagonists are themselves far from comprehensive (Aristotle but not Cicero, Descartes but not Vico or Condillac, Coleridge but not von Humboldt, Derrida but not Foucault, without so much as a cameo appearance by Freud, Lacan, or Kristeva), is it quite clear that the six stories would have been unaffected by the dialogue of additional characters? And what of less traditional, less bookish forms of contemporary rhetorical thought, contributions to digital or visual rhetoric for example? Does the scheme

DOI: 10.7330/9780874219364.c008

adequately embrace them? Truth to tell, I don't know. But I do know that nothing embraces everything.

What I would claim for my conceptual framework and its anthology of representative texts is the heuristic power available from thinking with the aid of what I. A. Richards (1955) famously called "speculative instruments" (in a book by the same name). While Richards never provides an especially clear or satisfying definition of the "speculative instrument," his idea has generally to do with the turning of language upon itself to produce thinking about thinking or the interpretation of an interpretation (Plato has a theory of rhetorical practice; I have a theory about Plato's theory and about his place in a constellation of theories—such is life in the funhouse of language). By playing with levels of semantic generality, we can create knowledge about our knowledge, an exercise enabling critical reflection. Burke's pentad is a good example of a speculative instrument—a device with which to think, a framework within which to assess, compare, and classify interpretations formed at other levels of generality but also, just as important, a set of formative principles with which to create those interpretations in the first place. The pentad enjoys greater explanatory power than my six grounds of meaningfulness because it functions as an exhaustive or enclosed set of higher order abstractions (scene, agent, and so on) while my set of alternative grounds is open ended, each ground dialectically related to the texts from which I've abstracted it, the ensemble in principle allowing expansion. But taken together, the grounds of meaningfulness similarly constitute a speculative instrument, enabling both the interpretation of ranges of texts that fall within their explanatory power and also the categorizing of texts within an overarching framework. While it remains true that the dispersion of historical statements about rhetoric comprises an intellectual bazaar, the ability to relate one statement to another by appeal to a higher level of generality provides gratifying potential for the orderly, if also contingent and provisional, differentiation of voices. As a speculative instrument, my set of conceptual oppositions can marshal and sort a considerable range of philosophic opinion, from the sophists to Derrida, while also focusing textual interpretations by appeal to recurring themes—with the understanding, of course, that in the end the idea is to eat the Jello, not the mold.

This speculative instrument can assist our thinking about rhetoric in a couple of different ways. For one, it offers a map of certain ideological (specifically epistemological) contours of European discourse theory, depicting what Stephen Toulmin might characterize as the "warrants" of Western practice (essentially a competition of warrants). I don't claim that my invoking of familiar motifs in Western philosophy—taken from classical metaphysics, Enlightenment rationalism, romanticism, pragmatism, socialism, and others—has been a thunderbolt of inspiration. But I would say that scholarly work devoted to the history of rhetoric has not routinely explored how different arguments about discourse manifest those ideologies, proceed from those warrants, and may be distinguished in their terms. There are, for example, basic differences between Greco-Roman concepts of invention and romantic concepts of creativity or imagination, even though both are broadly concerned with the discovery of what to say. Recognizing how classical metaphysics informs invention theory, representing the topoi or loci as literally places in the memory from which to retrieve already available argumentative materials, can serve to explain how Greco-Roman rhetoric differs fundamentally from romantic theories that assume the possibility of new ideas derived from formative acts of mind. The map of contrasting ideologies organizes the philosophical terrain of European discourse theory not by appeal to the details of Aristotle's rhetoric versus the details of Coleridge's but by appeal to prior intellectual convictions that not only sharply delineate one perspective from the other but also offer bases for differentiating concepts that, however similar they may appear, are peculiar to each. The warrant of mimesis is different from the warrant of originality. By extension, the history of Western rhetoric features, from this point of view, not a single tradition from Plato to the present but multiple traditions notably at odds with each other, a circumstance contributing to the complexity of public discourse today as it has been shaped by ideological crosscurrents.

At the same time, returning to a theme briefly introduced in chapter 1, the depiction of this philosophical terrain presumes that a map of Europe is not also a map of China or India or Africa, even where conceptual overlaps seem to occur. Rhetoric, like language itself, is global, but its features, like those of language, are culturally specific, so my contrasting *Western* ideologies are intended to have only local implications. The idea of "face," for example, appears across cultures as one dimension of politeness strategy (Scollon and Scollon 2001, 44 *f.*), and English speakers are familiar with notions of "losing face" and "saving face" in public discourse. But the more culturally specific distinction between *mianzi* ("social reputation") and *lian* ("moral character") in Chinese has no precise parallel in the West, let alone some explicit Western sociological or rhetorical concept to which it owes its origin. "Losing face" carries more social weight in Chinese communication, entailing not just embarrassment but potentially disgrace and loss of moral authority. Similarly, the concept of *nommo*, mentioned in chapter 1, which Molefi Asante (1987, 17) describes as the power of the spoken word in some African societies to create communal cohesiveness, balance, and harmony, presumes a distinctively African understanding of the world, "an interpretation of discourse based on Afrocentric values where *nommo* as word-force is a central concept." Seeking to understand or categorize concepts like *lian* and *nommo* by appeal to my framework of explicitly European ideologies (for instance, by explaining *nommo* as a hybrid of magical and sociological rhetoric) is worse than intellectual distortion: it's also cultural chauvinism. This is not to devalue comparative rhetorical studies. Xing Lu among others has argued persuasively about the importance of finding a "language of ambiguous similarity" in order to capture both sameness and difference in comparisons of Greek and Chinese rhetoric (Lu 2011, 92). Cultures are not mutually opaque or there could be no cross-cultural communication or understanding. But comparing cultural maps does not entail superimposing one on the other. My map is explicitly European and therefore does not accommodate the features of a different cultural terrain. Moreover, I have pointedly avoided the suggestion of similarities or parallels with non-European thought, even at risk of appearing to ignore the diversity of world rhetorics, for the simple reason that it hasn't been my purpose to undertake a comparative analysis. It should be sufficient, given a different intent, to acknowledge and guard against the potential for latent occidental imperialism in overextending the reach of my anthology.

So much for what I haven't attempted to do. What I *have* attempted—and this is the second application of my speculative instrument—is to suggest the roles and interplay of discursive ideologies in the communicative exchanges of everyday life, from the individual language practices of George and Louise described in chapter 1 to the discourses in which their uses of language are situated. Rhetorical theory and the history of rhetoric are finally of interest in themselves only to theorists and historians, harmless academic drudges like Samuel Johnson's lexicographer. Where they matter is in their commentary and their largely tacit influence on practice—understood not as mere technical rules but as the intellectual, political, and ethical fabric of public communication. Ideologies articulate ways of being in the world, and the six perspectives on rhetoric I've identified here, understood as ideological crosscurrents, have materially shaped European, including American, discursive practices. American culture owes much, for instance, to Enlightenment thought of the seventeenth and eighteenth centuries, a tradition encompassing the rise of science but also the epistemological and political arguments culminating in the romantic movement and the French Revolution. The intellectual values associated with these crosscurrents, from rigorous empirical investigation to freedom and human rights to the power of creative imagination, saturate not only our scientific but also our legal, political, medical, educational, and other discourses. Those values are not simple, however, since the subject/object dualism at the center of seventeenth- and eighteenth-century European thought, from Descartes to Kant, has yielded the array of dynamic oppositions (like nature/self, reason/imagination, and mechanism/organism) reflected in the perspectives of objectivism and expressivism described in chapters 4 and 5. The values privileged in these perspectives readily polarize, offering contrastive choices, or even contradictory impulses, fused together in the formation of our ideals, institutions, and communal practices.

Consider American education as a representative discourse: it is at once democratic and meritocratic, the romantic rhetoric of expressivism—suffused with the spirit of individual creativity, human freedom, the right to access, and the possibility of self-improvement ("Be all that you can be")—standing in stark, mostly unreflective opposition to the scientific rhetoric of educational outcomes assessment dedicated to creating hierarchies of ability and expertise (less suited to personal development than to the needs of the workforce) by appeal to empirical measures of competence. "Be all that you can be . . . but in the context of your inherent cognitive limitations." Invoking mechanical metaphors, we track students into ability and curricular groupings, a gesture of social engineering; but we also insist without cynicism and with no sense of contradiction on equality of opportunity. Invoking the botanical metaphors of romanticism, we celebrate the individual child's growth but we also prepare her for the stultifying assembly line or the groupthink of corporate middle management. We encourage creativity and spontaneity but also deliver course content by lecture, seek teacher-proof textbooks, and test knowledge (really the retention of data) by appeal to objective examinations. We want students to read for pleasure but we teach word-attack skills. Basics curricula vie with art and dance (although funding decisions don't make it much of a contest); Montessori meets the regimented drill-on-skill of the academic sweatshop. We value and seek to reward intellectual and imaginative development, but we also quantify student achievement (and teacher productivity) as though they could be measured as surely as we measure the masses of subatomic particles or the wind strength of tornadoes. At the worst, while we truly want to "Leave no child behind" we also find "objective" ways to justify the unequal distribution of wealth, enabling us to live more comfortably than we should with the "savage inequalities" that Jonathan Kozol (1991) documents in the schools of impoverished communities.

Nor are Enlightenment rationalism and post-Enlightenment romanticism the only traditions contributing tangled ideological content to our culture, including our educational discourse. It's no less important to recognize a powerful religious heritage featuring equally dynamic ranges of value from intensely personal experiences of the sacred (the magical perspective) to the doctrinal orthodoxy of established churches and time-honored truths (the ontological perspective). The rationalist traditions of the Enlightenment play off against traditions of belief and metaphysical commitment with far longer European pedigrees than that of empirical science. And so we argue about whether schools should be aggressively religious or restrictively secular, whether tax dollars should support charter schools, whether students should pray as well as recite the Pledge of Allegiance (and if so, whose prayers?), whether the curriculum should include creationism side by side with evolution, whether we should read *Huckleberry Finn*, or *Beloved*, or the Bible, whether there's a place in schools for sex education or LGBT clubs. Ontological verities, "One nation, under God," "All men are created equal," "God bless America," "English first," "No child left behind," "freedom of speech," live uneasily with each other while in the background, despite the ostensibly inclusive ambitions of public education, darker metaphysical commitments fuel arguments for ethnocentrism, misogyny, homophobia, discrimination, and xenophobia. "Send me your tired and poor" confronts "First secure the borders." "All men are equal" confronts "separate but equal." "No child left behind" says under its breath "unless he lacks a green card." In addition to the mix of scientific rationality, romantic individualism, religious enthusiasm, and metaphysical certainty there are ideological counterpoints to hegemonic values that express themselves as intellectual irreverence, critique, and dissent. Activists advocate for multicultural classrooms and mainstreaming instead of ability groups, for Hispanic and African American authors in the literary canon, for more women in science, for less high-stakes testing. Leftist scholars, expressing Marxist (sociological) and/or postmodern arguments, propose critical and oppositional pedagogies challenging the corporatization of schools, neoliberalism, late capitalism, economic injustice, and political disenfranchisement. Functional literacy confronts political literacy. Postmodern teachers modify traditional lectures and term papers by playing with social media and hypertext, and they subvert traditional course contents, along with the cultural assumptions that support them, in classes where the heroes, instead of Shakespeare, French history, opera, and business management, are as likely to be video games, Boy George, punk, anime, gangsta rap, and Lady Gaga. Put all the competing educational themes and narratives together and the result is Burke's rhetorical "scramble," people and groups jockeying for position and privilege through the expression of their commitments. Ideological oppositions are woven into the material fabric of discourse, not just in education but across the spectrum of our social institutions.

The abstract and artificially differentiated ideological counterpoints depicted in previous chapters are best understood, therefore, as an active interplay of the contrastive themes comprising our cultural experience, the articulation in material speech and writing of an array of competing values—sacred/profane, reason/emotion, belief/knowledge, certainty/skepticism, fact/fiction, truth/lie, individual/society, liberal/conservative, tradition/progress, freedom/restraint, work/play, authority/self-determination, altruism/self-interest, reverence/iconoclasm—enough binaries to keep Derrida busy for the first millennium of his eternal life. Rhetoric endlessly mediates these values in the spheres of actual public discourse, creating webs of meaning that give our institutions, along with our individual behaviors, their distinctive character. Different possibilities for action attach to different grounds of meaningfulness: magical rhetoric valorizes belief, faith, and spiritual transcendence; ontological rhetoric valorizes certainty, stability, and commitment; objectivist rhetoric valorizes dispassionate knowledge and technological progress; expressivist rhetoric valorizes freedom, individualism, and creativity; sociological rhetoric valorizes justice, collective responsibility, struggle for change; and deconstructive rhetoric valorizes irreverence and critique, the powerful mischief of play. No perspective encompasses all values, solves all problems, or answers all questions: magical and ontological rhetoric defend certainty (such as belief in God or country) but willingly ratify intolerance (the Inquisition and the deportation of "aliens"); objectivist rhetoric defends dispassionate empirical curiosity (the atom) but can also encourage passionate technological hubris (the atom bomb); expressivist rhetoric can champion personal rights while promoting egocentrism; sociological rhetoric can promote community ethos while suppressing individual initiative and ingenuity; and deconstructive rhetoric can subvert hegemonic ideas or institutions while lacking the energy and determined commitment, the confident sense of agency, necessary to sponsor (or even envision) change for the better. These strengths and insufficiencies perpetually circulate through any pragmatics of discourse.

Notice that I'm indulging in rhetoric about rhetoric—making a self-interested case for my speculative instrument with as much bravado as I can muster. But with apologies to Plato (who does the same thing), that admission need not be cynical. The truth is simply that we must keep our wits about us in the funhouse of language, making our way resolutely, if seldom with perfect balance, across the tilting floors, through the turning barrels, and past the distorting mirrors of the discursive fields that comprise our lives. As rhetorical beings we live in and through language, creating, borrowing, using, misrepresenting, contradicting, and abandoning texts as our primary strategies for learning. Naturally, we're self-interested—what else could we be? Our obligation is not to transcend self-interest but to disclose it, our own along with that of others, for the sake of our continual liberation from each other's designs, cultivating belief and doubt with equal seriousness, negotiating our points of view, sustaining our discourses without presuming the sufficiency of any text or discursive ideology, past or present. The rule of the funhouse is "Keep moving or you'll fall down." My speculative instrument, both as conceptual map and as representation of rhetorical practice, should be seen for what it is, a potentially helpful but temporary stimulus for learning, better discarded when it has exhausted its usefulness than retained as a solemnly insistent metanarrative, or a superficially convenient SparkNotes gloss. My anthology of stories about Western discourse theory brings no transcendent rationality to the funhouse. It resides there, an illusion among illusions, and as with any text, the veil of its artifice is well worth lifting.

REFERENCES

Aristotle. 1907. *De Anima*. Translated by R. D. Hicks. London: Cambridge University Press.

Aristotle. 1952. *Metaphysics*. Translated by Richard Hope. Ann Arbor: University of Michigan Press.

Aristotle. 1961a. *Physics*. Translated by Richard Hope. Lincoln: University of Nebraska Press.

Aristotle. 1961b. *Poetics*. Translated by Francis Fergusson. New York: Hill and Wang.

Aristotle. 1973. *Categories, On Interpretation, Prior Analytics*. Translated by H. P. Cooke and H. Tredennick. Cambridge, MA: Harvard University Press.

Aristotle. 1991. *On Rhetoric*. Translated by George A. Kennedy. New York: Oxford University Press.

Aristotle. 2009. *Politics*. Translated by Benjamin Jowett. Cambridge, MA: Internet Classics Library.

Arnauld, Antoine. 1964. *The Art of Thinking*. Translated by James Georgeoff and Patricia James. Indianapolis: Bobbs-Merrill.

Asante, Molefi Kete. 1987. *The Afrocentric Idea*. Philadelphia: Temple University Press.

Augustine. 1958. *On Christian Doctrine*. Translated by D. W. Robertson, Jr. Indianapolis: Bobbs-Merrill.

Augustine. 1961. *Confessions*. Translated by R. S. Pine-Coffin. Baltimore: Penguin.

Barth, John. 1969. *Lost in the Funhouse*. New York: Bantam.

Bede. 1970. *The Ecclesiastical History of the English Nation*. Translated by J. Stevens. London: J. M. Dent.

Belenky, Mary Field, Blythe McVicker Clinchy, Nancy Rule Goldberger, and Jill Mattuck Tarule. 1986. *Women's Ways of Knowing: The Development of Self, Voice, and Mind*. New York: Basic Books.

Berger, Peter L., and Thomas Luckmann. 1967. *The Social Construction of Reality*. Garden City, NY: Doubleday.

Berkeley, George. 1982. *A Treatise Concerning the Principles of Human Knowledge*. Indianapolis: Hackett Publishing.

Burke, Kenneth. 1969a. *A Grammar of Motives*. Berkeley: University of California Press.

Burke, Kenneth. 1969b. *A Rhetoric of Motives*. Berkeley: University of California Press.

Carnap, Rudolf. (1947) 1956. *Meaning and Necessity: A Study in Semantics and Modal Logic*. Chicago: University of Chicago Press.

Cassirer, Ernst. 1946. *Language and Myth*. New York: Dover.

Cassirer, Ernst. 1955. *Philosophy of Symbolic Forms*. Translated by Ralph Manheim. 3 vols. New Haven: Yale UP.

Cassirer, Ernst. 1965. *An Essay on Man*. New Haven, CT: Yale University Press.

Cixous, Hélène. 1976. "The Laugh of the Medusa." Translated by Keith Cohen and Paula Cohen. *Signs* 1 (4): 875–93. http://dx.doi.org/10.1086/493306.

Coleridge, S. T. 1965. *Biographia Literaria*. London: Dent.

Derrida, Jacques. 1974. *Of Grammatology*. Translated by Gayatri Spivak. Baltimore: Johns Hopkins.

Derrida, Jacques. 1981. *Positions*. Translated by Alan Bass. Chicago: University of Chicago Press.

Descartes, Rene. 1960a. *Discourse on the Method of Rightly Conducting the Reason and Seeking Truth in the Field of Science*. In *Discourse on Method and Meditations*. Translated by Laurence J. Lafleur. Indianapolis: Bobbs-Merrill. 3–57.

DOI: 10.7330/9780874219364.c009

Descartes, Rene. 1960b. *The Meditations Concerning First Philosophy*. In *Discourse on Method and Meditations*. Translated by Laurence J. Lafleur. Indianapolis: Bobbs-Merrill. 61–143.

Dillon, J., and T. Gergel, eds. and trans. 2003. *The Greek Sophists*. London: Penguin.

Eagleton, Terry. 1983. *Literary Theory: An Introduction*. Minneapolis: University of Minnesota Press.

Eliade, Mircea. 1959. *The Sacred and the Profane*. New York: Harper & Row.

Frazier, James. 1959. *The New Golden Bough*. New York: New American Library.

Freire, Paulo. 1996. *The Pedagogy of the Oppressed*. London: Penguin.

Freud, Sigmund. 2000. *Totem and Taboo*. New York: Prometheus Books.

Geertz, Clifford. 1973. *The Interpretation of Cultures*. New York: Basic Books.

Gramsci, Antonio. 1971. *Selections from the Prison Notebooks*. Edited and translated by Quintin Hoare, and Geoffrey Nowell Smith. New York: International Publishers.

Hartley, David. 2011. *Observations on Man, his Frame, his Duty, and his Expectations*. Facsim. Rpt. London: British Library.

Hirsch, E. D. 1988. *Cultural Literacy: What Every American Needs to Know*. New York: Vintage.

Isaacson, Walter. 2007. *Einstein: His Life and Universe*. New York: Simon and Schuster.

James, William. 1964. *The Varieties of Religious Experience*. New York: New American Library.

Kant, Immanuel. 2008. *Critique of Pure Reason*. London: Penguin.

Kennedy, George. 1998. *Comparative Rhetoric: An Historical and Cross-Cultural Introduction*. New York: Oxford University Press.

Kennedy, George. 1999. *Classical Rhetoric and Its Christian and Secular Tradition from Ancient to Modern Times*. Chapel Hill: University of North Carolina Press.

Kozol, Jonathan. 1985. *Illiterate America*. New York: Anchor/Doubleday.

Kozol, Jonathan. 1991. *Savage Inequalities: Children in America's Schools*. New York: Harper.

Kuhn, Thomas. 1970. *The Structure of Scientific Revolutions*. 2nd ed. *International Encyclopedia of Unified Science*. Vol. 2, no. 2. Chicago: University of Chicago Press.

Langer, Susanne. 1973. *Philosophy in a New Key*. Cambridge, MA: Harvard University Press.

Langer, Susanne. 1946. Preface to *Language and Myth*, by Ernst Cassirer. Translated by Susanne Langer, vii-x. New York: Dover.

Lévi-Strauss, Claude. 1967. *Structural Anthropology*. New York: Doubleday.

Locke, John. 1965. *An Essay Concerning Human Understanding*. Edited by Maurice Cranston. New York: Macmillan.

Lorde, Audrey. 2007. "The Master's Tools Will Never Dismantle the Master's House." In *Sister Outsider: Essays and Speeches*, 110–114. Berkeley, CA: Crossing Press.

Lu, Xing. 2011. *Rhetoric in Ancient China, Fifth to Third Century B.C.E: A Comparison with Classical Greek Rhetoric*. Columbia: South Carolina University Press.

Lyotard, Jean-Francois. 1984. *The Post-Modern Condition: A Report on Knowledge*. Minneapolis: University of Minnesota Press.

Malinowski, Bronislaw. 1948. *Magic, Science, and Religion*. New York: Doubleday Anchor.

Marx, Karl. 1978a. "A Contribution to the Critique of Political Economy." In *The Marx-Engles Reader*. Edited by Robert C. Tucker, 3–6. New York: Norton.

Marx, Karl. 1978b. "Economic and Philosophical Manuscripts of 1844." In *The Marx-Engels Reader*, 2nd ed., edited by Robert C. Tucker and translated by Martin Milligan, 66–125. New York: Norton.

Marx, Karl. 1978c. "Foundations ('Grundrisse') of the Critique of Political Economy." In *The Marx-Engels Reader*, translated by Martin Nicolaus, 221–293. New York: Vintage.

Marx, Karl, and Friedrich Engels. 1978. "The German Ideology." In *The Marx-Engels Reader*, 2nd ed., edited by Robert C. Tucker and translated by S. Ryazanskaya, 146–200. New York: Norton.

Minh-ha, Trinh T. 1989. *Woman, Native, Other: Writing, Postcoloniality, and Feminism*. Indianapolis: University of Indiana Press.

Montaigne, Michele de. 1958. *The Complete Essays of Montaigne*. Translated by Donald M. Frame. Stanford, CA: Stanford University Press.

Nietzsche, Friedrich. 1957. *The Use and Abuse of History*. Translated by Adrian Collins. Indianapolis: Bobbs-Merrill.

Ogden, C. K., and I. A. Richards. 1923. *The Meaning of Meaning*. New York: Harcourt, Brace, and World.

Piaget, Jean. 2002. *The Language and Thought of the Child*. Translated by Marjorie, and Ruth Gabain. Third edition. London: Routledge.

Plato. 1953. *Ion*. In *The Dialogues of Plato*, 4th ed., translated and edited by Benjamin Jowett. New York: Oxford University Press.

Plato. 1956. *Phaedrus*. Translated by W. C. Helmbold and W. G. Rabinowitz. Indianapolis: Bobbs-Merrill.

Plato. 1960. *Republic*. Translated by H. D. P. Lee. Baltimore: Penguin.

Plato. 1970. *Cratylus*. Translated by H. N. Fowler. Cambridge: Harvard University Press.

Plato. 1975. *Gorgias*. Translated by W. R. M. Lamb. Cambridge: Harvard University Press.

Plato. 2003a. "Protagoras" (excerpts). In *The Greek Sophists*. Edited and translated by John Dillon, and Tania Gergel, 22–32. London: Penguin.

Plato. 2003b. "Theaetetus" (excerpts). In *The Greek Sophists*. Edited and translated by John Dillon, and Tania Gergel, 10–12. London: Penguin.

Popper, Karl. 2007. *The Logic of Scientific Discovery*. New York: Routledge.

Richards, I. A. 1955. *Speculative Instruments*. New York: Harcourt.

Rorty, Richard. 1989. *Contingency, Irony, and Solidarity*. New York: Cambridge University Press. http://dx.doi.org/10.1017/CBO9780511804397.

Sapir, Edward. 1964. *Culture, Language, and Personality*. Berkeley: University of California Press.

Saussure, Ferdinand de. 1959. *Course in General Linguistics*. Translated by Wade Baskin. New York: McGraw-Hill.

Scalia, Antonin. 1998. *A Matter of Interpretation: Federal Courts and the Law*. Princeton: Princeton University Press.

Scalia, Antonin. 2008. *District of Columbia v. Heller*, 554 U.S. __, 128 S. Ct. 2783, 171 L. Ed. 2d 637.

Scollon, Ron, and Suzanne Wong Scollon. 2001. *Intercultural Communication*. 2nd ed. Malden, MA: Blackwell Publishers.

Spivak, Gayatri. 1974. Preface to *Of Grammatology*, by Jacques Derrida, lxxvi-lxxvii. Translated by Gayatri Spivak. Baltimore: Johns Hopkins.

Sterne Laurence. 1940. *Tristram Shandy*. New York: Odyssey Press.

Teresa of Avila. 2008. *The Book of Life*. Translated by Kieran Kavanaugh and Otilio Rodriguez. Indianapolis: Hackett.

Toulmin, Stephen. 1980. *The Uses of Argument*. New York: Cambridge University Press.

Volosinov, V. N. 1973. *Marxism and the Philosophy of Language*. Translated by Ladislav Matejka and I. R. Titunik. Cambridge: Harvard University Press.

Vygotsky, Lev. 1962. *Thought and Language*. Translated by Eugenia Hanfmann and Gertrude Vakar. Cambridge: Massachusetts Institute of Technology Press. http://dx.doi.org/10.1037/11193-000.

Williams, Raymond. 1985. *Marxism and Literature*. New York: Oxford University Press.

Wittgenstein, Ludwig. 1968. *Philosophical Investigations*. Translated by G. E. M. Anscombe. New York: Macmillan.

Wittgenstein, Ludwig. 1974. *Tractatus Logico-Philosophicus*. Translated by C. K. Ogden. London: Routledge.

ABOUT THE AUTHOR

C. H. KNOBLAUCH is professor of English at the University of North Carolina–Charlotte. His work on the writing process, critical pedagogy, and the Western rhetorical tradition has been influential in the field of rhetoric and composition for decades.